MAJOR ISSUES IN AMERICAN HISTORY

GENERAL EDITOR
A. S. EISENSTADT, Brooklyn College

CONDUCTING THE DIPLOMACY OF THE NEW NATION, 1793–1815
Patrick C. T. White

THE NEGRO QUESTION: FROM SLAVERY TO CASTE, 1863–1910
Otto H. Olsen

CREATING AN AMERICAN EMPIRE, 1865–1914
Milton Plesur

THE NEW IMMIGRATION
John J. Appel

REFORMING AMERICAN LIFE IN THE PROGRESSIVE ERA
H. Landon Warner

THE UNCERTAIN WORLD OF NORMALCY: THE 1920s
Paul A. Carter

CREATING AN
AMERICAN EMPIRE,
1865–1914

A JEROME S. OZER BOOK

published by PITMAN PUBLISHING CORPORATION

New York * Toronto * London * Tel Aviv

CREATING AN AMERICAN EMPIRE, 1865–1914

EDITED BY

Milton Plesur
State University of New York at Buffalo

Library of Congress Catalog Card No. 76 — 133004

Designed by Lenni Schur

Manufactured in the United States of America

I wish to record my appreciation to my colleague, Professor Selig Adler, Samuel Paul Capen Professor of American History at the State University of New York at Buffalo. His sage comments and suggestions were most helpful. Mr. Arthur Markowitz, a doctoral student in my department, assisted me in seeking out materials and I wish to acknowledge with gratitude his service. I am also appreciative of a travel grant I received from the Research Foundation of the State University of New York.

FOREWORD

The study of history in our classrooms too often proceeds merely from the perspective of the present. Hindsight becomes the great arbiter for settling the past's problems. In our standard textbooks, we judge rather than encounter the past; we instruct it with lessons learned from later developments. In such textbooks, the study of history tends to become a tidy arrangement of certain consequences that arose out of certain causes. As a result, the student can grasp only meagerly the sense that every past was its own present, alive with its own problems, wavering among the alternatives for solving these problems, uncertain about the future. With the security of hindsight and distance, the student is not sufficiently able to consider that a decade he sees as *then* was once a vital and challenging *now,* that its roads into the future were many, that there was nothing inevitable about the one it followed, and that many voices spoke and many forces were at work in affecting its decision to travel one road or another.

The study of American history has tended in recent decades, in yet another way, to remove the classroom from the past itself. It is not merely that we have been proceeding, in our textbooks, to perceive the past from a perspective that is settled and certain, but also that, in our supplementary materials, we have been reading not the past itself but how our major historians are perennially changing their interpretations of it. In this way, too, we are supplanting a study of the past with a study of latter-day commentators on it and, all too often, of commentators on the commentators. The original, vital language of the past itself has, it is fair to say, lost a good deal in the translation.

The *Major Issues in American History* series undertakes above all to restore the fresh, lively contact between the student of the past and the past he is studying. Each of the volumes in the series consists of fifteen or more essays written by earlier generations of Americans on issues of great importance in their times. The different volumes of the series tap a variety of primary sources, but mainly the rich store of our great periodical literature, in which the foremost leaders of American life, our publicists, literary figures, and statesmen addressed themselves to the major problems confronting their respective eras. The men and women who speak in these selections offer various reasons or qualifications for doing so: their intimate knowledge of the problem they are speaking of, their sophisticated perception of its nature, their deep persuasion about its urgency, their strong convictions about how to resolve it.

The selections in each volume seek to lay out the larger dimensions of the major issue with which it is concerned, to recapture the sense of the issue's contemporaneity and urgency, and to afford answers to questions such as the following: What are the nature and significance of the issue? How and why did the issue arise? How should it be resolved? What alternatives are there to achieve its resolution, and what difficulties does the pursuit of each of these alternatives present? Every age is alive with problems, doubts, and controversies, and the selections in each of the volumes seek to convey what these were, in the full measure of the immediacy and liveliness with which the age experienced them. In sum, the central aim of the series is to vitalize the study of the American past by means of *important contemporary essays on major issues.*

Each of the volumes has been edited by a specialist on the issue with which the volume is concerned. Each volume has several principal features designed to enhance its use by the student in his pursuit of a meaningful, rewarding study of the American past. The editor's introductory essay undertakes to present the issue in a broader perspective, indicating how it arose, what were its essential themes and substance, how the controversy it engendered proceeded, what proposals were made for its resolution, how it was ultimately settled, and what were its impact and historical significance. The headnotes for each of the selections extend the introductory essay, offering details about the author of the selection, what occasioned its writing, what the other sides of the controversy were, and the specific historical context in which the selection appeared. The bibliographical essay at the end of the volume offers a critical appraisal of the literature, primary and secondary, dealing with the issue under discussion. Selective rather than comprehensive, it affords the student the basis for a further exploration of the subject. Each volume has, moreover, a chronology which sets the major issue in the context of its times, relating it to the principal events of the age. It is a special point of the series, finally, that the selections have, wherever possible, been reprinted in their entirety. It is important that a spokesman of an earlier age be permitted to present his views in all their completeness and that the student give the past the full hearing it merits.

The *Major Issues in American History* series is meant for use in both basic and advanced courses in American history. The series extends the study of the American past in several ways. It takes the student beyond the confines of the textbook, with its pat formulations and neat divisions, to the reality of the past. Without in any way discounting the importance of what they are saying, it also takes the student beyond the perennial controversies among latter-day and recent historians about what the past signified. It sets the student down in the lively context of a major issue or crisis which earlier Americans had to face, and it compels him to take his place among them in facing and resolving it. Above all, it encourages him to venture out on his own into the realm of the American past and to develop those qualities of perception and judgment that make the study of history the challenging enterprise it is.

A. S. EISENSTADT
Brooklyn College

CONTENTS

A SELECTIVE
CHRONOLOGY

1866 Secretary Seward demands removal of all French troops from Mexico.
Fenians, an Irish brotherhood aimed at achieving Irish independence, raid Canada.

1867 Maximilian, French-supported Emperor of Mexico, executed.
Alaska purchased from Russia.
Midway Islands occupied.
Treaty for cession of Virgin Islands (Danish West Indies) negotiated; dies in Senate.

1868 Burlingame Treaty regulates Chinese labor coming to the United States.

1870 Senate rejects treaty of annexation of Santo Domingo.

1871 Treaty of Washington provides for submission of Anglo-American disputes to arbitration.

1872 *Alabama* Claims Settlement (*Alabama* was a British-built Confederate raider).

1873 Spain captures arms-running ship, *Virginius*, illegally flying the American flag; U.S. secures indemnity.

1875 Commercial reciprocity treaty signed with Hawaii.

1877 Secretary of War authorizes U.S. troops to cross Mexican border.

1878 Treaty of Amity and Commerce with Samoa. U.S. also receives nonexclusive rights to Pago-Pago.

1880 Treaty to restrict Chinese immigration.

1881 Secretary of State Blaine plans Latin-American Conference; cancelled by successor.

1882 U.S.-Korean Treaty of Amity and Commerce signed.

1884   Frelinghuysen-Zavala Treaty, violating Clayton-Bulwer Treaty, signed; dies in Senate.

Berlin Conference on Congo participated in by U.S. Not ratified.

1887   Reciprocity Treaty with Hawaii; Pearl Harbor received as base.

U.S., British, German agreement over Samoa; conference terminated without reaching decision.

1888   Bayard-Chamberlain Treaty (U.S.-Great Britain) provides for agreement over Canadian fisheries question; rejected by Senate.

1889   Berlin Conference on the Samoan protectorate provides for U.S., British, German control.

Pan-American Conference convened by Secretary Blaine; Pan-American Union established.

1892   Anglo-American controversy over sealing in Bering Sea; International Tribunal met in 1893 declared against the U.S.

1893   Hawaiian Revolution and abortive Annexation Treaty.

1895   Controversy between Venezuela and Great Britain over boundary line of British Guiana. U.S. invokes Monroe Doctrine. Resolved peacefully.

Cuban revolt against Spain arouses American sympathy; U.S. accords belligerent status to revolutionaries.

1898   Spanish-American War; U.S. acquires overseas territory.

Hawaii annexed to U.S. by Joint Resolution.

1899   Philippine leader, Aguinaldo, leads revolt against U.S.

Secretary of State John Hay enunciates First Open Door Note aimed at securing equal commercial opportunity in China.

United States, Great Britain, and Germany agree to division of Samoan area. U.S. and Germany divide territory while Britain relinquishes control.

First International Peace Conference at the Hague; Permanent Court of International Arbitration established.

1900   Foraker Act provides for civil government in Puerto Rico.

The Boxers, an anti-foreign Chinese revolutionary group, rebel against foreigners. After the rebellion was squashed, Secretary Hay issues a Second Open Door Note asking that Chinese territorial sovereignty be assured.

1901   Platt Amendment in effect makes Cuba a protectorate of the U.S.

Hay-Pauncefote Treaty signed after an earlier effort; so-called second such Treaty abrogates the Clayton-Bulwer Treaty (1850) and permits U.S. to construct and control an isthmian canal.

1902   Blockade and bombardment of Venezuela by Britain, Germany, and Italy; Roosevelt's arbitration offer accepted.

1903   Hay-Herran Treaty with Colombia whereby she relinquished sovereignty over a proposed Panama canal zone.

Panama revolt against Colombia; U.S. recognition of Panama after Roosevelt orders warships to maintain free transit across the isthmus.

Hay-Bunau-Varilla Treaty grants to the U.S. use and control of a canal zone in Panama.

1904 Alaskan Boundary Dispute with Britain settled.

Roosevelt Corollary to the Monroe Doctrine justifies preventive intervention in Western Hemisphere nations to forestall foreign intervention.

1905 Taft-Katsura Agreement stipulates U.S. would not interfere with Japanese ambitions in Korea in return for Japanese promise to disclaim conquest in the Philippines.

President Roosevelt arranges for the Portsmouth, New Hampshire Peace Conference, concluding the Russo-Japanese War.

1906 Roosevelt secures German acceptance of the Algeciras Conference affirming the independence and territorial integrity of Morocco.

Roosevelt signs a "Gentlemen's Agreement" with Japan limiting emigration of laborers to U.S. San Francisco School Board eventually rescinded its segregation order against Japanese children.

1907 Visit of American fleet on a world cruise.

Second Hague Peace Conference called by Russia. U.S. efforts for establishment of a world court unsuccessful.

1908 Root-Takahira Agreement provides that Japan and the U.S. would maintain the Pacific status quo, respect each other's territorial possessions, uphold the Open Door, and support Chinese independence.

1909 President Taft inaugurates "Dollar Diplomacy" policy in Asia and Latin America.

1910 Newfoundland and North Atlantic Fisheries dispute settled.

1911 U.S. Marines intervene in Nicaragua in consequence of a revolt; Senate fails to act on agreement which would have in effect made Nicaragua an American protectorate.

Canadian reciprocity treaty signed but not approved by Canada.

1912 Lodge Corollary to the Monroe Doctrine declares that the U.S. viewed with concern the possession of strategic areas in the Western Hemisphere by a foreign corporation or association, extending the Monroe doctrine to non-European powers (a Japanese syndicate prompted the Corollary) and foreign companies.

1913 Secretary of State Bryan negotiates "cooling-off" treaties with 30 nations providing for the referral of disputes to an investigating commission; resort to armed conflict prohibited until the report was submitted.

Wilson assumes policy of "watchful waiting" toward the Mexican Government of Huerta, which had assumed power as a result of revolution.

1914 Huerta's troops arrest a U.S. party at Tampico which had gone ashore in a restricted area to secure supplies; an apology was demanded and forthcoming, except for a flag salute.

U.S. troops landed at Vera Cruz because German ship supposedly approaching with munitions. Bombardment occurs. The ABC (Argentina, Brazil, Chile) Powers mediate the dispute at Niagara Falls, Ontario.

Senate repeals a bill exempting U.S. coastwise shipping from payment of tolls at Panama Canal. Such an act was in violation of Hay-Pauncefote Treaty according all nations free and open transit.

INTRODUCTION

From the surrender of Grant at Appomattox Court House in 1865 to Admiral George Dewey's conquest of Manila in the Philippines in 1898, American interest in foreign affairs oscillated between enthusiasm for expansion and reluctance to spread overseas. By 1900, the United States had acquired a far-flung empire that stretched from the Caribbean to the Orient without full realization of its new responsibilities and power. Our interests expanded so rapidly in Latin America and the Far East that when war came in 1914, the destiny of the New World had already been irretrievably linked with that of the Old.

For approximately five years after the Civil War, American expansionists were still under the spell of a manifest destiny to spread their civilization abroad. Moreover, the recent Civil War experience had highlighted the need for military and naval bases and quickened curiosity about remote lands. But, the temptations to expand were checked by cost consciousness, the problem of defending vulnerable territory in the event of war, concern about adding more nonwhites to the racial mix, and the ticklish constitutional questions certain to be raised by adding alien peoples within our constitutional frame.

William H. Seward, Secretary of State from 1861 to 1869 had an appetite for expansion. The only fruits of his grandiose ideas proved to be spacious Alaska and tiny Midway Island. The purchase of Alaska from Russia, however, was a milestone, for the United States for the first time acquired noncontiguous territory that thrust its power through the Aleutians to the borders of Siberia. To the southward, naval needs led only to an abortive attempt to acquire Samaná Bay in Santo Domingo. Despite talk of Washington's interest in Cuba, Puerto Rico, the

Danish West Indies, Hawaii, Canada, land for an isthmian canal, and an ephemeral interest in Africa and Korea, no concrete results were forthcoming. This concern, some of it only political election-time clap-trap, carried with it no sense of urgency. Thus, it differed sharply from the enthusiasm that marked expansionism in the ages of Polk and McKinley.

The principle of hemispheric solidarity stirred more interest. As the Union victory became imminent, Seward made it clear to Emperor Napoleon III that the United States would no longer tolerate a French puppet on the imperial throne of Mexico. Actually, Maximilian's fall came not as a result of American threats, but rather because France, increasingly anxious about Prussia's activity in Europe, lost interest in its unpopular Mexican venture. Yet, Seward's strong stand meant in practice the incorporation of the Monroe Doctrine, in theory if not in name, into the Republican creed. Careful not to mention the Doctrine specifically, he referred to America's established policy of opposing the interference of Europe in establishing monarchial institutions in the New World. Popular approbation resulted and the Maximilian Affair rein-forced the concept of the Monroe Doctrine.

While the administration of President Andrew Johnson succeeded in its Alaskan and Mexican diplomacy, Americans remained largely indifferent to the wider world. As a result, historians until recently have wasted few words on diplomatic matters occurring between the ad-ministrations of Grant and Harrison. The writers who have worked in this field left the impression of two decades of lethargic diplomacy resulting from preoccupation with domestic problems — Reconstruction, the last frontier, rapid industrialization and urbanization, and the "new" immigration. During the latter decades of the nineteenth century, Pres-idents often congratulated the country for its lack of interest in overseas adventure. Public opinion reflected the fashionable arguments of the day — the sacred isolationist ideals blessed by Washington and Jefferson, the condemnation of European imperialism as inherently wicked, and the value to the United States of the absense of strong neighbors. In view of this failure to achieve popular support, it is not surprising that so many postwar expansionist schemes failed. Those peaceful Victorian years were marked by only ephemeral and superficial foreign crises. The membership card to the exclusive Great Power club in those years was the acquisition of territory, but until the 1890s, America seemed perfectly content to remain outside looking in.

Actually, the United States had more interest in "practical politics" than the older writers suspected. Tradition has it that nineteenth century national isolationism gave way to contemporary global interventionism as a result of our war with Spain, but in truth the stimulus for our 1898 expansionist splurge lay rooted in the 1870s and 1880s. Statesmen of that lackadaisical period paved the way for empire, and a slow but steady drift toward imperialism prepared the nation for overseas adventure. In parallel fashion, economic growth led to political entanglements and the "large spirit" of the day, an expansionist posture rationalized in terms congenial to a business civilization. As our industrial economy outproduced the needs of the domestic market, the search for new outlets for American goods began. This meant in turn, need for an adequate navy to protect our far-flung commerce, and such a fleet necessitated global bases and fueling stations. Under these circumstances, it was only a matter of time before the United States would pierce the Isthmus of Panama to insure the safety of both of our coasts.

These developments are mirrored in the subtle attitudinal changes and intellectual speculations on expansionism from American writers and other leaders of civic thought, who argued that Americans were God's chosen, elected to hold a torch aloft to light the way to freedom and progress for all mankind. Such ideas, more often than not, embraced a mix of destiny, mission, and even racism in order to rationalize territorial expansion. For instance, the historian John Fiske, who purveyed British Social Darwinism to America, predicted in 1885 that someday the Stars and Stripes would fly from pole to pole. Only then, Fiske foretold, would civilization truly triumph in backward regions. Another herald of American imperialism was the missionary, Josiah Strong, who in his best-selling *Our Country* stressed the need for domestic evangelization, to be followed by a "thunderous" conversion to Protestantism as a precious gift to the heathen from the Anglo-Saxon colonizers. Still another prophet of expansion was the naval theorist, Alfred Thayer Mahan, who preached the tri-fold blessings of a favorable balance of trade, tariff reciprocity, and a strong navy. A few years later, the historian Brooks Adams, member of the famous family of public servants and author of the theory that civilization rose and fell according to growth and decline of commerce, pointed out that throughout the ages centers of world civilizations had developed at geographic junctions crossed by international trade arteries. He warned that if North America failed to take advantage of its favored position, the fulcrum of power would shift eastward in the direction of Germany or Russia. Only an American thrust into Asia, Adams reasoned, would offset this dire possibility. Even the apostle of American frontier democracy, Frederick Jackson Turner, sought new frontiers beyond our oceans to compensate for the disappearance of free land at home.

An unshakeable belief in the salutary effects of business supremacy also inclined to project American interests overseas. President Hayes' Secretary of State, William M. Evarts, advanced our commercial empire by inaugurating systematic consular reports aimed to provide forward-looking merchants with a firsthand analysis of foreign investment opportunities. The tariff issue, that hardy perennial of American politics, stimulated thoughts about overseas commerce for Republican protectionist orators, who stressed the baneful effects of cheap-labor foreign competition. The post-1870 European quest for remote markets became everyday news copy in the United States just as London's domination of world finance and trade was questioned in the light of what effects such control should have on our own waxing economic interests. Meanwhile, American participation in international fairs and exhibitions, dating from 1851, proved that Yankee know-how matched the technological skills of any nation on earth. Businessmen, anxious to expand their markets, and State Department officials, smarting at real and fancied insults from abroad, joined forces to best the Old World powers who regarded the United States as a johnny-come-lately on the stage of world affairs.

The right arm of diplomacy and commerce was the naval and merchant fleet. While a refurbished merchant marine was needed for overseas carriage, our new warships supported enlarged foreign interests. The sad realization that the once glory-covered American navy had succumbed to rot and rust aroused much comment and complaint. Penny-pinching Congressmen from rural areas had long regarded military expenditures as a gigantic waste, but by the mid-1880s both political parties began to have some second thoughts on the subject. This reassessment resulted in the creation of a naval advisory board, Congressional appropriations for the construction of powerful steel ships, and the establishment of the Newport naval war college, a postgraduate adjunct of Annapolis.

Protestant small-town America of the Cleveland era found missionaries a topic of major interest. More often than not, the only contact these rural folk had with alien cultures was the annual forwarding of the church's "penny boxes" to missionaries in China or Togoland. Long before Rudyard Kipling beckoned his race to take up the "white man's burden," American missionaries were active in the field, furnishing valuable information to both government and business. At the same time, these voluntary exiles interpreted far-off lands and strange cultures to the people at home. The religious press taught lessons in national destiny and racial superiority, as well as roads to salvation, and the evangelical-minded editors of these papers promoted and made apologies for imperialism.

Participation in international conferences also served to broaden the national horizon. Washington cooperated in the standardization of weights, measures, and coinage, belatedly joined the International Red Cross, participated in the International Postal Union, and helped fix the Prime Meridian at Greenwich. For a country preoccupied with domestic problems and weighted down by the isolationist albatross, the United States displayed a lively interest in many forms of international cooperation.

The increasing use of foreign settings by American writers reflected an awakened interest in other cultures. American artists were drawn to Europe in ever larger numbers, so much so that a spate of widely read travel books came from the gifted pens of writers such as Mark

Twain, William Dean Howells, and Henry James. The very knowledge of civilizations that so contrasted with Main Street helped break down our ingrained provincialism.

As economic expansion brought recovery from the Panic of 1873, vastly improved steamships made highways of the oceans. The summer season of 1877 saw about 30,000 Americans in Europe. Young people from affluent families made the customary Grand Tour and students and artists went abroad in ever greater numbers to study in such recognized centers of culture and learning as Berlin, Göttingen, and Heidelberg. Undoubtedly Germany exerted the greatest influence on American higher education, for it was here that our leading scientists, physicians, and professors learned or perfected their skills.

Americans at that time were increasingly curious about things foreign. As they looked outward, Americans were prone to regard European militarism and colonialism as illustrations of Old World degeneracy. Americans felt their own tranquility stood in sharp contrast with continental militarism. They looked askance at European ways, but there was a paradoxical twist to this attitude for we began, in post Civil War days, to pay a new deference to the Old World. This was especially true of such restless and sensitive souls as the writer Henry James, who sought to escape from our soot-filled cities and American acquisitiveness. Such intellectuals oftentimes could appreciate European culture, whether expatriates or not, and yet could also remain loyal to American institutions.

In contrast to our ambivalence toward Europe, where our concerns were primarily economic and cultural, American interest in Latin America was more economic and imperialist in nature. There we wanted naval bases, an American-owned canal, and the relaxation of tariff barriers. What came to be popularly called Pan-Americanism meant in those days United States leadership within the framework of the Monroe Doctrine. Between 1879 and 1884, the War of the Pacific occurred between Chile against both Peru and Bolivia. Chile, the eventual victor, demanded the valuable Peruvian nitrate beds. Secretary Blaine, in the interests of peace and stability, resented any possible European control of Chilean and Peruvian markets, and also opposed territorial cessions that might come in the Americas. American policy was singularly unsuccessful because Chile had won the war, Blaine had no public support for his policies, and our envoys in both Chile and Peru were quite undiplomatic. As a result of Secretary Blaine's Pan-American Conference, held in Washington in 1889–1890, a Central American Union was formed to facilitate commerce, further the cause of republicanism, and forestall possible European intervention. In time, Pan-Americanism was to evolve into the Good Neighbor Policy of the New Deal era, but the early enthusiasm for the policy resulted more from its commercial possibilities than from any genuine desire for true partnership with our southern neighbors. The United States evinced general interest in all areas south of the border, but our Isthmian policy took on special significance as public enthusiasm anticipated the joining of the oceans.

In the mid-1890s, a dispute arose between America and Great Britain over the boundary line separating British Guiana and Venezuela. In this conflict Secretary of State Olney warned Britain that in the Western hemisphere "[our] fiat is law." London replied in effect that the Monroe Doctrine lacked international sanction, but the war fever ebbed as England retreated less from fear of American bluster than because of the need of friendship to countervail the rising German menace that was suddenly apparent as the Venezuelan crisis became full blown. The American public — Republican and Democratic — rallied behind President Grover Cleveland.

As the century neared its end, the trade of such potentially vital regions as Samoa, Hawaii, the Congo, Canada, and Asia received increased attention both in the press and in diplomatic circles. An American sailor-diplomat, Robert W. Shufeldt, in the course of a world-wide naval mission, publicized Africa as a commercial prize and opened Korea to Western influence. Invariably, the United States regarded foreign expansionist schemes — real or imagined — with exaggerated suspicion. Rivalry over Samoa resulted, after years of travail, in a joint American-German control. Hawaii, long accepted as an American geographic outpost and object of sporadic annexationist attempts, was formally included in our Pacific sphere of interest by Secretary of State James G. Blaine in a well-publicized diplomatic paper. One tangible result of this concern was the acquisition of a base at Pearl Harbor, but many years elapsed before it was fortified. At the beginning of the 1890s, the influential American element in Hawaii led a revolt against the natives, who understandably wanted "Hawaii for the Hawaiians." This clash led in 1898 to the annexation of the islands by the United States.

While America had a romantic, Mikado-like image of the Orient, there were practical concerns as well. From the 1840s, Washington favored an Open Door policy and the maintenance of the territorial integrity of the Asiatic nations. Here as elsewhere, we acted either to exclude Europe or else to moderate foreign appetites for land. There was similar preoccupation with certain parts of Africa. Despite a growing economic interest and our special moral responsibility toward Liberia (founded by former American slaves), the African fever did not mount sufficiently to overcome our traditional isolationist reserve. Hence, the Conference in Berlin (1884–1885), called to settle such Congo problems as freedom of trade, outlawing the slave traffic, and neutralizing the area in wartime, failed to overcome the ingrained nonentanglement bias of the Capitol Hill politicos. The American delegate was sternly instructed to confine his attention only to commercial matters and not to bicker over Africa's political future.

Thus, while certain older historians held that the diplomacy of the 1870s and 1880s was a low point or nadir in the annals of American

foreign policy, such writers as Professors Walter LaFeber and David M.
Pletcher (see Bibliographical Essay) feel that it was during this period
that we broadened our world concerns with increasing economic entanglements and the defense of American primacy in certain areas where
it seemed to be threatened by foreign encroachments.

The Spanish-American War established the United States as a
formidable world power with all the fashionable imperialist trappings
of the day. The causes of this conflict lay in the Cuban situation where
concessions from Spain, won after a decade of revolt (1868–1878), proved
ephemeral. Insurrection broke out again in 1895, a development has-
tened by the loss of the preferential American market as a result of
the tariff of 1894 and economic distress concomitant to the 1893 business
slump. While most big business opposed a declaration of war, business
interests, as we have seen, were not indifferent to expansion. Both
politicians and commercial men saw foreign developments in terms
of economic satisfaction. Dewey's victory at Manila Bay and the now
possible lure of Far Eastern riches confirmed their feeling that overseas
markets insured American prosperity. Businessmen were never united
in opposition to intervention in Cuba as once supposed, and many
of them were also anxious to end the suspense stemming from McKinley's vaccilation on the Cuban issue.

Historians are not in entire agreement as to precisely how McKinley
drifted into war, but the majority argue that while the President sincerely
desired peace, he was not firm enough to withstand the pressures that
swirled around him. Some authorities suggest that he chose war, less
from want of a backbone than from a shrewd realization that grass-roots
opinion, to which he invariably lent a close ear, wanted to intervene
in Cuba. The President, a stronger executive than once believed, was
the master of his own decision, but with added patience, McKinley
might well have preserved peace. However, the war spirit was too strong,
the demagogues were too numerous, and, as cynics noted, the next
presidential election was too near. Moral revulsion against Spain's be-
havior in Cuba and enthusiasm for imperialism took us into the war
and allowed us to rationalize this step.

Spain's weakness outweighed American inefficiency and bumbling,
and so the United States wrested the remnants of Spain's colonial empire
from her grip in a little over a hundred days. The war fought to liberate
Cuba from Spain ended with Americans in possession of the Philippines,
Puerto Rico, and Guam. The nation was soon forced to deal with some
urgent questions raised in the Senate treaty debate. Anti-imperialists
doubted the wisdom of acquiring remote territory for commercial exploitation, they looked askance at the propriety of assuming dominion
of "less civilized" peoples, and they questioned the constitutionality
of governing territories without promise of incorporation into the Union.
Many opposed the very idea of a republic turning imperialist. The new
duties and responsibilities, the fresh policies and programs, and the

obvious dangers and involvements were pondered by the Senators and those of their constituents familiar with their current events. The Anti-Imperialist League, dominated by a New England intellectual elite, and whose strongest voice was that of Senator George F. Hoar of Massachusetts, eloquently opposed the acquisition of distant territory and American entrance into the perilous game of world politics. The League argued against territorial expansion in strange and remote areas of the world on grounds of both policy and morality. Hence, for America to follow an imperialist course amounted to a betrayal of our fundamental precepts.

Enough Democratic Senators followed the advice of William Jennings Bryan to approve the treaty thus ending the war. Bryan wanted to subordinate the issue of imperialism to that of free silver in the election of 1900, but when the Democrats attempted to make imperialism the "paramount" issue in the campaign, it failed to catch fire. McKinley's impressive victory was not a mandate for expansion, for his triumph was, in the main, due to the return of good times. After the election, the anti-imperialist movement faded and lost its strength. The hard core of anti-imperialists, more often than not aging Mugwumps of the 1884 vintage, displayed more concern with the morality and justice of policy than with the hard-rock decisions that imperialism precipitated. Their pressure group did provide a conscience, reminding the nation of its basic purposes and forcing a reappraisal of our policies. Under such circumstances we began our experiment as a colonial power. A group of Supreme Court decisions, referred to as the Insular Cases, stated that the Constitution did not follow the flag, that the Constitution did not automatically apply to the people of an annexed territory, nor did it confer on them citizenship, but that it was for Congress to specifically extend such provisions as it saw fit. If the Constitution did not necessarily follow the flag, other advantages and a good many disadvantages did.

By the turn of the century the United States was involved in the Caribbean and the Pacific to a degree no one would have prophesied a decade earlier. The annexation of distant colonies gave America a stake in the world balance of power at a time when this balance was losing its equilibrium. Our first important diplomatic actions as a result of our new overseas interests came in the Orient. The Open Door Policy (1899–1900), which proclaimed America's desire for equality of trade opportunity in China and the protection of that nation's territorial sovereignty, was a direct response to the carving out of spheres of influence in China on the part of the Great Powers. As a result, Secretary of State John Hay's pronouncements launched the United States on a path that was eventually to lead to Pearl Harbor and a history of questionable Far Eastern involvements.

The initial years of the twentieth century found the United States even more involved in Oriental affairs. Theodore Roosevelt brought

together both sides in the Russo-Japanese War (1904–1905), and the
Portsmouth, New Hampshire settlement led Tokyo to blame the United
States for her getting less from defeated Russia than expected. Thereafter,
Roosevelt paid close attention to American-Japanese diplomacy. In the
Taft-Katsura Agreement of 1905, Japan disavowed any designs on the
Philippines in return for American recognition of Japanese hegemony
in Korea. The following year President Roosevelt personally intervened
to ease tensions over the San Francisco School Board's discrimination
against Japanese children, and following protracted diplomacy, there
resulted a "Gentleman's Agreement" whereby Japan agreed not to issue
passports to any more laborers seeking entry to the United States. The
visit to Japan of America's "Great White Fleet" as part of a world tour
was T.R.'s way of flexing American naval muscles in the face of mounting
tensions with Japan. There followed, in 1908, the Root-Takahira agreement which helped pave the way for a détente. While the Taft administration has been closely identified with "Dollar Diplomacy" in both
Asia and Latin America — governmental encouragement of foreign investment and trade — the results of this policy were disappointing because American business was hardly responsive. Viewed from today's
perspective, Roosevelt was a much more far-sighted diplomat than his
hand-picked successor.

The long, dramatic voyage of the U.S.S. *Oregon* from the Pacific
coast around the Horn for Caribbean duty during the Spanish-American
War, made an Isthmian canal — American owned and operated — a prime
necessity. The Clayton-Bulwer Treaty (1850), which barred Britain and
the United States from exclusive rights in a canal across Panama, was
finally abrogated. By 1901, the second Hay-Pauncefote Treaty granted
America exclusive control providing only that the United States not
fortify the canal. A timely revolution in Panama against Colombia supported, if not encouraged, by President Roosevelt gave us the opportunity to begin digging our "Big Ditch," thus resolving the generation-old
dialogue over a Nicaragua versus a Panama route.

The necessity of defending Panama subsequently led to even
further involvements in adjacent areas. In those days, Caribbean "banana" republics were chronically in debt. Fearing that western European
nations would use force to collect these debts, Roosevelt added his
famous corollary to the Monroe Doctrine (1904) which declared that
American police power might be required in the Western Hemisphere
in order to forestall intervention by other nations. As the President
explained in a message to the Senate in 1905:

> The United States ... under the Monroe doctrine ... can not see any
> European power seize and permanently occupy the territory of one of
> these republics; and yet such seizure of territory, disguised or undis-
> guised, may eventually offer the only way in which the power in question
> can collect any debts, unless there is interference on the part of the
> United States.

These preventive measures were applied first in Santo Domingo and thereafter in several other Latin American states. Political and economic interventions were stepped up under the Taft and Wilson administrations. Taft's major Latin American concern was Nicaragua, and in 1912 marines intervened in a revolution there with the result that, as in Santo Domingo, there was American fiscal supervision. While Wilson originally condemned such actions as arbitrary, in practice he too followed them.

The Wilson administration was also to grapple with a vexing Mexican problem, a country where, in the course of its great revolution, noble objectives were thwarted by misguided tactics. From 1877 to 1911 Americans got along splendidly with the dictator Porfirio Díaz, whose economic policies encouraged American investments. Francisco Madero led a revolt in 1911 that ushered in a decade of chaos and unrest bound to jeopardize American nationals and their property rights in Mexico. In fact, the United States was brought to the verge of war with Mexico on several occasions and only mediation by the so-called ABC Powers (Argentina, Brazil, Chile) prevented hostilities. Relations were not to stabilize with our nearest southern neighbor until the eve of the Great Depression.

To sum up, when Europe went to war in 1914, the United States was already deeply involved in Latin American and Asian affairs. The Open Door in Asia remained a constant if illusory goal. South of the Rio Grande, a genuine "good neighbor" policy was not to come until we formally abandoned our interventionism a quarter of a century later. Although World War I thrust the United States to the center of the world stage, the Senate's rejection of the Treaty of Versailles — and with it American membership in the League of Nations — revealed that this country was not prepared to assume global leadership or to abandon isolationism. In retrospect, it is clear that we were still ambivalent about the results of our 1898 venture into political imperialism and Great Power status. Economic imperialism, the concomitant of a greatly enlarged world commerce, was much more to our taste. The anti-imperialists of 1898 were correct in predicting that American expansionism in the regions of the Caribbean and the Pacific would lead to a myriad of troubles. Today it is apparent that the acquisition of the Philippines and Asian responsibilities set off a chain reaction that led to three out of four wars fought thus far in the present century.

The issue of political and economic expansion forms one of the central questions of American history. The essential expansive outlook of the Gilded Age led to empire and world involvement. Despite a repeated denial of territorial ambition, the United States was caught in the web of *Realpolitik*. In a sense the wordy debates over expansionism were academic, for given our resources and the accelerated pace of world events in the twentieth century, the United States could not escape the obligations of power. In pondering today's perplexities, it is essential to realize that the first steps that led to our present complex position were taken in an age all too often described as tranquil and placid.

PART I

EXPANDING
HORIZONS
1865–1890

1

A NEWSPAPER PRO-MOTES WORLD-WIDE CONCERNS

 The men who opposed expansion during the Gilded Age were both numerous and vociferous. They reasoned, not without merit, that the United States had enough domestic problems to solve and unfilled land to settle without assuming additional burdens. The New York *Herald,* edited by James Gordon Bennett (1841–1918), was almost unique among the metropolitan newspapers in calling for a more expansive world view. Bennett increased the *Herald*'s popularity by distinguished reporting during the Civil War; by dispatching H. M. Stanley to Africa on several reportorial assignments, including the famous expedition which "discovered" Livingstone; by establishing a Paris edition; and by supporting George W. DeLong and the ill-fated Arctic exploration of the *Jeannette* (1879–1881). The *Herald* urged the "new" post-Civil War America to acquire and govern distant territory, thus adopting the trappings of a Great Power. The excerpt which follows mirrors the growing desire of the eastern seaboard for involvement in world affairs, a desire that eventually burdened the country with empire.

THE OLD REGIME AND THE NEW: OUR MANIFEST DESTINY

... Preposterous ..., in the United States at this day, "with all our modern improvements," is the fear entertained by our old time, slow-coach conservatives, that with the expansion of our boundaries the cohesion of States and sections must be more and more weakened until they fall to pieces. From the empire of Assyria down to our late Southern rebellion the fatal examples of too much territory are held up to warn us against this greatest of dangers to a great nation. But the difficulties which thus affected the territorial enlargement of any government under the old *regime* of dromedaries, horses and sailing vessels, as the means of intercommunication, have been swept away by the introduction in harness of steam and electricity. Within the last twenty-five years these two powerful agents of modern development and national cohesion have worked out, in this country, the most amazing political revolution in the history of mankind. ...

Steam, electricity, an independent press and universal education have enabled the loyal North to disarm the rebellious South, and thus was the old effete democracy displaced by the present republican party. Now, with the powerful additions to the Union cause of universal liberty, universal suffrage and civil and political equality, what have we to fear from the extension of our boundaries, though we absorb the Esquimaux of Behring Strait and the mixed breeds of Mexico? Our vast acquisition of territory in 1848, from Mexico, was regarded at first as only a howling wilderness but to-day what developments of wealth and prosperity have we in the gold mines and vineyards of California, in the silver mountains and rock salt of Nevada, in the golden rocks of Colorado, in the copper of New Mexico and in the wheat fields of Utah! And our fellow citizens of Spanish descent acquired with these Territories have, under our institutions, been models of law and order.

With our telegraphs, railroads, steamships and boats, the Union of to-day, extending from ocean to ocean, is far more compact and nearer to the centre, from its remotest extremities, than was the original Union limited to the Atlantic coast between Massachusetts

FROM The New York *Herald*, April 17, 1867.

and Georgia. With connecting railroads the city of Mexico can be brought nearer to Washington than was Chicago thirty years ago. What has finally broken up all that puzzling catalogue of petty German States, Duchies and free cities handed down from the Middle Ages? Railroads and telegraphs, fusing their people into one homogeneous mass. Under this new age little nationalities and the dividing lines of races and languages must disappear as the connecting agents of steam and electricity are extended. With these agents, and with an independent press, our common schools, universal liberty, suffrage and political equality (always "excepting Indians not taxed"), our constitution is broad enough, long enough and strong enough to hold the North American continent and its islands on both sides. "The Union as it was" went down with the old democratic party, which went down with the rebellion and slavery; the Union as it is is a Union of liberty and equality, enterprise, progress and continuous expansion. The solid masses of an educated people have taken the place of cliques of politicians. Our rural districts speak for themselves, and through the mediums of telegraphs, railroads and an independent press, they speak the same voice from Maine to Oregon.

Manifest destiny, under all these advantages, marks out the North American continent as the future map of the United States. Men of the present generation may live to hear in Congress that the Speaker has appointed a member each from New York, Quebec, New Archangel, San Francisco, the city of Mexico, Panama, Havana, Hayti and Jamaica as the House Committee on Foreign Affairs. If within the last six years we have put down a rebellion of over half a million of armed men, liberated four millions of slaves, reconquered eight hundred thousand square miles of territory, and purchased four hundred and fifty thousand square miles more, how long will it take us to absorb all North America?

2
CANAL INTERESTS

Henry Clay Taylor (1845–1904) pursued a naval career that began during the Civil War and lasted for thirty-five years, except for two years when he worked for the Nicaragua Canal Company. He commanded the *Indiana* during the Spanish-American War, and thereafter served as superintendent of the Naval War College and head of the North Atlantic Squadron. In 1902 he became Chief of the Bureau of Navigation.

Among Taylor's writing was *The General Question of Isthmian Transit* (1887), in which he argued that Christopher Columbus had not been mistaken in his westward quest for a new route to the Indies despite the fact that his way was blocked by the New World. But, Taylor predicted, the wisdom of the great explorer's gamble would be vindicated only when the oceans were linked by a water passage. An isthmian canal made eminent sense since both European and American shipping could then have a convenient route to the Far East. Taylor's article, "The Control of the Pacific," persuasively argues that an American canal piercing Nicaragua would insure control of the Pacific. Both in an official and private capacity Taylor helped spread the "canal fever" so popular in his day. Certainly no facet of our foreign policy so stimulated the public imagination as much as the canal question.

THE CONTROL OF THE PACIFIC

Henry C. Taylor

It may reasonably be supposed that in the course of time the States of our west coast will dominate the Pacific Ocean, but it will be long before their population and resources justify this expectation. For the next half-century this control will depend principally upon the use and ownership of a canal across the narrow lands that connect us with South America. Chili and Peru are much nearer to our eastern ports than to San Francisco, their longitude being the same as that of New York; and, with a canal across Central America, swift steamships would make Callao and Panama almost the neighbors of New Orleans and Mobile. It is with the circumstances of such a canal, therefore, and with the various interests that group themselves about such a possible transit, that we must principally concern ourselves, when, looking at the probabilities of the time to come, we endeavor to assign properly the future control of the Pacific.

Of the two great isthmuses of the world, it seems natural that Suez should first receive the attention of modern commerce. Some surprise might, indeed, be felt that the Suez problem was not attacked and solved long before that of the American isthmus. The reason is apparent, when we reflect that steam vessels are comparatively modern inventions, and that the Suez Canal is not of service to sailing ships, owing to the calms, baffling winds, and intense heat which prevail throughout the length of the Red Sea, for more than a thousand miles. Sailing vessels from Europe to India or China must continue to use the route around the Cape of Good Hope in preference to the Suez Canal. It was not, therefore, until steamships became numerous upon the ocean highways that a canal joining the Mediterranean and the Red Sea became justified by existing facts. The shores on both sides of Central America, with few exceptions, present, on the contrary, very favorable conditions of wind and weather for the approach of sailing ships; and, had steamships not been introduced, the question of cutting the American isthmus would have preceded by many years the construction of a canal at Suez. The weather and the prevailing winds will continue to be important factors in the canal problem. Much of the world's merchandise is still transported in sailing vessels, and in steamers of a class which must economize coal and be governed to a great extent, in the selection of routes, by the winds they are to encounter.

FROM *The Forum,* III (June, 1887), pp. 407–16.

In considering the interchange of products between the countries of the Pacific and those of the Atlantic, the difficulties and perils of the passage around Cape Horn or through the Straits of Magellan present themselves as the most serious that shipping has to encounter. Twenty degrees farther to the south than its companion cape of Africa, Cape Horn thrusts its bleak rocks far out toward the ice-fields of the Antarctic, and into the most tempestuous region known to seamen. Rich must be the products of countries to tempt shipping to seek them by a route so dangerous and expensive. How rich these products are may be inferred from the rapid increase in the number of vessels visiting the Pacific shores. The official reports of the United States Bureau of Statistics show the number of ships trading from our eastern coast and from Europe to the North and South Pacific to be, in the year 1879, 2,647, of an aggregate tonnage of 2,671,886 tons. The same reports show, in the year 1885, the total number of ships to be 4,139, of a tonnage of 4,252,434. This remarkable growth of trade will be more than repeated in the coming years. The industrial development of our Pacific States, the settlement of Alaska, the growing importance of Chili, assure this. Thus, should a canal through Central America be provided at the earliest possible moment, say in 1892, we might feel assured that shipping to the amount of from six to seven million tons annually would at once avail itself of this means of shortening and cheapening voyages. So much for the direct and immediate benefits to commerce; as for secondary and more remote advantages, the possibilities are, indeed, vast. The lumber trade between Alaska and the countries bordering on the Atlantic, checked at present by the expensive freights, would quickly assume large proportions. The guano and nitrate trade of the west coast of South America, already large, in defiance of almost prohibitory transportation charges, is capable of indefinite expansion if favored by the presence of such a Central American canal. It is questionable wisdom, from a business point of view, to construct canals or railroads for the purpose of developing and building up business, unless sufficient trade already exists to justify the cost of their construction; but, when there already awaits the opening of a canal a shipping three times greater than is needed to justify the cost of its construction, the mind may be permitted to measure in advance the great volume of business in those new branches of commerce which shorter lines of transportation would call into existence.

What nations will receive most benefit from such a transit between the seas? From a commercial standpoint and in the light of existing facts, the United States would not stand first. Great Britain would for the moment gain the greatest advantage. The ships which her enterprise sends around South America, to Chili and Peru, the manufactures they transport, the native products she receives in return, in fact, all of her trade north of Valparaiso, would be benefited by the canal. Much of the English trade with China, Japan, Australia, and New Zealand would use this line of travel. The sailing craft and slow freight steamers, especially when outward bound from home ports, would make the quickest and cheapest voyage possible by way of a Central American canal, being, during four-fifths of the whole voyage, in the region of favoring trade winds, blowing them smoothly and rapidly to their destination.

Germany has already a large trade with the South Sea, and has practically monopolized the commerce of the west coast of Mexico. It is safe to say that German merchants, after paying canal tolls, would double their present annual gains; and that the opening of a canal would be speedily followed by a great increase in the German shipping using it, and in the general proportions of the German trade with the Pacific. So too, the interests of Spain in the Philippine Islands, of France in Tonquin and at Otaheite, of Holland in Java, of Russia in Eastern Siberia, would cause the canal to be a source of much profit to the shipping of these nations.

It is not surprising that other shipping than American should be the immediate gainers, when we reflect how few ships still carry our flag upon the high seas, and when we find that, of the four millions of tonnage referred to above, over two millions is recorded as vessels clearing "from European ports in trade around Cape Horn with foreign countries other than the United States." We have to consider also that between our own ports on the Atlantic and Pacific, the trans-continental railroads have been effective competitors with the distance, delay, and expense of the Cape Horn route; thus reducing the number of American ships employed, and hence making the advantage to our commerce, immediately upon the opening of a canal, less apparent, in any tabular statement, than that derived by some other nations.

Returning to the comparison of the advantages gained by foreign shipping over our own, we find those advantages existing only at the moment of opening the canal. Immediately afterward, the value of our proximity to Central America would be felt, and would give us overwhelming odds against European shipping. To the question, "Do we control the Pacific?" our statistics answer decidedly, "No;" but to the question, "Shall we control the Pacific?" the inauguration of a Central American canal would give loud affirmative response

that would be understood throughout the world. The manufactures
of our eastern States, the products issuing from Cincinnati, St. Louis,
New Orleans, and Mobile, would quickly find their way by such
a route to profitable markets on the west coast, from Acapulco, in
Mexico, to Valparaiso, in Chili. Competition of merchandise brought
from London and Hamburg, with our goods, favored by the quickness
and ease of transportation, would be hopeless. Our trade once established along the Pacific coast, it would soon reach out strongly
among the Pacific islands, for the advantage of time, distance, and
favorable weather would still be with us. Nor would these favorable
conditions cease before reaching New Zealand and Australia, between which countries and New Orleans and New York an active
traffic would soon establish itself. Thus, with our Pacific States
holding their proper influence in the Sandwich Islands and the North
Pacific, the question, "Who shall control the Pacific?" would be
practically answered in favor of the United States. It is not within
the province of this article to discuss the revival of American shipping, but the writer cannot refrain from asking here, what surer
method can be suggested of attaining that much-desired revival, in
a natural and healthy manner, than by the opening of this inter-
oceanic canal?

The political and international aspects of the situation must
not be disregarded. No trade can flourish if dominated and repressed
by the power, military, naval, or diplomatic, of a foreign nation.
How shall we, then, protect our future commerce, without departing
too far from our republican traditions of a small army and navy,
and without involving ourselves too much in international complications? This question at once suggests that of the proper geographical
location of the canal. The two subjects are interdependent and must
be discussed jointly. There have been different opinions as to the
best route for interoceanic communication. Since the days of Columbus the dispute has been going on. It is sufficient, however,
for the scope of this discussion, to know that twenty years ago the
United States Government, urged on by the demands of commerce,
and weary of the general ignorance concerning a matter so closely
related to the country's welfare, determined to inform itself
thoroughly as to the whole subject, and to decide once for all what
routes for a ship canal across Central America were possible, and,
of these, which one would be the most desirable. To obtain this
information the best energies and intelligence of the government
were directed for several years, and exploration and surveying work
was done, representing the judicious expenditure of millions of

dollars. The Atrato River, San Blas, and Panama lines, the Nicaragua Lake routes, and those of the Tehuantepec Isthmus, all were thoroughly examined.

These examinations of the various localities were exhaustive. Under the name of reconnaissance and preliminary work, surveys of considerable thoroughness were prosecuted in many localities; and to establish more positively certain facts connected with the different routes, and to remove all doubt, new parties were sent into the field after the original plan of work was concluded. This continued until several years had been occupied in the work, and until the government possessed at last absolute and indisputable data on which to base a decision. When thus confronted with the facts one decision was alone possible. The only practicable method of connecting the oceans was by means of a lock canal across Nicaragua, using the lake as a summit level. Other plans and lines were fully considered and discussed. By the Atrato and Napipi rivers the line included a great tunnel for ships. Some other routes had the same defect. The Isthmus of Panama, regarded as impossible for a sea-level canal, promised to develop serious difficulties in supplying with sufficient water the summit levels of any proposed lock canal in that vicinity, and this isthmus was therefore regarded as out of the count of practicable methods and lines. The Isthmus of Tehuantepec, in Mexico, was found to be impracticable for a canal of any kind, the mountain range which traverses that isthmus having nowhere less than seven hundred feet elevation to be overcome. Nicaragua, on the contrary, was found to be a route singularly well adapted for a canal, and possessing natural advantages in a remarkable degree. Lake Nicaragua, a great body of fresh water, one hundred and five feet above sea level, offers itself as a most convenient summit level, and the river San Juan, through which the lake drains into the Caribbean Sea, constitutes a natural line of approach from that sea to the lake. Between the lake and the Pacific there intervenes an isthmus fifteen miles in width, with an elevation of only forty feet above the former, and with several natural lines for a lock canal to connect the lake with the ocean.

It will always be one of the marvels of history that, after these thorough surveys had been made by our government, two routes, already pronounced impracticable, should have been seriously thought of, much less attempted. The work of cutting the isthmus at Panama, undertaken by the energetic but unwise De Lesseps, has now been nominally prosecuted for several years; and with a debt of three hundred millions of dollars, and about ten per cent. of

the work completed, the world is just beginning to realize that the
task is an impracticable one, and that the failure of this scheme,
the collapse of this greatest of all financial bubbles known to history,
is now close at hand. The Tehuantepec Ship Railway scheme rivals
the Panama Canal in its disregard of the insurmountable obstacles
with which nature has barred its way; and by the abandonment
of this project, which now happily appears probable, the country
will be saved great financial loss and a bitter disappointment.

As to the political aspect of these two routes, it may be said
that had nature permitted a canal at Tehuantepec, its nearness to
us would have made our control of it an easy matter. Its eastern
entrance being in the Gulf of Mexico, quite near our Gulf ports,
would have made that body of water, even more than now, an
American lake; and its position in Mexican territory would tend
to strengthen the friendship between that republic and ourselves.
A ship railway, however, lacking the interior basins of a canal, where
fleets might await important events, would possess little of the political importance attaching to a canal. As to Panama, its distance from
our borders is greater than either Nicaragua or Tehuantepec, and
this isthmus belongs to a South American state, which is one of
the political divisions of the United States of Colombia. That republic
is even now fearing the aggressions of Venezuela, which state, under
General Guzman Blanco, looks forward confidently to a consolidation
of all the neighboring states under its own authority, and with the
able and distinguished Blanco as permanent chief of the confed-
eration. The commercial disadvantages are those of Suez. The calms
which extend many hundred miles to the westward of Panama in
the Pacific would interfere seriously with the use of the canal by
sailing ships. The climate is proverbially bad, and the locality has
few products upon which trade could be based. There could not
grow up about the canal any great center of business; local circumstances forbid it. The canal would be, like the one at Suez, a passage-way, and nothing more. These difficulties, political and commercial, need not occupy us seriously, for M. de Lesseps has already
convinced the world that nature does not contemplate a canal at
Panama, and that man cannot in this case overcome nature's obstacles. No one can see without regret the financial disaster now
overhanging the French people. The debt of the Panama Canal
Company amounts to about three hundred millions of dollars, and
the interest upon this debt, plus the fixed charges of the administration, is sixteen million dollars annually. This sum must be paid,
although not an hour's work should be done on the canal. The case

is indeed desperate. Among the many sad consequences of this impending evil will be its effect upon the mind of the business world, which will be turned for the moment against all projects for connecting the oceans. This cannot last, of course. Commerce will not cease to demand a passage-way for its shipping; and it is most fortunate that America and Europe have at last begun to recognize that such a passage-way is simple and practicable by way of Nicaragua. Here we should be spared that ignorance of the situation which has cost the French so dear at Panama. The Nicaragua route has been so often surveyed, and with such care, that every detail of the river and lake, of weather and climate, of geological formation and character of people, is intimately known. Clear and reasonable estimates, based on these careful surveys, have been submitted to some of the most famous canal engineers of the present day for their criticism and revision, and have received their cordial approval.

A liberal allowance for the construction of this great work has thus been settled upon as fifty million dollars. To this, fifty per cent. has been added to allow for all possible contingencies, and seventy-five millions is announced as the final cost of the canal, completed, and open to shipping of the largest class, and capable of transferring from sea to sea thirty vessels per day. The demand upon the capacity of the canal when first opened would be an average of about six ships per day, of three thousand tons each, or eighteen thousand tons daily, amounting to about six and a half millions of tons per year. This tonnage, at the rates now charged at Suez, of two dollars and a half per ton, will produce an annual receipt from tolls amounting to sixteen and a quarter millions of dollars. A liberal allowance for the maintenance of the canal is half a million a year, and we may allow more than a million, and still be well within the mark in saying that the canal when first opened will pay at once five per cent annually on three hundred million dollars, from the tonnage then awaiting transit. At Panama the maintenance and preservation of a canal for traffic, against the land-slides and freshets of that isthmus, is believed by many able engineers to be impossible at any cost; while at Tehuantepec, the running expense of a ship railway, judging by other less costly railways, would not fall short of eighty per cent. of the gross receipts.

In considering the revenue of a canal, no account has been made of the business in those branches of trade that its presence would call into existence. This increase in tonnage would occur in the case of any possible line for a canal in Central America, and would soon compel the enlargement of its capacity; but it would be especially marked in the case of a Nicaragua canal, by the singularly fortunate circumstances of that location. Lake Nicaragua, the summit level, drains a water-shed of exceptional fertility and salubrity. The northeast trade winds, the lofty mountain peaks, the expanse of deep cold water in the lake, moderate the tropical temperature, and produce a climate most favorable to health and the enjoyment of life; the western half of this region having been long renowned as a sanitarium.

These trade winds in the Caribbean and the Atlantic favor the sailing craft and freight steamers in their approach to the eastern entrance of the canal, while the Yucatan Channel and the Gulf Stream offer favorable routes of departure for our eastern seaboard and for Europe. The winds about the western entrance, though not so regular, afford also easy approach to and exit from the canal. The summit level, the lake itself, ninety miles by forty-five in extent, is provided for us by nature, and this great water-power is at our service for the work of construction on the lower levels; and, when the canal is completed, it will furnish the motive force for extensive manufactories, established here at this great *entrepôt* of the products of all nations.

It is the lake that gives to this route a political and international importance unique and significant. The nation that controls this canal under terms of amity with Nicaragua will here find rest and refreshment for its fleets. Here may the delays of warlike complications, so injurious in sea water to the iron-hulled frigates of our time, so fatal to their speed, be safely endured without loss of efficiency; the crews growing healthier, the ships more clean-limbed and speedier, in this great fresh-water sea. Hence may issue squadrons in the height of vigor and discipline, striking rapid and effective blows in both oceans, and returning to refit in this sheltered stronghold, and to draw from it nourishment and fresh strength for a renewal of hostilities. There cannot be imagined a more potent factor in deciding threatened difficulties or in securing an honorable peace with a powerful enemy than the presence in this healthy and capacious water-fortress of a strong fleet, prepared, at a telegraphic sign from the home government, to issue fully equipped from either entrance for instant service in the Atlantic or Pacific. So vast would be the power of the nation that controlled this transit, and so strong the international jealousies thus created, that it may be considered fortunate that this enterprise should now be moving forward as a purely commercial project, independent of the aid of any government; its only international feature being that London, Amsterdam, and Berlin are joined with New York, Chicago, and San Francisco in insuring its pecuniary success.

Thus, although the opening of a maritime canal through Nicaragua will give to the United States the control of the Pacific, it will be welcomed by the merchants of every country, creating for their commerce steady currents and a healthy circulation; and, by its existence alone, preventing those stagnations of trade so injurious to the financial prosperity of nations and to the happiness of their people.

3

THE CHURCH PRO-MOTES OVERSEAS ECONOMIC INTERESTS

Although the principal task of overseas missionaries was to propagate the gospel, their activities extended into a variety of other fields, particularly the promotion of foreign trade and commerce. The work of the Reverend Frank Field Ellinwood (1826–1908), a leading Presbyterian, illustrates the varied concerns of the overseas missionary. Mr. Ellinwood, who began his ministry in the 1850s, served as Corresponding Secretary of the Board of Foreign Missions of the Presbyterian Church for thirty years. His chief overseas duty was in the Orient and the propagation of his views on Asia helped to widen American knowledge and understanding of that region. Among his writings were *Oriental Religions and Christianity* (1892), *Our Relations to the Mongolian Race* (1884), and *Questions and Phases of Modern Missions* (1899).

In the following selection, Ellinwood stresses the then novel, yet obvious, relationship between spreading the gospel and enhancing foreign trade. Missionaries such as Ellinwood helped promote a more cosmopolitan outlook and a more sophisticated understanding of world problems, thus weakening the cultural isolationism of the American hinterland.

THE RELATIONS OF MISSIONS AND COMMERCE

Frank F. Ellinwood

Paul at Ephesus encountered not only the general opposition of the world, the flesh, and the devil, but he had special trouble with an unprincipled craftsman. At Phillippi, also, he found a stock company making merchandise of a half-demented girl whose conversion interfered with their business. And from that day to this, human rapacity has again and again thrust itself across the path of philanthropy and beneficence.

We do not forget that legitimate commerce has been a great factor in the development of civilization and even in the progress of the gospel. The growth of the early Church followed the lines of trade across the Mediterranean, and on the Continent of Europe Latin Christianity penetrated the forest homes of stalwart races where Roman arms and merchandise had opened the way. Secular enterprise has built the great Christian cities of our Western hemisphere, and opened mission fields everywhere in the chief islands of the sea. The California of to-day could not have been created by missionary effort alone, and the magnificent spectacle of a British Empire in Southern Asia, with its Bible, its schools and colleges, its law and order, its manifold enlightenment and moral elevation, could not have existed but for the long and sometimes questionable career of the East India Company.

But there is no universal law in the case. Civilization, even in its rougher forms, has not always preceded the missionary movement. Often it has proved a hindrance. Throughout British America, mission stations have followed the factories of the fur traders; but in Hawaii, Samoa, Fiji, and Madagascar, missionary labor has led the way. Centuries ago, also, missionaries from Ireland and Iona, penetrating not only England and Scotland, but many portions of the Continent, were unattended by secular enterprise, and yet their influence was so strong and deep that Europe and the world have felt it and rejoiced in it ever since. Those hordes of Northmen whom Britain could not resist, nor the armies of Charlemagne conquer or even check, were tamed at last by the simple, aggressive influence of the gospel, unattended by either military or commercial power.

Three things have been found almost universally true: first, that the gospel has always elevated the character and established

FROM *The Missionary Review of the World*, XI (December, 1888), pp. 881-7.

the power of our civilization in whatever lands its influence has reached. More than once has it been confessed that England could scarcely have retained her Indian possessions but for the conservative influence of those Christian missions which measurably restrained the injustice of rulers, while it promoted the enlightenment and the loyalty of native princes and peoples.

The second principle, which is generally true, is that the first contacts of commerce, and especially during the period of rough adventure and lawlessness, are evil. Whether adventurers have gone before or have followed the missionary, their influence has caused a blight. Whale-fishermen in Tahiti and Hawaii, convicts in Tasmania, kidnappers in Melanesia, slave traders in Congo, opium dealers in China, and whiskey venders among the Indian tribes of North America — all have proved a curse.

It is impossible to exaggerate the hindrances which have been thrown in the way of the gospel by these influences. And the distinctions which are made in our own lands between the Christian name and the wrongs and vices that prevail in the general community, cannot be appreciated by those who see us at a distance, and mainly on our worst side. Judging from the wholesale classifications of their own religious systems, they naturally identify the name European or American with the generic name of Christian.

Moreover, while here at home most men are under conventional restraints, adventurers in distant marts, removed from influences of home, too often give loose rein to their lowest instincts, throw off allegiance to Christian influences, and become hostile to missionaries and to missionary effort. They are hostile because the high principles and clean lives of missionaries carry with them an implied condemnation of their own shameless vices.

I wish it were possible to feel that governments, as such, had been wholly free from wrongs to inferior races. But there is no one of the so-called Christian nations which can cast the first stone at another. All have been guilty, more or less. These facts become more serious when we consider that to these nations our lost world chiefly looks for the blessed gospel.

The early American colonies had Christian missions for one great motive in their settlement. There it might have been expected that commerce and evangelization would proceed hand in hand, and that William Penn's beautiful dream of brotherhood would be realized, but although we have had in the last 250 years three heathen races on whom to exercise our gifts — the Indian, the African and the Mongolian — we have abused them all, and each in a different way. Our record is sad and disgraceful, and we are in no mood to read lectures to other Christian nations. But we are ready to unite with them, heart and hand, in any measures of amendment.

There are consolations in this dark history, as there are in the coolie traffic of the South Pacific. One is, that all this time the Christian Church, or at least portions of it, have realized the wrong, and have done what they could to save the people from destruction and lead them unto eternal life. There have never been more beautiful exemplifications of Christian love than those which were exhibited by Moravian missionaries through all the early history of our dealings with the American Indians. And thousands of our own people have followed their worthy example. Never in the whole history of martyrdom has one seemed to follow so nearly in the footsteps of the vicarious Redeemer, and so to fill up the remainder of His suffering even unto death, as the saintly Patteson, who literally died for the sins of unscrupulous kidnappers, of the Caucasian race.

A third principle is, that improvement generally follows as commerce becomes established. There is much comfort in this. The first rough adventurers are at length followed by a better class. Homes are established by Christian merchants; fathers who are solicitous for the moral atmosphere which surrounds their children, exert a wholesome influence; the missionary is no longer sneered at, but is supported; vice that was open and shameless is frowned upon. The church and school have arrived. In many a land where the first wave of our civilization seemed to cast up only mire and dirt, order, intelligence and religion at length prevailed.

There was a time in San Francisco when the courts of justice were paralyzed, and when the right-minded citizens felt constrained to send to Hawaii for a missionary to return and establish a Christian church in his own land. Even saloon-keepers joined in the call, alleging that without a church and Christian institutions no man's life was safe.

In all new mining fields, whether in America, or Australia, or South Africa, the first contact has been demoralizing, and yet in those same settlements, when order had been established, when the Christian family had arrived, when a church and a schoolhouse, and a Christian press and Christian influence had obtained a footing, all was changed. And dark as the problem of civilization in Africa now is, and urgent as may be the duty imposed upon us to save the present generation, we do not hesitate to prophesy that European civilization in West Africa a-half century hence will be full of life and light. Even at the worst, we are by no means disposed to hand

Africa over to Islam, which in all these centuries has done so little for the heathen tribes — which, by degrading woman, has tended to destroy the family, and, therefore, the State, and which has depopulated every country that it has ever controlled. The only hope of Africa is in our Christian civilization.

But if missions are to prosper in the future, it will be important to promote a more just sentiment toward inferior races. The time should soon come when races like the American Indians, or the Maoris of New Zealand, should be allowed equal natural rights with Caucasians. The time should soon come — if missions are to be a success — when might shall not make right, but weaker nations shall be treated as one European nation would treat another. The time should soon come when treaties with a country like Japan shall not be made and enforced merely for the convenience or profit of the great Powers, but shall have the same regard for even-handed justice as if the Japanese navies were thundering at our gates. The time should come when all commerce shall be so regulated that it shall not curse the nations with which we have to do. We have often counted upon improvements in inter-communication as factors in the advancement of the human race and as agencies of Redemption, but of late we are sometimes rather appalled than cheered. For example, the fond hopes which we cherished five years ago in regard to the opening of the Congo, have been sadly clouded over. And the fact that the Congo State is under international control would seem to render it a proper subject of consideration in this International Conference.

Allow me to call special attention to this subject. Whatever may be thought of the propriety of discussing here the abuses that may exist in the colonies of separate European powers, there can be no doubt of our privilege and duty in this case. The Valley of the Congo is common ground, and moreover, it is a vast mission field. Directly across the path of our progress in the evangelization of the Dark Continent lies this gigantic evil of the liquor trade. At the very gateway of our missionary enterprise croaches this hydra, whose hideous proportions no flight of poetic imagination can exaggerate. I need not give the statistics nor discuss the details which have become so familiar, but success or failure in African missions is concerned in this issue. The toils and sufferings of our brave missionaries appeal to us. How can we continue to send our heroic Hanningtons, and Combers, and Parkers, and yet neglect the very first duty which we owe to Africa? The honor of the Christian name is at stake. Those who persist in ignoring the distinction between so-called Christian nations and the Christian Church, are arraigning the Church for neglect in this matter. They are parading the conservative influence of Islam as the best hope of Africa, and are cursing the day that our Christian civilization disturbed its reign.

It seems desirable to treat this question on broad grounds which will enlist the sympathies of the largest possible constituency. The issue before us is not the temperance question with which many of us are accustomed to deal. It has all the enormity of systematic cruelty to children; it is a conspiracy by representatives of civilized nations against simple tribes of men who know not what they do. On such an issue the humane and pitiful of every name — Protestant or Catholic, Christian or unchristian — should unite their common protest.

The proofs that the rum traffic among the African tribes tends to destroy all other departments of trade, are so numerous and so well known that I need not dwell upon them. It is enough that this accursed evil blights all hope of the present generation, that even those who had begun to gather about them the comforts of civilization have gone back to barbarism — that women who had learned something of modesty have again discarded clothing that all their resources may be expended for drink. But the evil is not confined to the present; it incapacitates the people for future commerce and thrift; it casts a blight upon those whose hopes have been turned toward Central Africa as a great field of true commerce. Never before has Christendom made so gratuitous a concession to the sordid gains of a few unscrupulous business firms — one which involved so great a cost to national honor, to the fair name of the Christian Church, and to the best interests of millions of mankind.

No doubt great discouragements beset this question, and many whose sympathies are really touched are nevertheless hopeless of results. We may be very sure that the representatives of the liquor traffic are quietly but effectively exerting their influence to thwart every effort made in the interest of humanity. I am informed that at Washington an agent is employed by the "liquor interests," whose whole time and energy are employed to baffle all attempts supposed to conflict with their business.

But, on the other hand, what are some of our encouragements to effort?

First, the fact that so much has already been done to arouse public sentiment on the subject. I refer to the various public meetings which have been held in London, and especially to the formation of a working committee representing the Missionary Societies of Great Britain.

Second, that the constituencies represented here are so vast and may be so influential. Mr. W. T. Hornaday, of Washington, D. C., has pertinently asked: "Who are the more powerful, the traders who desire to enrich themselves out of the palm oil purchased with gin, or the Christian nations which were represented at the Berlin Conference, with their 388,000,000 of Christians? America has sixty-five foreign missionary societies; Great Britain seventy-two, and the Continent of Europe fifty-seven, not including those of the Roman Catholic Church. Are they not strong enough to cope with the rum traffic on the Congo?"

A third encouragement is found in the fact that a united movement by the Christian Church is in the line of true commercial interest. All enlightened statesmanship should be on our side. The Royal African Company, trading on the Niger, has already restricted the rum traffic on that river as a matter of business policy; as the only hope, in fact, of promoting legitimate commerce.

Fourth. We find encouragement even in the counsels of the Berlin Conference. Count De Launy of Italy, Sir Edward Malet of India, Mr. Kasson of the United States, and Count Van der Straten of Belgium plead for restriction. And the Conference itself finally adopted a sort of compromise, by expressing "a wish that some understanding should be arrived at between the Governments to regulate the traffic in spirituous liquors." Even the representatives of France and Germany, though not voting for restriction by the great Powers, expressed the belief that "the Congo Government, in any measures which it might deem it wise to adopt, would find the Powers ready to cooperate to this end." *And the Congo Government, represented by the King of the Belgians, is more than ready to do all that the sentiment of the nations will sustain him in doing.*

Have we not, then, great reason to believe that a united plea of all Christendom would be listened to by the contracting Powers? I say a united plea, for separate national movements are considered wellnigh useless. Each Government would feel that its own individual action would only cut off its subjects from the profit of the trade, and throw it into other hands, without at all diminishing the devastations which we deplore. It must be an international movement to be successful. The same Powers that made the original treaty can revise it, and we represent those Powers.

But the strongest consideration which presses upon us is found in a most touching appeal which comes from an unexpected source. A line of action has been suggested, providentially and significantly, by a Mohammedan prince in West Africa. I marvel that so little heed has been given to his words. The Emir of Nupe, speaking for his own dominions, sent many months ago the following stirring message to Bishop Crowther of the Niger Mission:

"It is not a long matter," runs the appeal, "it is about *barasa* (rum). It has ruined our country; it has ruined our people very much; it has made our people mad." And then, in the name of God and the Prophet, he beseeches Bishop Crowther to ask the Committee of the Church Missionary Society to petition the Government to prevent bringing *barasa* into his land. May we not consider this an appeal not merely to the Church Missionary Society but to all missionary societies in this Conference, and to the churches which they represent? Has not this Mohammedan prince struck a keynote for this great occasion? What particular measures shall be adopted it is for the wisdom of this great body to decide. May God direct its councils!

And what if we should not fully succeed? Let us suppose the very worst; yet one thing is certain, at least, the reproach of the Christian name will have been removed. It can no longer be said that the Church is sitting at her ease while the powers of darkness seem to triumph.

And lastly, there is one great power supreme over all, which we may believe is wholly on our side, and to that our petitions should arise as with the voice of one earnest and importunate soul. Africa is a vineyard which God has given to His Son for a possession, and the cause of African missions is a vine of His own right hand's planting. Let us pray, therefore, "that the boar out of the wood" shall not waste it, and "the wild beast of the field" shall not devour it.

4

COMMERCIAL USES
OF THE FLEET

The right arm of diplomacy and commerce was the American naval and merchant marine fleet. Nationalist-minded thinkers became concerned after 1865 because these vital props of government and business were weakened and seemed to be held in low esteem. The clarion call for revitalized American power on the high seas — both military and commercial — was sounded clearly by Commodore Robert W. Shufeldt (1822–1895). Shufeldt began his naval career in the Mexican War days. In the 1870s he helped reorganize the naval apprentice system and, in diplomatic affairs, represented the United States and Great Britain in the solution of a Liberian boundary dispute.

Shufeldt commanded a world tour beginning in the late 1870s during the course of which he popularized the commercial potentialities of the Congo. On the same trip, he "opened" Korea to American commerce, following an earlier abortive attempt by Rear Admiral John Rodgers in 1871 to implement closer trade possibilities and secure protection for American missionaries in that country. After tortuous negotiations and much intrigue among China, Japan, and Russia over the Korean peninsula, a treaty — the first with a Western power — was signed in May, 1882. It provided for concessions to American trade and for most-favored-nation tariff status.

Shufeldt's celebrated article, quoted below, is a classic portrayal of the nonmilitary purposes of the Navy. The statement, which originated as a request to Representative Leopold Morse of the House of Representatives Naval Committee, summarizes the importance of the Navy's peacetime tasks at a time when such functions were little understood by penny-pinching lawmakers.

THE RELATION OF THE NAVY TO THE COMMERCE OF THE UNITED STATES

Robert W. Shufeldt

No nation can be really great without an external commerce. China, for instance, with four hundred million people, has no status in the world as a nation. No account is taken of her in the relation of nations to each other. She is simply an aggregation of people without external force. This is owing to the fact of her exclusiveness — the absence of interchange of ideas through the absence of interchange of commodities in her own ships and under her own flag.

The United States, strange as it may appear, is pursuing a policy which, at no distant day, will make her in like manner as formidable beyond her limits as China or as a turtle in a shell.

With an immense internal trade, we are fast losing its legitimate results, viz., intercourse with the world under our own flag — in other words, we are sowing the seed while others are gathering the fruit. We surrender our commercial power on our very coasts to our commercial rivals, thereby courting the contempt of nations and cultivating our own insignificance. But, in addition to this fact, which is true as a matter of political economy, we are urged imperatively to the re-creation of our commerce through the absolute necessity of procuring a market for our surplus products.

At least one-third of our mechanical and agricultural products are now in excess of our own wants, and we must *export* these products or *deport* the people who are creating them. *It is a question of starving millions.*

Since the introduction of steam upon the ocean, experience has proved to Great Britain and other commercial powers, that capital will not invest in steam navigation without some security from the Government against total loss. The risk in seeking trade, together with the large investment required to inaugurate it, frightens the capitalist; but let the enterprise obtain a footing, then it continues by virtue of its merits and capabilities, or if it fails for want of them at the end of, say, five or ten years, it no longer deserves support.

FROM *The Relation of the Navy to the Commerce of the United States* (Washington, 1878).

In no other way can our commerce be re-established or our prestige restored upon the ocean. In no other way can the country be relieved of its surplus products, or an additional impetus be given to its industries.

Owing to the maladministration of *one* steamship company the idea of a subsidized line of steam packets has become odious to the American people; but it becomes the legislators of the country to boldly confront a prejudice when the public good clearly demands it, only guarding our legislation in such manner that the faults or crimes of one company shall not operate to the injury of others.

This can be avoided by granting subsidies to specific routes in proportion to the normal amount of trade and the maritime risks. No general law should be considered. It seems as if the cost of *marine insurance* upon the capital invested would form a just estimate for a government subsidy. At the present time this would amount to about 8 per cent. per annum. No subsidy should extend beyond ten years.

Granting, then, that subsidized steamship lines are essential to the commercial prosperity of the country and our real greatness as a nation, it follows that these steamships should be so constructed that while they are *commerce savers* in time of peace, they may become *commerce destroyers* in time of war. In other words, they become part of a navy, utilized in commercial pursuits in time of peace. By the very necessities of the work they are expected to perform, the mail packet *must* be very fast, faster than the fighting ship, pure and simple, can be made, and combine the other qualities essential for a man-of-war.

These mail steamers thus become the skirmishers of the ocean in time of war, as useful to the friend and as fatal to the foe, owing to their great speed, as the more ponderous regular war ships. They are also transports ready made for troops and stores.

But these are not the only qualities which connect the mail-packet service to the Navy proper. During the late war the Navy drew from the merchant marine *four thousand five hundred officers* — deck officers and engineers. This is, perhaps, not the place to eulogize these men who jumped as it were into fighting gear at a moment's warning from the peaceful pursuits of commerce to the intricate duties of the man-of-war. How creditably the new duties were performed and how vital they were to success, the Navy and the country have often acknowledged. That these men did not possess the military training of the regular, no one denies, but the records of that war show that wherever the fight was the thickest or the gale the heaviest, there they were in the midst of them. But this is not all. During the war *sixty thousand men*, the rank and file of the Navy, came in from the merchant service. Should another war come upon us — and, if any, it is to be hoped a foreign war — where are these ships, these officers and men to come from, unless the mercantile marine of the country is restored to its former prestige? Are we to hire some belligerent to fight our battles? Is the boundless empire of the ocean, is the sceptre of the sea, to pass entirely from our hands under a policy which fears to risk a dollar for the chance of gaining a thousand? Are the United States and China to be joint apostles of inertness and consequent insignificance upon the world's great battle field — the mighty deep?

But if the mercantile marine is so essential to the Navy it is safe to say that the Navy is no less indispensable to commerce. The Navy is, indeed, the pioneer of commerce.

In the pursuit of new channels the trader seeks not only the unfrequented paths upon the ocean, but the unfrequented ports of the world. He needs the constant protection of the flag and the gun. He deals with barbarous tribes — with men who appreciate only the argument of physical force. The old paths of commerce are well known, but as manufactures increase, new markets must be found and new roads opened. The man-of-war precedes the merchantman and impresses rude people with the sense of the power of the flag which covers the one and the other.

It is hardly necessary to remind you of the history of the American Navy; it is interwoven with commercial enterprise upon the sea and linked to every act which has made the nation great. It suppressed piracy in the Mediterranean when even the great nations of Europe were paying tribute to the Barbary powers. It swept the West India islands and adjacent seas clear of the pirate hordes, which had hitherto defied England, France, and Spain. It went into the war of 1812 with the motto of "free trade and sailors' rights," and came out of that war with this principle vindicated against "all comers." It was during this war that Porter opened the trade of the Pacific Ocean to the whaling fleet of America, and incidentally to general American commerce. It conquered California, and added it by almost bloodless victories to the galaxy of States — this under Stockton. It opened the Empire of Japan to America and the world, starting a new era in the East, and adding another nation to the great family of civilized peoples — this under Perry.

Travel where you may over the boundless sea, you will find the American flag has been there before you, and the American

Navy has left its imprint on every shore — no less in peace than in war. Wilkes in the South Seas; Kane, Hartstene, De Haven, in the Arctic regions; Berryman and Belknap defining telegraphic plateaus; Lull, Selfridge, Collins and Shufeldt, piercing the Cordilleras in search of inter-oceanic routes; Herndon and Gibbon across the continent of South America and down the Amazon; Maury, the geographer of the seas, with his wind and current charts, making the paths of commerce plain to the commonest understanding; Jenkins, the founder of the light-house system, dotting the coast of America with its lights, buoys, and beacons, now as safe to the mariner as the gas-lighted street to the wayfarer; the Coast Survey, with its unequalled charts and sailing directions for thousands of miles of shore, and bay and river; Wyman, in the Hydrographic Office, watching every discovery of shoal or rock upon the ocean, and warning the somewhat heedless mariner of his danger. Nor should we forget the National Observatory, with its insignificant means and dilapidated buildings, yet holding its place among the scientific institutions of the world.

All this, while acting as the police of every sea, the Navy has done in the aid and for the aggrandizement of American commerce.

Nor has this mission ended, nor will it ever end, unless Congress cripples this arm of the national defense. Last year the United States had upon the ocean, in the shape of products of export and import, property to the amount of $1,132,000,000. This immense sum involving the credit of thousands of individuals, and in no small degree the prosperity of the nation itself, was more or less directly under the guardianship of the Navy — its officers and men.

But the connection of the Navy with commerce does not end here. It is educating five or six hundred American boys per annum; many of whom at the age of twenty-one years will go into the merchant service, thoroughly disciplined and drilled to become its officers and seamen, taught to believe in the flag which floats over them, and proud of the country of their birth. These boys are saved from idleness, and perhaps from vice and crime, to become hardy and brave men. The first tap of the drum which signals danger to the nation will rally them around the flag. Do not these facts compensate in a great degree for the expense of maintaining a navy? If they do not, then this nation is a mere myth, and national progress an utter absurdity. I, for one, however, still believe in the inherent greatness of our people. I believe that our merchant marine and our Navy are joint apostles, destined to carry all over the world the creed upon which its institutions are founded, and under which its marvellous growth in a century of existence has been assured. Actuated by these considerations, I have to recommend:

First. A subisdy to steamship lines for carrying the mails on certain specified routes at specific rates. I am opposed to any general law which may enable any one company to bid for all routes; ships to be built of iron, three thousand tons and upwards; to be manned by American seamen, and compelled to take as apprentices five boys to every one thousand tons of burden; and to have a speed of thirteen knots. These ships to be inspected when ready for sea, and annually thereafter, by a board of naval officers, who are to report to the Secretary of the Navy, and he to inform the Postmaster General whenever the ships do not come up to the requirements of their contract.

Second. I have to suggest such a re-organization of the executive departments of the Government as may be necessary to place all governmental maritime interests under one department, to be designated as the Marine Department, the head of which is to be styled the "Secretary of Marine."

At present I find the following distinctive branches of the public service under the control of the Secretary of the Treasury as mere additions to an overgrown and cumbersome department, viz., Light-House service, Coast Survey, Revenue Marine and Life-Saving service.

It needs no argument to prove the advantages which would accrue to the country, both in effectiveness and economy, if these duties, so intimately connected with the sea, could be transferred to a marine department. Much of this duty is now performed by naval officers who are under the orders of the Secretary of the Treasury. The "Revenue Marine" officers should be transferred to the Navy proper on some principle of assimilated rank and the vessels be made to form a part and parcel of the Navy itself. The "Life-Saving Service" should also form a "Coast Guard" and be placed under Naval laws and discipline.

The unification of these various branches under one head would not only create harmony, so essential to efficiency, but, in my opinion, would result, as I have said before, in a measurable economy of money and materials.

These services have grown up without any organized plan, and the founders of them deserve great credit for what they have accomplished under many obstacles and prejudices; but it seems to me the time is now opportune for a simplification of a complex system without violating the obligations which the Government has incurred toward any body of men.

The *"Navy pension fund"* should also be under the absolute control of the "Secretary of Marine," and all claims upon it adjudicated by him. It is manifest that these claims should be adjusted in the department where the records are filed.

The *"Signal Service,"* now under the War Department, belongs, by the nature of its duties in connection with commerce, to the Marine Department; and the officers of the Navy employed in the Live-Saving and Coast-Guard service, could and should perform all of its duties so far as the sea and lake coast are concerned.

Third. The *training of boys* for the Navy, and incidentally for the merchant service, should be made a permanent institution, imperative upon the Navy Department, and no longer subject to the judgment or discretion of any individual Secretary. It should become one of the institutions of the country, as much so as our public school system.

The "rank and file" of the Navy has hitherto been neglected as if education was not as important to the seaman as to the officer — each in his sphere. The statue books of our legislation show an absence of law either for the protection or improvement of this class of our citizens, strangely inconsistent with our institutions. There is no other country in the world which does not foster its seamen as a class of its people who contribute in a large degree to its prosperity in time of peace and to its protection in time of war.

These suggestions, which, if adopted, would employ every graduate of the naval academy in a way improving to himself and useful to the country, are, nevertheless, only hints to the committee who have our Naval affairs in charge. They have occurred to me in the course of study of the subject which you asked me to consider, viz., "the relation of the Navy to the commerce of the United States." This subject has grown on my hands until, while I see great possibilities of good in legislation upon this subject, I realize how much it needs the study of any legislator who desires to advance the interests of the whole country.

5

A GRANDIOSE BUT ABORTIVE EXPAN-SIONIST PLAN

One of the outstanding demagogues of American history, Benjamin F. Butler of Massachusetts (1818–1893), turned the country's attention north-ward at every possible opportunity. He longingly anticipated the day when the Stars and Stripes would fly over all the territory from the Rio Grande to the North Pole. We are not certain whether Butler took these grandiose schemes seriously, or was merely making political capital by baiting Britain for the benefit of his Irish-American constituency.

After supporting the Southern Democrats in 1860, Butler became a Union General and was best known for his ruthless occupation of Baltimore early in the war. He was in command in New Orleans follow-ing the fall of that city to the Union, and his rule there earned him the nickname of "Beast." Later, as a Representative, he "managed" the impeachment trial of President Andrew Johnson for the House Radicals before the Senate. Butler served in Congress from 1867–1875 and again from 1877–1879. Three years later he was elected Governor of Mas-sachusetts and in 1884 was nominated by both the Anti-Monopoly and Greenback parties for President.

While some enthusiasts favored territorial expansion northward across the border, our interests in Canada were largely commercial. Canadian-American relations were continuously vexed by the fisheries dispute, the longest-lasting diplomatic dispute in our history. Despite the sabre-rattling typified by Butler, the most effective pressure for closer American-Canadian relations stemmed from cool-headed businessmen who had industrial rather than territorial appetites.

SHOULD THERE BE A UNION OF THE ENGLISH-SPEAKING PEOPLES OF THE EARTH?

Benjamin F. Butler

... All know the fact that two English-speaking nations lie here side by side, divided by a conventional line only of more than six thousand miles in length. One the Dominion of Canada, a dependency of a European monarchy; the other the mightiest of republics, now beyond all peradventure a *Nation,* whose duty and mission it is to maintain the principles of self-government of the people of all nations. Our own military power and strength, our financial and commercial condition, our enormous resources and their extent, are fully known and considered, and we are approaching an exhaustive census which shall make known all these to the world in their minutest detail, so that pondering upon them we may arrive at certain just conclusions as to what our future may be.

But how is it with our neighbor on the northern side of this astronomical line? Are such kindred subjects concerning her as fully understood as they should be? because we are compelled to take into consideration how far her future may be a controlling element in our own.

We hear men, some of whom hold positions which statesmen should fill, speak of the annexation of Canada to this country with the same levity as one in the ordinary walks of life might speak of the jointing of a tail to a dog, — a little difficult to do, but of itself a very small matter.

How should this be spoken of if the tail might happen to be larger than the dog? In my belief this frivolous talk, belittling alike to Canada and insulting to the might and power of Great Britain, is one of the chief obstacles to what every patriot in the United States, and every Englishman in Canada, if not in the empire, must, if the question is fully understood, greatly desire, — the union of these two great English-speaking peoples on this continent, which must happen if democracy is not to be a failure, so that this continent shall be the home and exemplar of English freedom and of the

FROM *Should There Be a Union of the English-Speaking Peoples of the Earth?* A dissertation, delivered before the alumni of Colby University . . ., July 2, 1889 (Boston, 1889).

English language, as modified and improved by American genius and American enterprise.

The first great fact to be taken into contemplation when we speak so lightly of the annexation of Canada is her immense area, which includes 40 per cent. of all the possessions of Great Britain, wherever situated on the globe.

If Disraeli had made the Queen of Great Britain Empress of Canada, which he would have done if he had considered the facts as we are about to discuss them and the relation of Canada to the rest of Great Britain, the British empire would indeed have been like in extent to the empire of Rome.

Empress of India indeed! There is room for three British Indian possessions within the Dominion of Canada and enough territory left over out of which the area of Great Britain might be five times taken.

Modern empires are pigmies to it, for there is room in Canada to carve out nine German empires.

Victoria, Empress of Canada! If the Dominion can be held in the future generations, which are but hours in the lifetime of nations, the English Empress would be the ruler of the greatest and most powerful English-speaking people, civilized and Christianized, such as nowhere exists now, but must exist in the future, if the laws by which the growth of nations continue, under which they have been laid out and begun. . . .

Canada and her surrounding waters contain quite one-half of all the fresh water of the globe. Please bear this great fact in mind, for, I repeat, it is a foundation of the resources to make one of the greatest nations on earth.

The general idea when thinking of Canada is that her high latitudes must be regions of Arctic cold. Cursory thought takes but little else than this into consideration when dealing with matters of climate. Humboldt says that many other matters which we cannot here stop to specify must be taken into consideration in determining the temperature of a given portion of the earth's surface, and its adaptability to the culture of the cereals, roots, and vegetables that go to support human life.

I may be permitted to mention one, however, which has very much to do with climate. A condition which most sensibly affects climate, and is most rarely taken into consideration, is *altitude*; that is, the height of the given lands and waters above the level of the sea. The waters of Lake Superior, among the very highest fresh waters of Canada, are six hundred feet only above tide-water.

These waters of Lake Superior are rarely, if ever, to any considerable extent frozen over. The immense body of waters known as Hudson's bay, one thousand miles long and six hundred miles wide, thrust deep into the centre of Canada, and which, in ordinary comprehension, being connected with the waters of the Arctic ocean, is deemed to be wholly frozen over for a great part of the year, averages three or four degrees higher temperature than the waters on the south-western shores of Lake Superior. This higher temperature is, perhaps, due to the fact that Hudson's bay is tide-water. And we must remember that on the south-western shores of Lake Superior lie Michigan, Wisconsin, and Minnesota *of our North-west.*

Do we claim any States more flourishing, any land more fruitful, or any part of the United States which has made greater progress than the great North-west to which the Star of Empire takes its way?

It is supposed these upper cold and sterile regions require nothing either to be carried to them or brought from them. They have scarcely entered into our calculations as a portion of the peopled globe. Yet, let me give you another statistical fact.

Cast your eye in imagination on the map, and you will observe a strait connecting the chain of lakes below with Lake Superior. Our Government has dug a small canal for the purposes of navigation, to obliterate the falls of *"Sault Ste. Marie."* It was not thought of much significance when built. Its navigation would only supply the frozen regions of the North and the shores of Lake Superior, the vessels to pass through it carrying up tools, such as the settlers wanted, some necessaries mayhap, and other supplies, and bringing back perchance some furs and a little lumber — almost a doubtful experiment at best.

But let us see how much is needed in that sterile territory of the far North-west. In 1888 that canal carried north and brought south articles and productions which are most needful for the support of the human race, including *twenty-three million* bushels of wheat, *six million four hundred and eleven thousand four hundred and twenty-three* tons of freight, while the Suez canal, over which the greatest nations of Europe and Africa have quarrelled, and which is fed by the commerce of two hemispheres, carried *six million six hundred and forty thousand eight hundred and thirty* tons, but took twelve months to do it in, while the little canal of the falls of *Sault Ste. Marie* had but seven in which to do nearly an equal amount.

The lands of Canada not fertile! She has quite one-quarter more land fitted for wheat cultivation than has the whole United States. The average production of wheat per acre in the United States in the year 1887 was a little over twelve bushels, while in the same year in Manitoba, where we hardly realize there is aught to support life, the yield was *twelve million five hundred thousand* bushels, at an average of twenty-seven bushels to the acre.

It may be safely said, — for I will trouble you with a few more statistics, — that leaving out the worn-out wheat lands of the United States, Canada has twice the extent of unworn-out lands, which produce an average of more than twice the number of bushels to the acre than are produced by the average lands of the United States, and on some lands of Canada wheat has been raised in the largest producing quantities for twenty years in succession without a fertilizer.

You may ask, and I will turn aside from the thread of my discussion to answer, "Why should these lands be better wheat-producing lands than those of the United States?" Because that climate is colder in the winter and hotter in the summer. The dry, cold air of winter freezes the ground to a given and permanently frozen depth, destroying quite all insect life unfavorable to the growth of vegetation. In the growing season the hot sun pours down upon and warms the ground to a given depth; the rootlets of the wheat penetrate toward a line of frost which continually exudes moisture, and the two hours' longer day in summer, warming the growing plants which never feel the need of moisture from refreshing showers, gives a crop of wheat in abundance unequalled in the world.

If I have not already convinced you of the resources of Canada, I will add that she has more timber in herself than she and the United States can need of every possible description in one hundred years. She has more iron and coal in her borders than any other country yet known to the world. She has more copper than any other country, if not all others. The northern shores of Lake Superior are more capable of the production of that metal than the southern.

I have brought to your attention the resources of Canada, not with that particularity of detail that I might well do, because time forbids, and my only object is to convince you of the startling facts of the increasing power of the north-west of Canada as it joins upon us, and to bring further to your attention the increase of our own country in power and strength by the enterprise of its inhabitants, from the fecundity in production of children, with all the adjuncts and accompaniments for a reduction of unoccupied and unexplored territory, proceeding from the Middle and Northwestern States, not only to the north-western parts of our own territory, but to Canada.

The political effect of this great increase of national power has suddenly developed itself by the admission of four new States into the Union, in addition to Iowa, Wisconsin, Michigan, and Minnesota, to which the nation will soon look as a great factor in the direction of its political affairs, all of which are on the very north westernmost part of our territory.

As we have a fixed line at the North, the great tide of emigration which is still flowing to the North-west flows over into Canada, where the settlers find an equal climate and a congenial people.

Comparing the progress of our other territories lying in more temperate climes with that of the bleak North-west, the results reached are exceedingly interesting and striking, demanding all a patriot's careful study of the future.

In 1848 the United States became possessed of a very large tract of country by conquest and purchase from Mexico. From that territory since that time we have only a part of Colorado, Nevada, and California, the latter being the most considerable State. Colorado has a climate which would seem almost at first glance, from its temperature, to be uninhabitable, especially with the accompaniments of droughts and blizzards. Nevada is hardly more than a respectable agricultural county in New England in population, and she came to a State simply from her silver mines, as California substantially did from her gold mines. The rest of this magnificent Mexican territory is blessed with the most healthy and congenial climate, and largely, as it has turned out, with a fertile soil, with plains on which cattle feed and roam to the number of millions, and mines of fabulous wealth.

From all this territory, which seems almost a paradise, *never a single State has come to increase our national power.*

Why not? Because of the rule, which is a universal one, that a climate which abounds in genial skies and warmth that enervates, and at the same time produces a vegetable and animal creation most luxuriantly, whether on the eastern shores of the Pacific or the western shores of the Atlantic Ocean, does not produce the men and women who make the energetic life-blood of the nation. Human experience has been that the climate that allows man to get enough for his personal comfort without any considerable exertion also makes that man pause at that point, and he will make scarce further exertion.

That rule is not confined to any race or color or condition of men.

We are accustomed to say that our Southern States have not increased because of slavery; but our Southern Territories have not increased, and we took great care to keep slavery out of them. They have every advantage, but the imperative law is that no men are fit for anything but those who must work in order to eat and be warm.

It will be seen, therefore, that looking in this direction the colored problem at the South is of no considerable importance. We cannot grow great in Southern climes, except, possibly, in numbers. If the colored race shall be so far prosperous as to maintain its great fecundity in children, black or white, all enterprise and energy are controlled by a climatic line.

If, hereafter, as we may hope and expect soon, we acquire Mexico and Central America, even to the isthmus, still the rule will hold that we may have accession of territory and of people, but not of any considerable power or strength of empire.

By her Indian possessions England got much of territory and much of people and great wealth; but from the people and land no accession of power to her empire has come, save in the northern part thereof, very lately, by the production of wheat to supply her home consumption. The increase of her military strength because thereof is simply an increase of weakness, requiring more white men to take care of such class of inhabitants than soldiers acquired, whose numbers in place thereof will make good that army.

We must keep in mind that Mexico has been inhabited by the Latin race more than twice as long as New York and New England have been settled. When Spain came into possession she was an empire in organization, with riches untold and men in nations. In a climate that permits generations to deteriorate, where is that power now?

The climatic advantages of Canada are that it is cold enough to compel everybody to work in order to live, and the land is fertile enough to give every man abundant returns for his labor.

Hence results the wealth of the nation and the enterprise of its people.

Can it happen otherwise, therefore, than that the men who hold the north-western part of our country and the south-western part of Canada, with an intermingling climate, — for the cattle of Montana and Dakota are driven across the line to Winnipeg, as a regulation of business, for what can be found growing there for the support of animal life in the winter, — that those men of congenitive race and corresponding habits of thought and independence of action will be brought together, so that the hold of a supposed loyalty to a far-off monarchy, which ere long may be no monarchy at all, cannot keep them apart.

The Monroe doctrine, as applied to the southern part of the continent, precludes this Government from tolerating, in so far as it may interfere, the establishment of any kingly government over a people on this continent. The same idea might preclude a foreign government from continuing a hold upon the allegiance of another class of men who will be soon immensely superior, both in numbers, strength, and power, to our fathers of the Revolution, so as to prevent them from declaring independence, their condition then being such that there can be no fear of any attempt to crush the will of such a people by arms, and no Germans for sale to aid the mother country in enslaving her people.

We have seen that the expansion of our country from ocean to ocean makes a limit to its extension east and west; that the proximity of the equator on the south may not add to us peoples which will increase our strength, our enterprise, or our capacity for self-government, and that we must look only to the north for that class and condition of men in whose hands we would be most willing to confide the future destiny of our country, with the confident hope that it shall revolutionize the world so far as any of its peoples are capable of receiving and maintaining the blessings of civil and religious liberty, controlled by laws enacted by popular intelligence.

Why did not Canada join with the rest of the country in declaring its independence of Great Britain? There was a time when all our colonies were most loyal to the crown, fighting its battles against France and Spain with a strength, fervor, and determination which was wonderful. The answer must be found in observing the elements which controlled Canada from the first. Canada was the most considerable of the colonies of France. Indeed, she had scarce any other colonies, except some unimportant islands. She was first on this continent, but her colonial organizations were like those of Mexico on the eastern shores of the Pacific.

Religious missions took charge of the colonies under the special auspices of the Romish Church, claiming their object to be the Christianization of the Indian tribes. Commencing at some of the easternmost islands of Canada, thence overflowing upon the mainlands at Cape Breton in Nova Scotia, the lines of colonization centred along the St. Lawrence and around the city of Quebec, which the military genius of France soon made the Gibraltar of America. Thence along the river, across the Great Lakes, they planted their missions on the Mississippi, descending that waterway toward New Orleans and Louisiana, where their second most important settlement was founded. The military foresight of their engineers contrived to plan a chain of forts along the St. Lawrence to the lakes, thence down the navigable rivers until they struck the Mississippi, thereby enclosing the whole British possessions of North America in that line which France believed she could maintain against Great Britain and her colonies by the aid of the Indian tribes, then supposed to be powerful enough for that purpose, and with whom France never had a war. The scheme was a magnificent one, and it was quite successfully, as at first, carried out. As we have said, Quebec was the most aggressive and enterprising part of that colony from the necessity of its climate and the consequent physical organization of its people. All of its inhabitants were of the devoutest sects of Catholics. The hand of the Jesuits was actively felt there longer than in most Catholic countries. It differed only in its thorough devotion to a government by the Almighty directly, a theocracy, from the New Englanders who were equally bigoted and devout, and insisted that their government was a theocracy, controlled from the hand of God himself, while the Canadian believed that his government was the same, only it came through the medium and agency of the Catholic Church.

Between these two colonies there was the most intense and uncompromising hatred. This was fanned into a flame which burned up every idea that anything that a New Englander could do was right, in the minds of the French, by what is known as the French and Indian War, commencing about 1755. The results of that war were exceedingly disastrous to the French power and to the French colonies in the North.

The French settlements in Nova Scotia and Breton, called Acadia, were seized upon, and the quiet, unoffending people were carried off by the soldiers of Massachusetts, distributed in Massachusetts, some in New Hampshire, some in the bleak island of Prince Edward, and some in North Carolina, and some even taken and disposed of in the French colony of New Orleans. Then came the fall of Louisburg, the next most considerable fortress to Quebec, and the incursions upon and occupation of the island of Newfoundland. Next came the attack upon Quebec, which was lost to the French by the Quixotic bravery of Montcalm, who threw away the advantage of holding the strong citadel by meeting Wolfe on the open field. This victory substantially ended that war, as far as America was concerned.

It had involved France, Spain, and England and all their colonies in every part of the world, and the treaty of 1762 — known as the treaty of Paris — was exceedingly destructive of French interests, by which many great and important religious questions were finally adjusted. It became imperative that the See of Rome should relinquish either her ecclesiastical rights and powers over her French subjects, or her Spanish subjects in America. Cuba had been seized by the English forces led by Massachusetts. Pensacola and Florida had been captured from the kingdom of Spain, and all the colonies of France in North America had been substantially surrendered to England. The colonization and settlements of the province of Quebec had been, as we have seen, substantially religious missions, including what lay farther south and west. All the line of posts by which France had meant to enclose the English colonies from Louisiana north had been lost and that scheme abandoned. The loss of the ever-faithful isle, Cuba, to Spain and the Church was one that could not be submitted to; so it was agreed that Florida should be relinquished by Spain, and Cuba released to her in its stead, and that the province of Quebec and all its dependencies on the mainland should be given to England, fishing rights in several of the eastern islands only being reserved to France, by which their Catholic population might be fed with fish in Lent, as also some two or three small islands among the West Indies. But the Church insisted that as the English colonies adjacent to the province of Quebec had been settled, especially New Hampshire and Massachusetts on the east, by people most fully and determinedly hostile to the Catholic Church, where Puritan New England contended with the Irish Calvinists of the covenant in furious hate of that religious establishment which they derided as the "whore of Babylon," the treaty could only be permitted to be signed after the most carefully considered and effective provision therein to protect Catholic rights and ecclesiastical powers, and some almost temporal, by the most solemn forms of a treaty between three nations, two of them children of the Church.

It is curious to observe how those religious quarrels have affected the conditions of Canada and the English colonies of North America and their descendants even to this day. When our fathers came to the conclusion to throw off their allegiance to Great Britain, agents were sent to Quebec to have Canada join with the English colonies in the endeavor to eject English government from the continent, and to a casual observer it would seem that there was every prospect of success, because the province of Quebec, which was substantially all there was then of political organized power in the Canadas, was, as it has been many times since, quite in a state of insurrection against Great Britain, and would delight in getting rid of British Domination altogether. But the Protestant New Englanders who led the rebellion had not reckoned with the Pope in the matter. He at once foresaw that if Canada joined the rebellion, and the rebellion did not succeed, all the rights of the Catholics under the treaty of Paris would be lost. If the revolution did succeed, then the province of Quebec was but a province of thirteen others who joined together to make a confederacy, and all the assurances that the Catholic Church would not be overthrown by the disciples of Cromwell were gone forever. Therefore Canada did not join the rebellion, and as nine-tenths of the inhabitants were Catholics she remained true to England, ...

The same condition of differences in religious opinion continues almost to the present hour. The strongest opposition to annexation appearing in Canada has always been found in the province of Quebec. The eastern provinces have in them a very considerable minority of favorers of annexation, as undoubtedly is their interest in every condition of commercial and financial concern. The vexing fishery question would have been settled long since by Nova Scotia, New Brunswick, Cape Breton, and Newfoundland, which has not yet become a part of the Dominion of Canada, had all those provinces stood with Newfoundland as they did in the early organization of the Dominion.

The Catholic opposition is very much ameliorated. When we made our treaty with Mexico of Guadaloupe Hidalgo, we gave very strong guarantees that the religious condition of our acquired territory should never be interfered with or church property disturbed, and Rome knows how religiously and carefully we have kept our pledged faith in that regard.

We have persecuted nobody in that territory for their religious opinion, save the Mormons.

Because of the strong Catholic element in the United States, there need not ever be the least fear that any treaty or act of Congress by which the rights of the Catholic people and Church in Canada may be guaranteed, would ever be disturbed. All apprehensions on the part of the people of any disturbánce of their religious rights or opinions have passed away, because within the last decade nearly half a million of French subjects have come to Puritan New England to make their home, and have found that their religious rights are as faithfully and well preserved to them here as at home. So it would now seem that if the Catholic Church shall look, as it might well do, to North America for a strong, powerful, and influential body of adherents, there should be formed and established a closer union between their Canadian adherents and those in the United

States in a government where both would protect the Church by their votes, instead of the adherents in Canada being left wholly without power to aid the Church in any political or governmental matter.

Why, then, is it necessary for statesman or priest to contemplate the declaration or enforcement of the independence of Canada, if there is a possibility of union of that country with the United States?

The problem seems to me to be this: Does Canada desire a union with the United States? If she so signifies her wish in a recognizable form, England has no power to prevent it. If Canada does not, then England has no power to enact it. She may throw Canada off as a dependency, but she cannot throw her upon the United States. Would not the more feasible, the more sensible, nay, the more statesmanlike and effective, manner of bringing together the United States and Canada, and ultimately both in a common bond of political union with Great Britain herself, especially as in a few years Great Britain may be a republic, the form of her government seeming to be not substantially in the way now, be to enter into negotiations for that purpose, carefully and in the most friendly spirit, the negotiators in charge having only one idea in common; that is, how can the three peoples best get together.

England and the United States are just recovering from irritations of unpleasant memories of the wars of the Revolution, of 1812, and of the late rebellion, and there is nothing to renew any unhappy controversy between the two nations save the fishery questions, which would readily settle themselves under a wise and sagacious diplomacy, which should be between the two nations, and not between this nation on the one side and Canada on the other. Our late attempted negotiations and enactments — for diplomacy they could not be called — will only result in raising ill feeling on the part of our neighbors, because of the annoying thought that for the first time in the history of diplomacy has a province been left to carry on a diplomatic struggle with a nation almost without the aid of the parent country, under a threat from the opposing nation that the consequences of failure or treaty were to be visited on the province alone. Why should not, instead of this paltry and narrow matter, the diplomacy be that negotiations should be approached with a view of uniting the two adjacent English-speaking peoples, lying side by side in America, in the same commercial and business relations between each other, with or without a zollverein, as may be determined, leaving Great Britain, whose institutions depend upon the same constitutional provisions, and whose laws of freedom give equal protection to their several peoples, later on, when her interest or safety demands, to come into like compact with the United States and Canada, a league against the world, if any part of the world should see fit to take such a stand, which none would or could successfully do.

Negotiations conducted on such a basis and for such an end could be carried on without touching the pride or arousing jealousies, with none but the kindest sentiments being evolved in either people. Concessions would not be required of either nation. They are coming together.

Two great navies to menace each other, with their enormous equipment and consequent expenditures and losses by decays, would at once be dispensed with. A small, inexpensive navy of each could bid the world defiance, and be used only to emphasize messages which might as well be sent by telegraph. All Europe and Asia joined together in battle array, if such a thing were possible, against the English-speaking people of the globe, would pause in dismay before any hostile step should be taken against such a united power.

Such a national combination would, within its own borders, have everything that would be necessary to carry on a defensive or offensive warfare, and its borders would be the compass of the globe.

Why should we not look to such a union as the means of spreading the Christian religion in its most enlightened form, permitting every sect equal rights to bring into its fold its own proselytes in its own way, against the atheism or agnosticism of an erring world?

Take another view: such a united power as I have sketched would save all the other nations of Europe from final and inevitable bankruptcy because of maintaining immense armies and navies, to the destruction of their people, to hold each other in check.

To that English-speaking league every nation would be obliged to submit for arbitrament every cause of differences, if not out of fear of its armed intervention, yet because of its holding the money of the world. No war could be carried on which that power should disapprove, and any nation might disarm who should be protected even by promise of financial aid from the pledge of the united English-speaking people of the earth.

With America and England uniting their means of production and transportation of that which sustains life and secures comfort, no want or famine could ever come; and within a century a universal language could pervade the world, thus relieving it from the punishment inflicted on mankind by the Lord Almighty at the tower of Babel.

6

A GRAND SCHEME FOR EXPANSION: DARWIN'S CONTRIBUTION

 John Fiske (1842–1901), librarian at Harvard University, was both a philosopher and historian. From his prolific pen came many works in American history which proved to be among the most popular of his time. Among his writings were *American Political Ideas* (1885), *The Critical Period of American History* (1888), *The War of Independence* (1889), and *The Mississippi Valley in the Civil War* (1900). Fiske did more to arouse interest in American history than almost any man of his time, but his writings, although charming and persuasive in style, were superficial and usually evolved from his lively lectures rather than profound scholarship.

Fiske turned his pen to explaining Darwinian principles and, as a firm believer in the concept of the "survival of the fittest" and "natural adaptation," he was instrumental in reconciling such ideas of traditional religion as the Creation with the new evolutionary principles of biology. Manifest Destiny — the dominion of "advanced" nations over "lesser breeds beneath the law" — was for Fiske the supreme example of Anglo-Saxon superiority. Viewed in this light, American expansionism served a needed mission for the underdeveloped peoples were in sore need of the benefits of white civilization. An extreme chauvinist, Fiske helped form the Immigration Restriction League in the 1890s which eventually achieved its goal in 1924 with the virtual closing of the gates to the "new" immigrant. The "new" Manifest Destiny, which paved the way for the expansionist splurge of 1898, owed much to this historian's oratory and prose.

MANIFEST DESTINY

John Fiske   We have seen how desirable it is that self-governing groups of men should be enabled to work together in permanent harmony and on a great scale. In this kind of political integration the work of civilization very largely consists. We have seen how in its most primitive form political society is made up of small self-governing groups that are perpetually at war with one another. Now the process of change which we call civilization means quite a number of things, but there is no doubt that it means primarily the gradual substitution of a state of peace for a state of war. This change is the condition precedent for all the other kinds of improvement that are connoted by such a term as "civilization." Manifestly the development of industry is largely dependent upon the cessation or restriction of warfare; and furthermore, as the industrial phase of civilization slowly supplants the military phase, men's characters undergo, through very slowly, a corresponding change. Men become less inclined to destroy life or to inflict pain; or to use the popular terminology, which happens to coincide precisely with that of the doctrine of evolution, they become less *brutal* and more *humane*. Obviously, then, the primary phase of the process called civilization is the general diminution of warfare. But we have seen that a general diminution of warfare is rendered possible only by the union of small political groups into larger groups that are kept together by community of interests, and that can adjust their mutual relations by legal discussion, without coming to blows. . . .

Let us consider now to what conclusions the rapidity and unabated steadiness of the increase of the English race in America must lead us as we go on to forecast the future. Carlyle somewhere speaks slightingly of the fact that the Americans double their numbers every twenty years, as if to have forty million dollar-hunters in the world were any better than to have twenty million dollar-hunters. The implication that Americans are nothing but dollar-hunters, and are thereby distinguishable from the rest of mankind, would not perhaps bear too elaborate scrutiny. But during the present paper we have been considering the gradual transfer of the preponderance of physical strength from the hands of the war-loving portion of the human race into the hands of the peace-loving portion — into the hands of the dollar-hunters, if you please, but out of the hands of the scalp-hunters. Obviously to double the numbers of a preeminently industrious, peaceful, orderly, and free-thinking commu-

FROM *Harper's New Monthly Magazine*, LXX (March, 1885), pp. 578–90.

nity is somewhat to increase the weight in the world of the tendencies that go toward making communities free and orderly and peaceful and industrious. So that, from this point of view, the fact we are speaking of is well worth considering, even for its physical dimensions. I do not know whether the United States could support a population everywhere as dense as that of Belgium, so I will suppose that, with ordinary improvement in cultivation and in the industrial arts, we might support a population half as dense as that of Belgium, and this is no doubt an extremely moderate supposition. Now a very simple operation in arithmetic will show that this means a population of fifteen hundred millions, or more than the population of the whole world at the present date. Another very simple operation in arithmetic will show that if we were to go on doubling our numbers even once in every twenty-five years, we should reach that stupendous figure at about the close of the twentieth century, that is, in the days of our great-great-grandchildren. I do not predict any such result, for there are discernible economic reasons for believing that there will be a diminution in the rate of increase. The rate must nevertheless continue to be very great in the absence of such causes as formerly retarded the growth of population in Europe. Our modern wars are hideous enough, no doubt, but they are short. They are settled with a few heavy blows, and the loss of life and property occasioned by them is but trifling when compared with the awful ruin and desolation wrought by the perpetual and protracted contests of antiquity and of the Middle Ages. Chronic warfare, both private and public, periodic famines, and sweeping pestilences like the Black Death — these were the things which formerly shortened human life and kept down population. In the absence of such causes, and with the abundant capacity of our country for feeding its people, I think it an extremely moderate statement if we say that by the end of the next century the English race in the United States will number at least six or seven hundred millions.

It used to be said that so huge a people as this could not be kept together as a single national aggregate, or, if kept together at all, could only be so by means of a powerful centralized government, like that of ancient Rome under the emperors. I think we are now prepared to see that this is a great mistake. If the Roman Empire could have possessed that political vitality in all its parts which is secured to the United States by the principles of equal representation and of limited State sovereignty, it might well have defied all the shocks which tribally organized barbarism could ever have directed against it. As it was, its strong centralized government did not save it from political disintegration. One of its weakest political features was precisely this, that its strong centralized government was a kind of close corporation, governing a score of provinces in its own interest rather than in the interest of the provincials. In contrast with such a system as that of the Roman Empire the skilfully elaborated American system of federalism appears as one of the most important contributions that the English race has made to the general work of civilization. The working out of this feature in our national constitution by Hamilton and Madison and their associates was the finest specimen of constructive statesmanship that the world has ever seen. Not that these statesmen originated the principle, but they gave form and expression to the principle which was latent in the circumstances under which the group of American colonies had grown up, and which suggested itself so forcibly that the clear vision of these thinkers did not fail to seize upon it as the fundamental principle upon which alone could the affairs of a great people, spreading over a vast continent, be kept in a condition approaching to something like permanent peace. Stated broadly, so as to acquire somewhat the force of a universal proposition, the principle of federalism is just this: that the people of a state shall have full and entire control of their own domestic affairs, which directly concern them only, and which they will naturally manage with more intelligence and with more zeal than any distant governing body could possibly exercise; but that, as regards matters of common concern between a group of states, a decision shall in every case be reached, not by brutal warfare or by weary diplomacy, but by the systematic legislation of a central government which represents both states and people, and whose decisions can always be enforced, if necessary, by the combined physical power of all the states. This principle, in various practical applications, is so familiar to Americans to-day that we seldom pause to admire it, any more than we stop to admire the air which we breathe or the sun which gives us light and life. Yet I believe that if no other political result than this could to-day be pointed out as coming from the colonization of America by Englishmen, we should still be justified in regarding that event as one of the most important in the history of mankind. For obviously the principle of federalism, as thus broadly stated, contains within itself the seeds of permanent peace between nations, and to this glorious end I believe it will come in the fullness of time.

And now we may begin to see distinctly what it was that the American goverment fought for in the late civil war — a point which at the time was by no means clearly apprehended outside the United

States. We used to hear it often said, while that war was going on, that we were fighting not so much for the emancipation of the negro as for the maintenance of our federal union; and I doubt not that to many who were burning to see our country purged of the folly and iniquity of negro slavery this may have seemed like taking a low and materialistic view of the case. From the stand-point of universal history it was nevertheless the correct and proper view. The emancipation of the negro, as an incidental result of the struggle, was no doubt a priceless gain, which was greeted warmly by all right-minded people. But deeper down than this question, far more subtly interwoven with the innermost fibres of our national well-being, far heavier laden, too, with weighty consequences for the future weal of all mankind, was the question whether this great pacific principle of union, joined with independence, should be overthrown by the first deep-seated social difficulty it had to en-counter, or should stand as an example of priceless value to other ages and to other lands. The solution was well worth the effort it cost. There have been many useless wars, but this was not one of them, for, more than most wars that have been, it was fought in the direct interest of peace, and the victory so dearly purchased and so humanely used was an earnest of future peace and happiness for the world.

The object, therefore, for which the American government fought was the perpetual maintenance of that peculiar state of things which the federal union had created — a state of things in which, throughout the whole vast territory over which the Union holds sway, questions between States, like questions between individuals, must be settled by legal argument and judicial decisions, and not by wager of battle. Far better to demonstrate this point once for all, at whatever cost, than to be burdened hereafter, like the states of Europe, with frontier fortresses and standing armies and all the barbaric apparatus of mutual suspicion! For so great an end did this most pacific people engage in an obstinate war, and never did any war so thoroughly illustrate how military power may be wielded by a people that has passed entirely from the military into the industrial stage of civili-zation. The events falsified all the predictions that were drawn from the contemplation of societies less advanced politically. It was thought that so peaceful a people could not raise a great army on demand; yet within a twelvemonth the government had raised five hundred thousand men by voluntary enlistment. It was thought that a territory involving military operations at points as far apart as Paris and Moscow could never be thoroughly conquered; yet in April,

1865, the Federal armies might have marched from end to end of the Gulf States without meeting any force to oppose them. It was thought that the maintenance of a great army would beget a military temper in the Americans, and lead to manifestations of Bonapartism — domestic usurpation and foreign aggression; yet the moment the work was done the great army vanished, and a force of twenty-five thousand men was found sufficient for the military needs of the whole country. It was thought that eleven States which had struggled so hard to escape from the federal tie could not be re-admitted to voluntary co-operation in the general government, but must henceforth be held as conquered territory — a most dangerous experiment for any free people to try; yet within a dozen years we find the old federal relations resumed in all their completeness, and the disunion party powerless and discredited in the very States where once it had wrought such mischief.

Such has been the result of the first great attempt to break up the federal union in America. It is not probable that another attempt can ever be made with anything like an equal chance of success. Here were eleven States, geographically contiguous, governed by groups of men who for half a century had pursued a well-defined policy in common, united among themselves, and marked off from most of the other States by a difference far more deeply rooted in the ground-work of society than any mere economic difference — the difference between slave labor and free labor. These eleven States, moreover, held such an economic relationship with England that they counted upon compelling the naval power of England to be used in their behalf. And, finally, it had not yet been demonstrated that the maintenance of the federal union was something for which the great mass of the people would cheerfully fight. Never could the experiment of secession be tried, apparently, under fairer auspices; yet how tremendous the defeat! It was a defeat that wrought conviction — the conviction that no matter how grave the political questions that may arise hereafter, they must be settled in accordance with the legal methods the Constitution has provided, and that no State can be allowed to break the peace. It is the thoroughness of this conviction that has so greatly facilitated the re-instatement of the revolted States in their old federal relations; and the good sense and good faith with which the Southern people, in spite of the chagrin of defeat, have accepted the situation and acted upon it, is something unprecedented in history, and calls for the warmest sympathy and admiration on the part of their brethren of the North. The federal principle in America has passed through this fearful ordeal and come out stronger than ever, and we trust it will not again be put to so severe a test. But, with this principle unimpaired, there is no reason why any further increase of population or of territory should overtask the resources of our government.

In the United States of America a century hence we shall therefore doubtless have a political aggregation immeasurably surpassing in power and dimensions any empire that has as yet existed. But we must now consider for a moment the probable future career of the English race in other parts of the world. The colonization of North America by Englishmen had its direct effects upon the eastern as well as upon the western side of the Atlantic. The immense growth of the commercial and naval strength of England between the time of Cromwell and the time of the elder Pitt was intimately connected with the colonization of North America and the establishment of plantations in the West Indies.

These circumstances reacted powerfully upon the material development of England, multiplying manifold the dimensions of her foreign trade, increasing proportionately her commercial marine, and giving her in the eighteenth century the dominion over the seas. Endowed with this maritime supremacy, she has with an unerring instinct proceeded to seize upon the keys of empire in all parts of the world — Gibraltar, Malta, the Isthmus of Suez, Aden, Ceylon, the coasts of Australia, island after island in the Pacific — every station, in short, that commands the pathways of maritime commerce, or guards the approaches to the barbarous countries which she is beginning to regard as in some way her natural heritage. Any well-filled album of postage stamps is an eloquent commentary on this maritime supremacy of England. It is enough to turn one's head to look over her colonial blue-books. The natural outcome of all this overflowing vitality it is not difficult to foresee. No one can carefully watch what is going on in Africa today without recognizing it as the same sort of thing which was going on in North America in the seventeenth century; and it can not fail to bring forth similar results in course of time. Here is a vast country, rich in beautiful scenery, and in resources of timber and minerals, with a salubrious climate and fertile soil, with great navigable rivers and inland lakes, which will not much longer be left in control of tawny lions and long-eared elephants, and negro fetich-worshippers. Already five flourishing English states have been established in the south, besides the settlements on the Gold Coast, and those at Aden commanding the Red Sea. English explorers work their way with infinite hardship through its untravelled wilds, and track the courses of the Congo and the Nile as their forefathers tracked the Potomac and the Hudson. The work of La Salle and Smith is finding its counterpart in the labors of Baker and Livingstone. Who can doubt that within two or three centuries the African continent will be occupied by a mighty nation of English descent, and covered with populous cities and flourishing farms, with railroads and telegraphs and free schools and other devices of civilization as yet undreamed of? If we look next to Australia we find a country of more than two-thirds the area of the United States, with a temperate climate and immense resources, agricultural and mineral, a country sparsely peopled by a race of irredeemable savages hardly above the level of brutes. Here England within the present century has planted five greatly thriving states, concerning which I have not time to say much, but one fact will serve for an example. When in America we wish to illustrate in one word the wonderful growth of our so-called Northwestern States, we refer to Chicago, a city of half a million inhabitants standing on a spot which fifty years ago was an uninhabited marsh. In Australia the city Melbourne was founded in 1837, the year when the present Queen of England began to reign, and the state of which it is the capital was hence called Victoria. This city, now just forty-eight years old, has a population half that of Chicago, has a public library of 200,000 volumes, and has a university with at least one professor of world-wide renown. When we see, by-the-way, within a period of five years, and at such remote points upon the earth's surface, such erudite and ponderous works in the English language issuing from the press as those of Professor Hearn of Melbourne, of Bishop Colenso of Natal, and of Mr. Hubert Bancroft of San Francisco, even such a little commonplace fact as this is fraught with wonderful significance when we think of all that it implies. Then there is New Zealand, with its climate of perpetual spring, where the English race is now multiplying faster than anywhere else in the world, unless it be in Texas and Minnesota. And there are in the Pacific Ocean many rich and fertile spots where we shall very soon see the same things going on.

It is not necessary to dwell upon such considerations as these. It is enough to point to the general conclusion that the work which the English race began when it colonized North America is destined to go on until every land on the earth's surface that is not already the seat of an old civilization shall become English in its language, in its religion, in its political habits and traditions, and to a predominant extent in the blood of its people. The day is at hand when four-fifths of the human race will trace its pedigree to English forefathers, as four-fifths of the white people in the United States trace their pedigree to-day. The race thus spread over both hemispheres, and from the rising to the setting sun, will not fail to keep that sovereignty of the sea and that commercial supremacy which it began to acquire when England first stretched its arm across the Atlantic to the shores of Virginia and Massachusetts. The language spoken by these great communities will not be sundered into dialects like the language of the ancient Romans, but perpetual intercommunication and the universal habit of reading and writing will preserve its integrity, and the world's business will be transacted by English-speaking people to so great an extent that whatever language any man may have learned in his infancy, he will find it necessary sooner or later to learn to express his thoughts in English. And in this way it is by no means improbable that, as Jacob Grimm long since predicted, the language of Shakespeare will ultimately become the language of mankind.

In view of these considerations as to the stupendous future of the English race, does it not seem very probable that in due course of time Europe, which has learned some valuable lessons from America already, will find it worth while to adopt the lesson of federalism in order to do away with the chances of useless warfare which remain so long as its different states owe no allegiance to any common authority? War, as we have seen, is with barbarous races both a necessity and a favorite occupation; as long as civilization comes in contact with barbarism it remains a too frequent necessity; but as between civilized and Christian nations it is an absurdity. For example, we sympathize keenly with wars such as that which Russia has lately concluded for setting free a kindred race and humbling the worthless barbarian who during four centuries has wrought such incalculable damage to the European world. But a sanguinary struggle for the Rhine frontier, between two civilized Christian nations who have each enough work to do in the world without engaging in such a strife as this, will, I am sure, be by-and-by condemned by the general opinion of mankind. Such questions will have to be settled by discussion in some sort of federal council or parliament if Europe would keep pace with America in the advance toward universal law and order. All will admit that such a state of things is a great desideratum. Let us see if it is really quite as utopian as it may seem at the first glance. No doubt the lord who dwelt in Haddon Hall in the fifteenth century would have thought it very absurd if you had told him that within four hundred years it would not be necessary for country gentlemen to live in great stone dungeons with little cross-barred windows and loop-holes from which to shoot at people going by. Yet to-day a country gentleman in Massachusetts may sleep securely without locking his front door.

We have not quite done away with robbery and murder, but we have at least made private warfare illegal; we have arrayed public opinion against it to such an extent that the police court usually makes short shrift for the misguided man who tries to wreak vengeance on his enemy. Is it too much to hope that by-and-by we may similarly put public warfare under the ban? I think not. Already in America, as we have seen, it has become customary to deal with questions between States just as we would deal with questions between individuals. This we have seen to be the real purport of American federalism. To have established such a system over one great continent is to have made a very good beginning toward establishing it over the world. To establish such a system in Europe will no doubt be difficult, for here we have to deal with an immense complication of prejudices, intensified by linguistic and ethnological differences. Nevertheless the pacific pressure exerted upon Europe by America is becoming so great that it will doubtless before long overcome all these obstacles. I refer to the industrial competition between the Old and the New World, which has become so conspicuous within the last ten years. Agriculturally Minnesota, Nebraska, and Kansas are already formidable competitors with England, France, and Germany; but this is but the beginning. It is but the first spray from the tremendous wave of economic competition that is gathering in the Mississippi Valley. Presently, as with increase of population labor grows cheaper in America, the competition in manufactures also will become as keen as it is now beginning to be in agriculture, as the recent industrial history of New England abundantly proves. Now this economic pressure exerted upon Europe by the United States will very soon become so great that it will be simply impossible for the states of Europe to keep up such military armaments as they are now maintaining. The disparity between the United States, with a standing army of only twenty-five thousand men, and the states of Europe, with their standing armies amounting to two or three millions of men, is something that can not be kept up. The economic competition will become so keen that European armies will have to be disbanded, the swords will have to be turned into ploughshares, and thus the victory of the industrial over the military type of civilization will at last become complete. But to disband the great armies of Europe will necessarily involve the forcing of the great states of Europe into some sort of federal relation, in which congresses will become more frequent, in which the principles of international law will acquire a more definite sanction, and in which the combined physical power of all the states will constitute (as it now does in America) a permanent threat against any state that dares for selfish reasons to break the peace. In some such way as this, I believe, the industrial development of the English race outside of Europe will by-and-by enforce federalism upon Europe. I do not ignore the difficulties that grow out of differences in language, race, and creed; but we have seen how Switzerland has long since triumphantly surmounted such difficulties on a small scale. To surmount them on a great scale will soon be the political problem of Europe, and it is America which has set the example and indicated the method.

Thus we may foresee in general how, by the gradual concentration of physical power into the hands of the most pacific communities, we may finally succeed in rendering warfare illegal all over the globe. As this process goes on, it may, after many more ages of political experience, become apparent that there is really no reason, in the nature of things, why the whole of mankind should not constitute politically one huge federation, each little group managing its local affairs in entire independence, but relegating all questions of international interest to the decision of one central tribunal supported by the public opinion of the entire human race. I believe that the time will come when such a state of things will exist upon the earth, when it will be possible (with our friends of the Paris dinner party) to speak of the United States as stretching from pole to pole, or with Tennyson to celebrate the "parliament of man and the federation of the world." Indeed, only when such a state of things has begun to be realized can civilization, as sharply demarcated from barbarism, be said to have fairly begun. Only then can the world be said to have become truly Christian. Many ages of toil and doubt and perplexity will no doubt pass by before such a desideratum is reached. Meanwhile it is pleasant to feel that the dispassionate contemplation of great masses of historical facts goes far toward confirming our faith in this ultimate triumph of good over evil. Our survey began with pictures of horrid slaughter and desolation; it ends with the picture of a world covered with cheerful homesteads, blessed with a Sabbath of perpetual peace.

7
A NEW ERA OF DIP-LOMATIC RELATIONS

 One of those who spoke out against American insularity was Edward John Phelps (1822–1900), lawyer, judge, and diplomat. A Vermont Democrat in a predominantly Republican state, and a renowned trial lawyer, Phelps argued the American cause in such international arbitrational disputes as the Alaska Fur Seal issue, the New England fisheries contest, and the Venezuela-Great Britain boundary dispute. Phelps also was active in investigating Ferdinand de Lesseps's connection with a proposed Panama Canal. From 1885 to 1889 Phelps was minister at the Court of St. James's, succeeding the popular poet and author, James Russell Lowell. Phelps's London mission proved extremely successful where his tact, charm, and kindly dignity won him many friends. During his long career he also served as President of the American Bar Association and professor of law at Yale University. *America and Europe: A Study of International Relations* (1886), and *Orations and Essays of Edward John Phelps: Diplomat and Statesman* (1901) constitute his principal writings. In the 1889 annual Phi Beta Kappa address at Harvard University, Phelps, recently returned from Britain, declared in ringing terms that "the New International Relations" signaled the end of American isolationism and the dawn of a new age of global cooperation.

INTERNATIONAL RELATIONS

Edward J. Phelps

... It is less with abstract principles that I care to deal to-day than with that immediate view of the subject of international relations which belongs to our own country and our own time. During almost all the first century of the independent history of America these relations have been of only occasional and limited importance. Far remote from the theatre of European diplomacy, with no invasion to fear, no balance of power to consider, no monarchical intrigues to be drawn into, and few foreign interests to protect, it has been at rare intervals that we have had much to do with other countries, except for the interchange of courtesies, the promotion of trade, or the gratification of curiosity. We have had nothing to fear and little to gain from them, and our country has become the unlimited asylum for the overflow of their people, to such an extent that we are in danger of losing our own nationality.

But those halcyon days of international independence have now gone by. A great change has come over the face of the world, and over our own situation. We have joined the Atlantic to the Pacific. Our population, our industries, our interests, our intercourse with the outside world have enormously increased. Steam-power, the telegraph, invention, competition, and the restless enterprise of the age have brought foreign countries to our door, and have carried us to theirs. Our people, with tireless and irrepressible footstep, overspread the world, and create everywhere new relations, new engagements, and new enterprises. Within a very short time we have been drawn into the discussion of grave and important questions, involving considerable and fast-growing interests: with Great Britain, touching the fisheries of Canada, the seal catching of the Behring Sea, the vague and undetermined boundaries of Alaska; with Germany, concerning the Samoan Islands; with France and Central America, about the Panama Canals; with South American governments, with Mexico, with Hayti, with China; and we have become charged with the protection of our citizens and their property in all known countries of the earth. Questions of this sort are usually difficult and delicate. To know precisely what our rights are is not always easy; to maintain them successfully is often harder. I allude

FROM *Orations and Essays of Edward John Phelps: Diplomat and Statesman*, J. G. McCullough, editor (New York and London, 1901), pp. 149–81.

to them only to illustrate my remark as to the growing importance of the subject.

It must be plain to the thoughtful observer that henceforth the variety, the intricacy, the magnitude of our foreign affairs, already considerable, must continually increase. To understand and administer them correctly, to protect the rights involved, to keep the national honor untarnished, and at the same time to avoid the embarrassment and injury of strained and interrupted relations, and the calamities of actual war, which, like disease and death, come usually when least expected, and may arise out of small immediate causes when the way has been prepared by mutual irritation and misunderstanding — this is to be in the future one of the largest, perhaps the very largest, of the functions of American government.

The time has come when, as it appears to me, we need to have established a distinctive, definite, wise, firm, and, above all, a consistent American policy in international concerns. Not one that is taken up and laid down hap-hazard, or that shifts and veers about with the exigencies of politics, the changes of party, or the competence or incompetence of temporary officials. Changing hands so often as our government does, we can have nothing worthy the name of a foreign policy, nothing that will either be respected abroad or effectual for its purpose, unless by the establishment of principles, of traditions, of modes of procedure such as shall stand the test of experience and the criticism of mankind, and that shall pass on unimpaired from administration to administration, from party to party, the common property of all, the inheritance of each from its predecessor. The changes of party do not affect the construction of the Constitution. That goes on irrespective of politics, uniform, consistent, permananet. It underlies all questions of government, a common and unchangeable foundation.

Such a policy, as I think wise and thoughtful men will agree, should have for its basis the opposite of the theory set forth by Lord Lytton. It should be founded in the highest morality and justice. It should prefer the right to the expedient, or, rather should find in the right what is always in the end the expedient. It should be neither aggressive, nor offensive, nor hasty, but fair towards others, as well as just towards ourselves, invading no right that we would not ourselves surrender, establishing no precedent that we might afterwards wish to evade. It should be the policy, so far as consistent with the national honor, of peace, of conciliation, dignity, and forbearance, free from the cheap braggadocio by which the applause of the mob is sometimes purchased, setting up no claims that we are not prepared to maintain, making no demand that we do not expect to insist upon. It is the great and powerful nation that can best afford to be just, and more than just, to be generous. But, on the other hand, upon the line thus deliberately adopted, the stand should be absolutely firm and unyielding. Caution in taking up a position is the best preparation for firmness in holding it. Any policy is better than a cowardly, a shifting, or a retreating one. Details, incidentals, disputed facts or figures, conflicting business interests, doubtful questions, these are the proper subjects of a compromise and of mutual concession. But a principle, a point of honor, the just and clear right of a citizen, once asserted, should never be surrendered or receded from.

It is idle to expect that a foreign policy of this kind, elevated, just, consistent, and resolute, can be maintained by our country unless the subject can be withdrawn from the field of party politics. No government can successfully carry forward any international relations at all in matters of consequence without the general support of the public sentiment of its own people. The house that appears to be divided against itself will command no respect. The ground that is taken by one administration will be repudiated by the next. Foreign governments will find, in case of dispute, their strongest ally in the opposition that ours has to contend with, and will speculate, in dealing with us, upon the changes of party that may present to them an entirely different front. And, aside from the effect of such partisan warfare abroad, the Executive cannot obtain at home that concurrence and assistance from co-ordinate departments that are necessary in order that any measures in the matter of foreign affairs should be effectual. . . .

I am far from maintaining that all measures of a government towards other nations should receive a blind and unreasoning approval, or that they should cease to be the proper subject of criticism and attempted improvement. I do not say that an administration may not be overthrown for the very defects and failures of its foreign policy, its incompetence, its neglect, its blunders. That might well occur in the conduct of a war, and yet every citizen be bound to support, as against the enemy, the very operations he disapproves. All I contend for is that questions relating to external affairs should be judged on their own merits, and not upon party grounds; that a government should be sustained abroad until a better one can be put in its place; and that it should be sustained in this particular at home till it is found to be in the wrong. We cannot afford to obtain party advantages at the expense of just foreign relations.

But for the maintenance of a more effectual foreign policy, it is not enough that it should be just and well considered, and that we should be united in support of it at home. We must likewise be known to be strong enough to enforce it. Nothing is more mistaken than the idea that we are always to hold our own among the nations of the earth, while human nature remains what it is, by the mere force of argument. That discussions of disputed questions should be able and skilful, that the resources of reason, the ties of friendship, the offices of courtesy, and the suggestions of mutual interest should be made the most of, and may often be sufficiently effective, is not to be questioned. But it is also true that they must sometimes fail if there is no other force behind them. It does not detract from the effect of an argument that he who makes it is in a situation to command attention as well as to invite it. Mere attorneyship was never yet a decisive power in international affairs. The nation which is only the petitioner for justice, with nothing to depend upon but logic and rhetoric, friendship and sentiment, may fare well enough in small matters, but will be likely to go to the wall in great ones. It is not only humiliating, but disastrous, when the state that marches up the hill has nothing for it but to march down again amid the derision of the world.

It is true, as has been observed, that all nations profess to be guided by the principles of justice, and that what they accept as international law has these principles for its foundation. No government admits any other rule of action, but they differ widely, under the stimulus of self-interest and the pressure of popular feeling, as to the application of it. Most people profess to be and mean to be law-abiding, yet without courts of justice society could not go on. And of what avail would be courts of justice without a sheriff to execute their decrees if resisted? What makes law a controlling force in civilized society is not so much the justice of its conclusions as the consciousness that the power of government stands behind them.

It is the nation which, however conciliatory and easy to be entreated, and however adverse to hostilities, is felt, nevertheless, to hold in reserve an ultimate power it is not safe to provoke, which commands respect. The force of argument is immensely strengthened when it is sustained by a background of artillery. That country is most likely to enjoy the blessings of peace which is in a condition to be most formidable in war. National strength means strength in the right quarter and the right way. It does not consist in power where it is not wanted. The science of war is said to depend upon bringing to bear a predominant force at the vital point, at the critical time. Of the invincible power of our country upon its own soil there can be no question. We have shown that we can gather a great army as rapidly as the snow comes on the wings of the winter wind, and disperse it again like the melting of the same snow in the spring. At home we may safely defy the world in arms, but by land we shall never be attacked. If we are ever so unfortunate as to be involved in war with any country great enough to go by the sea, the issue must be determined upon the sea, and not upon the shore. In this view what is our situation? Every seaport we have is absolutely at the mercy of any maritime nation in the world. We have no naval force that can cope with that of any such nation, or that could stand up at all before the great war ships and powerful artillery of the present time. We have no fortifications whatever, nor a single modern gun in position upon our coast, that would be effectual in defence against such an attack. Were we to assemble a million of men to defend New York or Boston against it, they would be powerless, and only available for slaughter. These are humiliating facts, not adapted to festive occasions, but they should be looked in the face. All the world knows them, and takes them into account. It is only against countries that have no navy that we are capable even of self-defence. When the point of controversy is in some other part of the world than ours, we are unable to place there any force that could successfully encounter that of a sea-going nation. For the protection of any distant interest, or the immediate redress of an injury or outrage, we are powerless. In short, we are the only nation pretending to be of the first class that is incapable either of offence or defence, except that sort of defence that will never be challenged or called into play.

There is still another view in which a naval force is a very important factor in foreign relations besides the strict requirements of offence and defence. There is a phrase that figures largely in the wake of a war, and when terms of peace have to be patched up — the *"statu quo ante bellum."* That is a condition often as important in the outset of a controversy as at the end of it. It may be prospective as well as retrospective. The presence of a competent force at the right point at the right moment sometimes prevents transactions that prove most troublesome after they have occurred. It serves to keep the peace that, once broken, is hard to mend. It is the prevention that is better than cure. Possession is said to be nine points of the law. That is as true between nations as between individuals. A wrong may be quickly set right on the spot, in a way that is likely to be acquiesced in; and very material advantage in subsequent discussion may result from a proper adjustment of the *statu quo* beforehand. More than once in recent times prolonged and heated discussion could have been avoided by our own government if it had possessed a force which, quietly and seasonably interposed, would have prevented wrongs, for which, once committed, it is not easy to obtain peaceable redress. And that is especially true in a case where diplomatic relations are with one country, and actual transactions with a dependency over which it has little control.

It may be thought that I am diverging from the subject I have been dealing with when I enter upon these considerations. But no remark I have made is more germane to my topic. Naval strength has become at this day the right arm of diplomacy, and the most important element in large and critical foreign relations. Moral power is an excellent thing. It is best to be right, and in the long run it is necessary to be right, however powerful a nation may be. But there are times when it is of small avail to be right if we are likewise impotent. A right arm without brains or conscience is never a desirable force, but brains and conscience without a right arm are not always an effectual one. I would propose, therefore, as one of the first steps towards such an international attitude as it seems to me our country should assume, and, having assumed maintain, that a naval force should be created that should leave us nothing to fear from collision with any other naval power in the world. For this no country has such facilities — an overflowing treasury, a sea-coast extensive enough to afford ship-yards for the world, inventive and mechanical genius and industry unsurpassed, a highly educated and well-selected body of naval officers, a people to whom seafaring is the gift of nature more than to any other people except those of their own race. Better to expend the whole surplus in the treasury, which is demoralizing the country and debauching its politics; better to create a ship-yard in every port, and to employ thousands of men in building ships and thousands more in sailing them, until our ancient prestige on the ocean is restored, than to remain in the condition where our only means of asserting disputed rights, or defending ourselves against attack, is the soft answer that turneth away wrath.

Of course, it is easy enough to misunderstand these suggestions. Nothing in the world is easier than to misunderstand, except to misrepresent. The one is natural to the dull man, the other is the most convenient weapon of the dishonest one. It is easy to say that a proposal to put a nation in a condition for self-defence is to advocate a career of war and bloodshed and aggression. But saying so does not make it so. That man is a fool, if there be such a man at the present day, who does not know that war is the greatest of calamities and sorrows, and the most destructive to all the best interests of humanity. To avoid the possibility of war is the first object of all foreign intercourse. To cultivate with other nations the free commerce, the amenities and the courtesies that are the fruits of peace, is the second. The views of mankind have undergone a vast change within the last century on the subject of war. It is no longer the game of kings, or of statesmen, or of ambitious soldiers. It is universally deprecated and dreaded among all civilized men.

With the present intercourse among nations, a mere paper war of three months' duration, between two great powers, even if not a shot should be ultimately fired, would work an incalculable injury in the interruption of business and travel, the derangement of finance, the disturbance of relations, the enormous expense of preparation, and the general alarm and excitement. War is, therefore, more and more to be feared, and will be more and more anxiously avoided. And yet it can never cease from off the earth. It will still and always remain the last resort of nations, and the last resort must sometimes be appealed to. The vast armaments still kept up by all the great European countries show the general consciousness of this. They are maintained, not for the purpose of making war, but of avoiding it. It is an armed neutrality that now pervades Europe.

There are humanitarians of excellent motives who seem to believe that war can be put an end to forever by the universal agreement of mankind to substitute arbitration in its stead. Theirs is a harmless effort, but not a promising one. Arbitration is one of the most plausible words in the English language. But it means one thing to those who have had much to do with it, and quite another to those who have not. The former usually ascertain that it signifies the trial and determination of controversies by those who have no acquaintance with that difficult business. Great as are the evils of litigation, arbitration has never had any perceptible effect in reducing it. Men are generally more ready to prescribe it for others than to accept it themselves. Nevertheless, imperfect remedy as it is, it will continue to be sometimes employed in a certain class of international questions, especially the adjustment of money claims, public and private. In such cases almost any disposition that is honorable is better than a continuance of the dispute. But the idea that it can ever be made the ultimate resort of nations in those more important quarrels that involve questions of principle or of honor, or that have stirred the blood and moved the passions of men, appears to me altogether chimerical. Could the battle of Waterloo have been avoided by an arbitration between Great Britain and Napoleon? Or would the world have been the better if that great quarrel had been so patched up? Would the American South have consented at the outset of the civil war to refer the question of the independence they claimed and expected to achieve — would the North have submitted the question whether we had a government not dissoluble by rebellion, to the arbitrament of some European potentate or political philosopher, to be argued by counsel, in the French language, at some watering-place on the Continent? States can never be brought to agree beforehand, in respect to prospective controversies that have not arisen and may never arise, to bind themselves to this method of adjustment. But were such a compact ever so solemnly made, it would never be carried out in the white heat which, when the occasion comes, melts into one current all the ingredients of national emotion. There is hardly a policy of insurance that does not contain a provision that, in case of dispute, it shall be submitted to arbitration. But when the loss has occurred, and a quarrel has arisen, and the parties are stirred by a sense of fancied wrong, who on either side ever pays attention to this solemn and formal agreement? Wars do not take place like murders, by malice aforethought. They are not arranged for beforehand, like matches at chess. They come when combustible materials have been allowed to accumulate, and irritated feeling to grow; when a match carelessly dropped, perhaps by an insignificant hand, at an unexpected moment, sets a flame that the high wind of public sentiment drives into a conflagration.

I have said, and I repeat it, that the policy of the United States should be that of an enlightened and Christian nation, deprecating war, and devoted to the arts, the industries, the humanities of peace, and ready to make sacrifices as well as efforts to preserve it. But the best way to accomplish that object in the different future now opening before us still remains to be thoughtfully considered, in the light of the history and the experience that will continue to repeat themselves, from time to time, as long as the world stands. . . .

PART II

THE IMPERIALISTS
AND THEIR CRITICS
THE *1890s*

8

THE OUTWARD THRUST: AMERICA'S DESTINY

Some thinkers, of whom the philosophically oriented John Fiske is an example, recognized the paradox of isolationism in a modern world of rapidly shrinking distances. Others, like Rear Admiral Alfred Thayer Mahan (1840–1914), were more pragmatic. Born at West Point, where his father taught, Mahan did more than anyone else in his generation to rekindle American interest in sea power. A prolific writer on naval problems and maritime history, his works included histories of the navy in the Revolution and the War of 1812, the naval implications of the South African Boer War, and a study of Admiral David Farragut.

In his most influential work, *The Influence of Sea Power Upon History 1660–1783* (1890), which made him world famous, Mahan contended that throughout history a country's might and prestige derived from the proper use of ocean highways and that the wise cultivation of sea power explained Britain's primacy in modern times. To Mahan, sea power is a prime requisite for a nation's greatness. For America, this strength would come from a rehabilitated merchant marine, the acquisition of global bases so that its navy could operate in remote waters, and overseas colonies. Although Mahan was not the sole architect of the "new" American navy, begun in the administration of President Chester Alan Arthur (1881–1885), he was the most widely read writer of the expansionist school. The "mercantile imperialism" that he preached received a sympathetic hearing by such rising politicos as Henry Cabot Lodge and Theodore Roosevelt. In an oft-quoted article in the *Atlantic Monthly* in 1890, included below, Mahan admonished his country to "look outward" if its true destiny was to be fulfilled. Mahan was accorded the historian's highest accolade when, in 1902, he was elected President of the American Historical Association.

THE UNITED STATES LOOKING OUTWARD

Alfred T. Mahan

Indications are not wanting of an approaching change in the thoughts and policy of Americans as to their relations with the world outside their own borders. For the past quarter of a century, the predominant idea, which has successfully asserted itself at the polls and shaped the course of the government, has been to preserve the home market for the home industries. The employer and the workman have alike been taught to look at the various economical measures proposed from this point of view, to regard with hostility any step favoring the intrusion of the foreign producer upon their own domain, and rather to demand increasingly rigorous measures of exclusion than to acquiesce in any loosening of the chain that binds the consumer to them. The inevitable consequence has followed, as in all cases when the mind or the eye is exclusively fixed in one direction, that the danger of loss or the prospect of advantage in another quarter has been overlooked; and although the abounding resources of the country have maintained the exports at a high figure, this flattering result has been due more to the superabundant bounty of Nature than to the demand of other nations for our protected manufactures.

For nearly the lifetime of a generation, therefore, American industries have been thus protected, until the practice has assumed the force of a tradition, and is clothed in the mail of conservatism. In their mutual relations, these industries resemble the activities of a modern ironclad that has heavy armor, but an inferior engine and no guns; mighty for defense, weak for offense. Within, the home market is secured; but outside, beyond the broad seas, there are the markets of the world, that can be entered and controlled only by a vigorous contest, to which the habit of trusting to protection by statute does not conduce.

At bottom, however, the temperament of the American people is essentially alien to such a sluggish attitude. Independently of all bias for or against protection, it is safe to predict that, when the opportunities for gain abroad are understood, the course of American enterprise will cleave a channel by which to reach them. Viewed broadly, it is a most welcome as well as significant fact that a prominent and influential advocate of protection, a leader of the party committed to its support, a keen reader of the signs of the

FROM *Atlantic Monthly,* LXVI (December, 1890), pp. 816–24.

times and of the drift of opinion, has identified himself with a line of policy which looks to nothing less than such modifications of the tariff as may expand the commerce of the United States to all quarters of the globe. Men of all parties can unite on the words of Mr. Blaine, as reported in a recent speech: "It is not an ambitious destiny for so great a country as ours to manufacture only what we can consume, or produce only what we can eat." In face of this utterance of so shrewd and able a public man, even the extreme character of the recent tariff legislation seems but a sign of the coming change, and brings to mind that famous Continental System, of which our own is the analogue, to support which Napoleon added legion to legion and enterprise to enterprise, till the fabric of the Empire itself crashed beneath the weight.

The interesting and significant feature of this changing attitude is the turning of the eyes outward, instead of inward only, to seek the welfare of the country. To affirm the importance of distant markets, and the relation to them of our own immense powers of production, implies logically the recognition of the link that joins the products and the markets, — that is, the carrying trade; the three together constituting that chain of maritime power to which Great Britain owes her wealth and greatness. Further, is it too much to say that, as two of these links, the shipping and the markets, are exterior to our own borders, the acknowledgment of them carries with it a view of the relations of the United States to the world radically distinct from the simple idea of self-sufferingness? We shall not follow far this line of thought before there will dawn the realization of America's unique position, facing the older worlds of the East and West, her shores lapped by the oceans which touch the one or the other, but which are common to her alone. . . .

There is no sound reason for believing that the world has passed into a period of assured peace outside the limits of Europe. Unsettled political conditions, such as exist in Hayti, Central America, and many of the Pacific islands, especially the Hawaiian group, when combined with great military or commercial importance, as is the case with most of these positions, involve, now as always, dangerous germs of quarrel, against which it is at least prudent to be prepared. Undoubtedly, the general temper of nations is more averse from war than it was of old. If no less selfish and grasping than our predecessors, we feel more dislike to the discomforts and sufferings attendant upon a breach of peace; but to retain that highly valued repose and the undisturbed enjoyment of the returns of commerce, it is necessary to argue upon somewhat equal terms of strength with an adversary. It is the preparedness of the enemy, and not acquiescence in the existing state of things, that now holds back the armies of Europe.

On the other hand, neither the sanctions of international law nor the justice of a cause can be depended upon for a fair settlement of differences, when they come into conflict with a strong political necessity on the one side opposed to comparative weakness on the other. In our still-pending dispute over the seal-fishing of Bering Sea, whatever may be thought of the strength of our argument, in view of generally admitted principles of international law, it is beyond doubt that our contention is reasonable, just, and in the interest of the world generally. But in the attempt to enforce it we have come into collision not only with national susceptibilities as to the honor of the flag, which we ourselves very strongly share, but also with a state governed by a powerful necessity, and exceedingly strong where we are particularly weak and exposed. Not only has Great Britain a mighty navy and we a long, defenseless seacoast, but it is a great commercial and political advantage to her that her larger colonies, and above all Canada, should feel that the power of the mother country is something which they need, and upon which they can count. The dispute is between the United States and Canada, not the United States and England; but it has been ably used by the latter to promote the solidarity of sympathy between herself and her colony. With the mother country alone an equitable arrangement, conducive to well-understood mutual interests, could readily be reached; but the purely local and peculiarly selfish wishes of Canadian fishermen dictate the policy of Great Britain, because Canada is the most important link uniting her to her colonies and maritime interests in the Pacific. In case of a European war, it is probable that the British navy will not be able to hold open the route through the Mediterranean to the East; but having a strong naval station at Halifax, and another at Esquimalt, on the Pacific, the two connected by the Canadian Pacific Railroad, England possesses an alternate line of communication far less exposed to maritime aggression than the former, or than the third route by the Cape of Good Hope, as well as two bases essential to the service of her commerce, or other naval operations, in the North Atlantic and the Pacific. Whatever arrangement of this question is finally reached, the fruit of Lord Salisbury's attitude can hardly fail to be a strengthening of the sentiments of attachment to, and reliance upon, the mother country, not only in Canada, but in the other great colonies. Such feelings of attachment and mutual dependence supply the living spirit, without which the nascent schemes for Imperial Federation are but dead mechanical contrivances; nor are they without influence upon such generally unsentimental considerations as those of buying and selling, and the course of trade.

This dispute, seemingly paltry, yet really serious, sudden in its appearance, and dependent for its issue upon other considerations than its own merits, may serve to convince us of many latent and yet unforeseen dangers to the peace of the western hemisphere, attendant upon the opening of a canal through the Central American Isthmus. In a general way, it is evident enough that this canal, by modifying the direction of trade routes, will induce a great increase of commercial activity and carrying trade throughout the Caribbean Sea; and that this now comparatively deserted nook of the ocean will, like the Red Sea, become a great thoroughfare of shipping, and attract, as never before in our day, the interest and ambition of maritime nations. Every position in that sea will have enhanced commercial and military value, and the canal itself will become a strategic centre of the most vital importance. Like the Canadian Pacific Railroad, it will be a link between the two oceans; but, unlike it, the use, unless most carefully guarded by treaties, will belong wholly to the belligerent which controls the sea by its naval power. In case of war, the United States will unquestionably command the Canadian Railroad, despite the deterrent force of operations by the hostile navy upon our seaboard; but no less unquestionably will she be impotent, as against any of the great maritime powers, to control the Central American canal. Militarily speaking, the piercing of the Isthmus is nothing but a disaster to the United States, in the present state of her military and naval preparation. It is especially dangerous to the Pacific coast; but the increased exposure of one part of our seaboard reacts unfavorably upon the whole military situation. Despite a certain great original superiority conferred by our geographical nearness and immense resources, — due, in other words, to our natural advantages, and not to our intelligent preparations, — the United States is woefully unready, not only in fact, but in purpose, to assert in the Caribbean and Central America a weight of influence proportioned to the extent of her interests. We have not the navy, and, what is worse, we are not willing to have the navy, that will weigh seriously in any disputes with those nations whose interests will there conflict with our own. We have not, and we are not anxious to provide, the defense of the seaboard which will leave the navy free for its work at sea. We have not, but many other powers have, positions, either within or on the borders of the Caribbean, which not only possess great natural advantages for the control of that sea, but have received and are receiving that artificial strength of fortification and armament which will make them practically inexpugnable. On the contrary, we have not on the Gulf of Mexico even the beginning of a navy yard which could serve as the base of our operations. Let me not be misunderstood. I am not regretting that we have not the means to meet on terms of equality the great navies of the Old World. I recognize, what few at least say, that, despite its great surplus revenue, this country is poor in proportion to its length of seaboard and its exposed points. That which I deplore, and which is a sober, just, and reasonable cause of deep national concern, is that the nation neither has nor cares to have its sea frontier so defended, and its navy of such power, as shall suffice, with the advantages of our position, to weigh seriously when inevitable discussions arise, — such as we have recently had about Samoa and Behring Sea, and which may at any moment come up about the Caribbean Sea or the canal. Is the United States, for instance, prepared to allow Germany to acquire the Dutch stronghold of Curaçoa, fronting the Atlantic outlet of both the proposed canals of Panama and Nicaragua? Is she prepared to acquiesce in any foreign power purchasing from Hayti a naval station on the Windward Passage, through which pass our steamer routes to the Isthmus? Would she acquiesce in a foreign protectorate over the Sandwich Islands, that great central station of the Pacific, equidistant from San Francisco, Samoa, and the Marquesas, and an important post on our lines of communication with both Australia and China? Or will it be maintained that any one of these questions, supposing it to arise, is so exclusively one-sided, the arguments of policy and right so exclusively with us, that the other party will at once yield his eager wish, and gracefully withdraw? Was it so at Samoa? Is it so as regards Behring Sea? The motto seen on so many ancient cannon, Ultima ratio regum, is not without its message to republics.

It is perfectly reasonable and legitimate, in estimating our needs of military preparation, to take into account the remoteness of the chief naval and military nations from our shores, and the consequent difficulty of maintaining operations at such a distance. It is equally proper, in framing our policy, to consider the jealousies of the European family of states, and their consequent unwillingness to incur the enmity of a people so strong as ourselves; their dread of our revenge in the future, as well as their inability to detach more than a certain part of their forces to our shores without losing much of their own weight in the councils of Europe. In truth, a careful determination of the force that Great Britain or France could probably spare for operations against our coasts, if the latter were suitably defended, without weakening their European position or unduly exposing their colonies and commerce, is the starting-point from which to calculate the strength of our own navy. If the latter be superior to the force that can thus be sent against it, and the coast be so defended as to leave the navy free to strike where it will, we can maintain our rights; not merely the rights which international law concedes, and which the moral sense of nations now supports, but also those equally real rights which, though not conferred by law, depend upon a clear preponderance of interest, upon obviously necessary policy, upon self-preservation, either total or partial. Were we now so situated in respect of military strength, we could secure our perfectly just claim as to the seal fisheries; not by seizing foreign ships on the open sea, but by the evident fact that, our cities being protected from maritime attack, our position and superior population lay open the Canadian Pacific, as well as the frontier of the Dominion, to do with as we please. Diplomats do not flourish such disagreeable truths in each other's faces; they look for a *modus vivendi*, and find it.

While, therefore, the advantages of our own position in the western hemisphere, and the disadvantages under which the operations of a European state would labor, are undeniable and just elements in the calculations of the statesman, it is folly to look upon them as sufficient for our security. Much more needs to be cast into the scale that it may incline in favor of our strength. They are mere defensive factors, and partial at that. Though distant, our shores can be reached; being defenseless, they can detain but a short time a force sent against them. With a probability of three months' peace in Europe, no maritime power would now fear to support its demands by a number of ships with which it would be loath indeed to part for a year.

Yet, were our sea frontier as strong as it now is weak, passive self-defense, whether in trade or war, would be but a poor policy, so long as this world continues to be one of struggle and vicissitude. All around us now is strife; "the struggle of life," "the race of life," are phrases so familiar that we do not feel their significance till we stop to think about them. Everywhere nation is arrayed against nation; our own no less than others. What is our protective system but an organized warfare? In carrying it on, it is true, we have only to use certain procedures which all states now concede to be a legal exercise of the national power, even though injurious to themselves.

It is lawful, they say, to do what we will with our own. Are our people, however, so unaggressive that they are likely not to want their own way in matters where their interests turn on points of disputed right, or so little sensitive as to submit quietly to encroachment by others, in quarters where they have long considered their own influence should prevail?

Our self-imposed isolation in the matter of markets, and the decline of our shipping interest in the last thirty years, have coincided singularly with an actual remoteness of this continent from the life of the rest of the world. The writer has before him a map of the North and South Atlantic oceans, showing the direction of the principal trade routes and the proportion of tonnage passing over each; and it is curious to note what deserted regions, comparatively, are the Gulf of Mexico, the Caribbean Sea, and the adjoining countries and islands. A broad band stretches from our northern Atlantic coast to the English Channel; another as broad from the British Islands to the East, through the Mediterranean and Red Sea, overflowing the borders of the latter in order to express the volume of trade. Around either cape — Good Hope and Horn — pass strips of about one fourth this width, joining near the equator, midway between Africa and South America. From the West Indies issues a thread indicating the present commerce of Great Britain with a region which once, in the Napoleonic wars, embraced one fourth of the whole trade of the Empire. The significance is unmistakable: Europe has now little interest in the Caribbean Sea.

When the Isthmus is pierced this isolation will pass away, and with it the indifference of foreign nations. From wheresoever they come and whithersoever they afterward go, all ships that use the canal will pass through the Caribbean. Whatever the effect produced upon the prosperity of the adjacent continent and islands by the thousand wants attendant upon maritime activity, around such a focus of trade will centre large commercial and political interests. To protect and develop its own, each nation will seek points of support and means of influence in a quarter where the United States has always been jealously sensitive to the intrusion of European powers. The precise value of the Monroe doctrine is very loosely understood by most Americans, but the effect of the familiar phase has been to develop a national sensitiveness, which is a more frequent cause of war than material interests; and over disputes caused by such feelings there will preside none of the calming influence due to the moral authority of international law, with its recognized principles, for the points in dispute will be of policy, of interest, not of conceded right. Already France and England are giving to ports held by them a degree of artificial strength uncalled for by their present importance. They look to the near future. Among the islands and on the mainland there are many positions of great importance, held now by weak or unstable states. Is the United States willing to see them sold to a powerful rival? But what right will she invoke against the transfer? She can allege but one, — that of her reasonable policy supported by her might.

Whether they will or no, Americans must now begin to look outward. The growing production of the country demands it. An increasing volume of public sentiment demands it. The position of the United States, between the two Old Worlds and the two great oceans, makes the same claim, which will soon be strengthened by the creation of the new link joining the Atlantic and Pacific. The tendency will be maintained and increased by the growth of the European colonies in the Pacific, by the advancing civilization of Japan, and by the rapid peopling of our Pacific States with men who have all the aggressive spirit of the advanced line of national progress. Nowhere does a vigorous foreign policy find more favor than among the people west of the Rocky Mountains.

It has been said that, in our present state of unpreparedness, a trans-isthmian canal will be a military disaster to the United States, and especially to the Pacific coast. When the canal is finished the Atlantic seaboard will be neither more nor less exposed than it now is; it will merely share with the country at large the increased danger of foreign complications with inadequate means to meet them. The danger of the Pacific coast will be greater by so much as the way between it and Europe is shortened through a passage which the stronger maritime power can control. The danger lies not merely in the greater facility for dispatching a hostile squadron from Europe, but also in the fact that a more powerful fleet than formerly can be maintained on that coast by a European power, because it can be so much more promptly called home in case of need. The greatest weakness of the Pacific ports, however, if wisely met by our government, will go far to insure our naval superiority there. The two chief centres, San Francisco and Puget Sound, owing to the width and the great depth of the entrances, cannot be effectively protected by torpedoes; and consequently, as fleets can always pass batteries through an unobstructed channel, they cannot obtain perfect security by means of fortifications only. Valuable as such works will be to them, they must be further garrisoned by coast-defense ships, whose part in repelling an enemy will be coördinated with that of the batteries. The sphere of action of such ships should not be permitted to extend far beyond the port to which they are allotted, and of whose defense they form an essential part; but within that sweep they will always be a powerful reinforcement to the seagoing navy, when the strategic conditions of a war cause hostilities to centre around their port. By sacrificing power to go long distances, the coast-defense ship gains proportionate weight of armor and guns; that is, of defensive and offensive strength. It therefore adds an element of unique value to the fleet with which it for a time acts. No foreign states, except Great Britain, have ports so near our Pacific coast as to bring it within the radius of action of their coast-defense ships; and it is very doubtful whether even Great Britain will put such ships at Vancouver Island, the chief value of which will be lost to her when the Canadian Pacific is severed, — a blow always in the power of this country. It is upon our Atlantic seaboard that the mistress of Halifax, of Bermuda, and of Jamaica will now defend Vancouver and the Canadian Pacific. In the present state of our seaboard defense she can do so absolutely. What is all Canada compared with our exposed great cities? Even were the coast fortified, she could still do so, if our navy be no stronger than is as yet designed. What harm can we do Canada proportionate to the injury we should suffer by the interruption of our coasting trade, and by a blockade of Boston, New York, the Delaware, and the Chesapeake? Such a blockade Great Britain certainly could made technically efficient, under the somewhat loose definitions of international law. Neutrals would accept it as such.

The military needs of the Pacific States, as well as their supreme importance to the whole country, are yet a matter of the future, but of a future so near that provision should immediately begin. To weigh their importance, consider what influence in the Pacific would be attributed to a nation comprising only the States of Washington, Oregon, and California, when filled with such men as now people them and are still pouring in, and controlling such maritime centres as San Francisco, Puget Sound, and the Columbia River. Can it be counted less because they are bound by the ties of blood and close political union to the great communities of the East? But such influence, to work without jar and friction, requires underlying military readiness, like the proverbial iron hand under the velvet glove. To provide this, three things are needful: First, protection of the chief harbors by fortifications and coast-defense ships, which gives defensive strength, provides security to the community within, and supplies the bases necessary to all military operations. Secondly, naval force, the arm of offensive power, which alone enables a country to extend its influence outward. Thirdly, it should be an inviolable resolution of our national policy that no European state should henceforth acquire a coaling position within three thousand miles of San Francisco, — a distance which includes the Sandwich and Galapagos islands and the coast of Central America. For fuel is the life of modern naval war; it is the food of the ship; without it the modern monsters of the deep die of inanition. Around it, therefore, cluster some of the most important considerations of naval strategy. In the Caribbean and the Atlantic we are confronted with many a foreign coal depot, and perhaps it is not an unmitigated misfortune that we, like Rome, find Carthage at our gates bidding us stand to our arms; but let us not acquiesce in an addition to our dangers, a further diversion of our strength, by being forestalled in the North Pacific.

In conclusion, while Great Britain is undoubtedly the most formidable of our possible enemies, both by her great navy and the strong positions she holds near our coasts, it must be added that a cordial understanding with that country is one of the first of our external interests. Both nations, doubtless, and properly, seek their own advantage; but both, also, are controlled by a sense of law and justice drawn from the same sources, and deep-rooted in their instincts. Whatever temporary aberration may occur, a return to mutual standards of right will certainly follow. Formal alliance between the two is out of the question, but a cordial recognition of the similarity of character and ideas will give birth to sympathy, which in turn will facilitate a coöperation beneficial to both; for, if sentimentality is weak, sentiment is strong.

9
NEW PACIFIC
INVOLVEMENTS

 Toward the end of the nineteenth century, the Orient began to figure more prominently in America's growing interest in foreign affairs. John Barrett (1866–1938), American minister to Siam from 1894 to 1898, predicted in the prestigious *North American Review* that the great commercial future of the country lay in the Far East. Barrett stressed trade advantages that would ensue but was ridiculed by some who did not recognize his foresight. A confirmed Orientophile, he stressed the importance of the territorial integrity of China, the Open Door, the abolition of spheres of influence, and competition with European countries for the Asiatic market. Barrett had a long and distinguished career in the American foreign service. After his tour of duty in Siam, he served as special war correspondent in Manila, commercial commissioner in Asia, American delegate to the Second Pan-American Conference, and minister to three Latin American countries. From 1907 to 1920 he was Director General of the Pan-American Union where he worked for closer commercial ties within the New World even as he had labored for more intimate Far Eastern relationships. Barrett was a prolific writer whose works included: *Admiral George Dewey* (1899), *Pan American Union — Peace, Friendship, Commerce* (1911), *The Panama Canal — What it is, what it means* (1913), and *The Call of South America* (1924).

AMERICA'S INTEREST IN EASTERN ASIA

John Barrett

There are few if any questions pertaining to the foreign interests of the United States which are to-day more important than the question: What is or what shall be its material policy in Eastern Asia?

In other terms, shall the Great Republic be a strong or weak factor, a known or an unknown quantity, in working out the complex problem that presents itself in the development of Japan, Korea, China and Siam? . . .

Frankly and truthfully stated — though not pleasing to our national pride — our country is not regarded by the Oriental people in their practical knowledge and relations as a Great Power in the common acceptance of the term; it is not placed in the same category with Great Britain, France, Germany and Russia. Theoretically only do they class it with these; they think of it with a vague, undefined conception — powerful perhaps but distant, grand in its home influence but having little concern in foreign affairs. To both the traveller and the permanent resident in the Orient this is constantly in evidence whether he be at a seaport or in the interior. A study of its cause finds speedy solution in our small and neglected maritime and trade interests. "Old Glory" is more of a curio to the Oriental than an emblem of progress and power. When the beautiful steam yacht of one of our millionaires anchored in Bangkok's harbor, the natives learned from what country it came by comparing its ensign with the flag that floated over the United States Legation! But this is not surprising in view of the fact that not one of the 517 merchant vessels that entered this busy port last year was American.

Yet in the light of results to be attained and of effects upon the ultimate standing of the races and nations of the world, it is not unreasonable to affirm that the United States has as great interest in the development of Eastern Asia as in that of South and Central America. It would be well if a fair share of the attention given to the latter countries and the energy exerted in exploiting them were diverted to that wonderful coast which reaches from Japan and Siberia to Java and Siam. Japan alone has more inhabitants than

FROM *North American Review*, CLXII (March, 1896), pp. 257–65.

all of South America; while the Nicaragua canal finds a greater argument for its construction in facilitating trade with the Orient than facilitating that with Western South America.

Get a map and look at that trans-Pacific coast; get reliable authorities and study its history, resources and conditions; get a ticket to cross the seas and travel from one end of it to the other; get acquainted with it thoroughly and not superficially; and then its possibilities as a powerful agent in shaping the history of men will be fully appreciated.

Extending right away for over 4,000 miles from Hakodate and Vladivostock to Bangkok and Singapore; peopled with 400,000,000 restless beings; busy with a great and growing commercial exchange; provided with capacious harbors and thriving *entrepots* of trade; intersected by mighty rivers and canals; possessed of uplands in which are found every mineral the earth produces, and of lowlands that are gardens of prodigal fertility; densely populated in certain sections; with vast resourceful areas unimproved; presenting the extremes of progress and retrogression, of energy and sloth, of advanced civilization and lowest barbarism; having histories and boasting of philosophies that antedate those of Christian nations; and possibly at this very hour on the verge of momentous events which may necessitate the remaking of the maps of the world; this section of Asia with all its phases and questions, indeed fascinates alike the diplomat and the tradesman, the politician and the economist, the conqueror and the peacemaker, the optimist and the pessimist.

What better indication can there be of what these countries can do than what they are doing? What better proof of the value of this field is wanted than the business it already possesses? What plainer evidence is at hand that the opportunity is not appreciated and improved by our own country than the comparison of its efforts and results with those of other lands? Statistics and figures are usually dry and uninteresting, except when they bring important facts to light. They are quoted here to answer the questions just asked.

The total foreign trade of Japan, Korea, China, and Siam in 1894, roughly stated, was $725,000,000,* of which the share of Japan and China was $665,000,000; of Siam and Korea, $60,000,000. Were the trade of European colonies of the coast added to the above total it would reach the grand sum of nearly $1,000,000,000.

* The figures given are silver dollars. All calculations and transactions of the Asiatic coast are in silver, and with the fluctuating value of the same in gold it would be unsatisfactory to give the returns in the latter coin.

Japan's foreign trade shows a remarkable increase from $64,400,000 in 1885 to $230,700,000 in 1894; that of China from $229,809,000 in 1885 to $435,300,000 in 1894; that of Siam, from $19,400,000 in 1892 to $42,000,000 in 1894.

In both Japan and China the imports from foreign countries exceed the exports, and show a greater increase than the latter from 1885 to 1894. Japanese imports increased from only $28,300,000 in 1885 to $117,400,000 in 1894, and her exports from $36,100,000 to $113,200,000 in 1894; China's imports developed in the same years from $132,300,000 to $243,150,000 and her exports from $97,500,000 to $192,150,000.

The excess of China over Japan is not large in view of the fact that China has eight times the population of Japan and her customs returns are made from 24 ports, against only six in Japan.

We have now seen how great is the volume of the trade of these countries and how extensively they purchase from other lands. The share of the United States in this commercial exchange is next to be noted. Japan's imports from the United States in 1894 amounted to $11,000,000 approximately, but imports from England were over $42,000,000, and yet Japan is almost 9,000 miles nearer San Francisco than London. Imports from other European countries reached nearly $16,000,000. In short, Japan's imports from all Europe were $58,000,-000, or five times in excess of her American imports. A careful examination of the schedule of imports, however, shows that the United States can produce and manufacture fully 60 per cent. of the goods represented by that $58,000,000.

In the matter of exports from Japan the showing is still more remarkable. Her exports to the United States in 1894 were over $43,000,000, or a balance against us of $32,000,000! Contrast this with England. Her purchases from Japan were only $6,000,000, or a splendid balance in her favor of $34,000,000! The United States provides Japan with her best market. The nearest approach is France with purchases of $19,000,000, which are largely silk remanufactured, and then sold perhaps as extensively in the United States as in other lands.

The moral from these figures is plain. If the exporters of the United States wishing to trade with Japan would show as much energy and interest as their brother importers who have their best men stationed in the Mikado's realm to buy the first qualities of teas, silks, and curios, they could develop a greater market, and either make the balance in favor of America or at least equalize the exchange.

In China is another object lesson of American opportunity neglected, another illustration of an unfavorable balance. China's imports from the United States in 1894 approximated $10,000,000, her exports $25,000,000, or a debit balance for the United States of $15,000,000. From England her imports were $45,000,000 against exports of $36,000,000, or a credit balance in favor of that kingdom of $9,000,000. A minute study of the schedule of China's imports from England and other European countries permits the same conclusion that obtains in a like inspection of Japan's imports; there is no valid reason in the nature of the goods themselves why a major per cent. of them should not come from the United States. Were this paper merely a technical one, I would quote liberally from the specific customs' returns of China, Japan, and Siam, to substantiate more fully this assertion, but this is the work of trade reports. Not only could a large proportion of these articles be exported from America, but an investigation of both wholesale and retail prices proves that the American products could be sold at a reasonable profit.

Whatever may be the exact hindrances, there is no question that the decadence and threatened extinction of our merchant marine is a mill-stone around the neck of our foreign commerce. Let American shipping interests, fostered by the helping hand of Congress, regain their hold of former days in these waters, and our trade with the Orient will increase with a pace that will warm the heart of the coldest blooded misanthrope.

The shipping returns of Japan well nigh impel the patriotic American to hide his face in shame. Into the ports of that little kingdom, just over the sea from California, Oregon and Washington, there entered in 1894 only 32 steamers flying the Stars and Stripes out of a total of 1,788, and this paltry number showed a decrease of five from 37 in 1893! Out of a total tonnage of 2,539,951, the steamers of that nation whose fleet once ruled the ocean wide could muster only 83,350. Along with our lonely 32 steamers were 850 British and 370 German. In sailing vessels our showing was somewhat better, but there we were outnumbered again by the British.

I hesitate to speak of our shipping in China lest I be accused of misrepresentation, but as it is the purpose of this article to tell the truth and awaken interest in the hunt for the Golden Fleece of far Cathay, I must make no exceptions. Shanghai is the most important port of China. In 1894, 2,844 merchant steamers with a tonnage of 3,304,918 entered that port but not one was American! Not one American trading steamer came to Newchwang out of 348;

not one to Tientsin of 645; not one to Cheefoo of 1,031; not one to Chinkiang of 1,493; not one to Foochow of 294; not one to Canton of 2,250. Kind Amoy only breaks the mournful record, where four lone steamers out of 822 found a haven in her quiet waters. Hong Kong of course is the terminal point of our few trans-Pacific steamer lines, but that is not strictly a Chinese port. A small number of sailing ships wandering up and down the coast, and a few men-of-war cruising here and there, alone carried our flag into China's waters. I have already mentioned how lonesome the Legation ensign is in Siam.

In face of all these facts and conditions it is as palpable as the sun in the sky that American maritime and trade interests in this part of the world are not only grossly neglected, but afford an opportunity for vigorous development that it is ludicrous and inconsistent to deny.

Who is to blame? If Congress, let it proceed to legislate the remedy. If shippers and exporters, manufacturers and merchants, let them enter upon a campaign of education and development. If the American people at large, let them awake to the fact that the principle of the survival of the fittest must apply to nations, that commerce is their life-giving energy, and that without such life blood the United States cannot be numbered among the fittest.

To the Nicaragua canal reference has already been made, but it is of sufficient importance to invite more consideration. Were any man who is now opposed to its construction to thoroughly study its bearing on our commercial relations with Eastern Asia and all the other countries of the Pacific seas, it is probable that he would be convinced of the error of his position. The best British trade experts openly state that its completion will place the United States in a position to control the markets of the Pacific. Mr. A. S. Colquhoun, whose life and energies seem to be devoted to the advancement of Great Britain's foreign trade, has recently in an exhaustive discussion shown how completely in the event of its construction can the United States dominate every market north of Hong Kong and south east of Java, that is, Japan, Korea, northern and central China, Australia, and New Zealand and the islands of Australasia. The extent of the present commerce and traffic between Europe and the Pacific is measured to a large extent by the greatly increasing business of the Suez canal. The tonnage passing through the canal in 1894 reached the enormous volume of 11,750,000 tons, and its receipts the astonishing figures of 75,500,000 francs or about 15,100,000 gold dollars. The Nicaragua canal may not show such traffic and revenues at first, but it will not have long to wait. It will enable the South not only to supply the increasing demand for raw cotton in Japan and China which is destined to reach a great figure in the near future, but it will place the manufacturing centres of the Atlantic seaboard and the Central West 1,200 to 2,000 miles nearer the great markets of Japan, Korea, and Northern China. In brief it will give manufacturing and productive America a clear basis of advantage in the matter of water routes and transportation. In 1894, the exports of the United States to all the countries of Eastern Asia did not reach $15,000,000 gold, while those of Europe exceeded $75,000,000. Two years after the Nicaragua canal is opened, I deem it no exaggeration to say that our trans-Pacific trade will exceed $75,000,000 or a sum almost sufficient to construct it.

To enumerate all the conditions, the lack of which have retarded the development of our Asiatic trade in the past, and the presence of which will materially assist it, would consume more space than is at the writer's disposal. That I may not be guilty, however, of diagnosing a disease without naming a remedy, a few suggestions are given as a result of considerable investigation.

Aside from the building up of our merchant marine and the opening of the Nicaragua Canal, are the following: the establishment of reliable branch American houses to handle all classes of American products; the sending of representatives possessing experience, tact, and thorough knowledge of their lines, both to study the Oriental demand and develop a market; Chambers of Commerce, Boards of Trade, banking and commercial agencies, obtaining full and truthful data on the demands of markets, the most direct and the cheapest routes, and the financial rating of Asiatic buyers; offering inducements similar and equal to those offered by European merchants, such as favorable terms of purchase and credit, opportunity and time to take advantage of advance in exchange; sending consignments on commission; packing and preparing goods with great care, sending only the best quality and at competitive rates, and securing prompt despatch; liberal advertising in the press of the leading ports; the establishment, where feasible, of papers under American control; Americans entering the employ of Asiatic governments, where hundreds of Europeans now have a monopoly and are quiet promoters of European interests; the possible sending of commercial missions, like those sent out by the Chambers of Commerce of French, British, and German manufacturing centres; the reasonable subsidizing of steamship lines, such as is now done with profit by the chief countries of Europe; maintaining an effective naval squadron to "show the flag" and protect American interests; and last, but assuredly not least, increasing the efficiency of legations and consulates by providing a sufficient and competent staff to perform the manifold duties incumbent upon them, proper buildings for offices, and sufficient allowances to maintain the same on an equality with those of other nations. A commercial *attaché* at each legation who could devote his entire time to his work would prove a valuable addition to the usual force, and his appointment a worthy innovation upon the present system.

In regard to the cheap labor of Japan and China, there is no doubt that it presents a grave question, but it is one that time alone can solve. It is not such as to debar or deter American producers and manufacturers from entering the field. The day is yet distant, if it ever comes, when there will not be a great demand for foreign products in Japan, China, Siam and Korea. Our commercial interests must not be kept from the conquest by the reports of retired manufacturers who have made their own fortunes at home and report impressions gained by superficial observations of leisurely travel; by correspondents who come in by one door, as it were, and go out by the next; or by alarmists who hold the sixpence of European competition and Asiatic cheap labor so near their eye that they cannot see any good beyond.

In conclusion, a word more can be appropriately said concerning what I would term the "Importance of the Asiatic Opportunity." China is on the point of great development. Such a land cannot remain in material darkness. With her rivers, her plains, her plateaux, her mountains, all suggestive of latent power and possibilities, she is now where the United States was sixty years ago before the era of marvellous advancement. The conditions of race and population are different, but the raw material is there. Japan has on foot gigantic schemes for the further improvement of her land and people, while rich and undeveloped Formosa is awaiting her best efforts. Korea has vast unimproved mineral and agricultural resources. Siam is a garden with only the paths laid out and a fringe of flowers along their sides. And yet the same lands are the home of histories, religions, philosophies and peoples that were ancient before the United States were born.

Curzon in his "Problems of the Far East," and Norman in "The Far East," the latest and most exhaustive works on Eastern Asia, after studying these countries long and carefully, have used stronger language than I have employed. Unless all signs fail, a new era is coming in modern history. A "Pacific Question" is developing apace. The Atlantic must share its glories and power with its sister sea. As the latter is mightier in extent than the former, it may yet be the scene of mightier events in shaping the world's history.

In the new adjustment of international relations and the rearrangement of the world's commerce which must inevitably result, it remains for our country to decide whether its hand will be strong or weak.

10
A CLERGYMAN DEFENDS WAR IN 1898

Lyman Abbott (1835–1922), a Congregational minister, labored as much for the propagation of his secular as his religious views. Abbott was associated with his fellow clergyman, Henry Ward Beecher, in editing the *Christian Union* (later *The Outlook*), and in 1881, became editor-in-chief of the magazine. Seven years later, Abbott succeeded Beecher as minister of the prestigious and influential Plymouth Congregational Church in Brooklyn, New York.

Through his prolific pen and his persuasive platform oratory, Abbott displayed an analytical ability that brought him both fame and fortune. A leading advocate of the "social gospel", the belief in the more humanitarian applications of religion, Abbott accepted its Darwinian corollary that the "survival of the fittest" and "natural selection" applied to nations as well as to individuals. This he preached with messianic fervor in a sermon delivered in Plymouth Church during the Spanish-American War. In "The Duty and Destiny of America," Abbott placed upon the United States the responsibility for the future of the alien peoples and lands which, he was certain, it would acquire at the conclusion of the war. Holding such beliefs it is little wonder that Abbott became a close associate of Theodore Roosevelt who, after his presidency, chose *The Outlook* to broadcast his views.

THE DUTY AND DESTINY OF AMERICA

SENSE OF
SELF-DECEPTION **Lyman**
AS A NATION, **Abbott**

 # REASON
OVER
FORCE

WAR W/. SPAIN =

1.) EMOTIONAL

2.) MILITARY

3.) ENCROACHING POWER

4.) NO "IMPROVEMENT" TO
THE CUBANS.

SELF-GOVT.
UNDER
"RIGHTEOUS
LAW"

LAW = CONSCIENCE

What are the distinguishing characteristics of American history; how do we differ, if at all, from other people? In the first place, we are on this continent forty-four independent sovereign states, and yet in a century there has been but one battle between these states. Why? Because we have contrived a method? No; not only that — because with that method we have possessed ourselves of a certain power of self-restraint and patience, and have said, when these sovereign and independent states get into controversies with one another, they shall not settle them by appeal to force, they shall settle them by appeal to reason, and we will have a tribunal which shall exercise that reason for us. And this one war between the states grew out of the refusal of certain of them to abide by that agreement. That is the first distinguishing characteristic of the American people. All writers, I think, on constitutional law recognize the fact that there never has been in human history anything analogous to our Supreme Court. And it is not merely a tribunal which we have created; there is a principle which we have embodied in our national life — that controversies between communities as well as controversies between individuals shall be settled by right and by reason, not by force of arms.

Along with that has gone another — that we will depend chiefly on right and reason and conscience for the maintenance of law. We call this country a country of self-government. What do we mean by that? We mean, primarily, this: that we believe that men have wisdom enough to judge for themselves and conscience enough to respect the rights of their neighbor; and so, while we have our police and our armed force, and now and again we must call them into activity, in the main we depend, in this country, not on the police, not on the militia, to maintain the supremacy of the law; we believe there is a power in the human conscience and we trust to that power; in other words, we believe that if a law is a righteous law it will enforce itself. Or, to put it still more truly, we believe that God stands behind every righteous law, and that we can trust God Himself, by the force and operation of conscience speaking in man, to enforce righteous laws.

There is no other country that compares to America in its application of this principle of self-government; that is, trust to the

FROM *The Plymouth Morning Pulpit*, I (June 15, 1898).

conscience of men respecting the rights of their neighbors. I wonder if it will not surprise you, as last night it surprised me, to be told that the oldest legislative hall in the world is in the United States. The issue lies between the old House of Representatives hall in Washington and the State House of Representatives in Boston, the former first planned, the latter first completed. It is true that the older representative body is not in the United States; we borrowed from England's House of Commons our House of Representatives; but it is also true that not until after our House of Representatives became recognized as the supreme and final power in the land did the House of Commons become recognized as the supreme and final power in Great Britain. Self-government, trust in the reason and the conscience of man, is a distinguishing characteristic of this nation.

BORROWINGS FROM ENGLAND.

1688 ?

Along with this is an attempt, at least, to give an equal and fair opportunity to all men. I do not say that we have accomplished this attempt with anything like fullness; but it lies more in our purpose, and is wrought more into our constitution and our organic life, than it is in the life and constitution of any other nation. In England, in France, in Germany, in Russia, in all European Powers, men are born more or less into classes and remain there; in this country a man is born an American; that is all. He is not born a porter nor a merchant nor a lawyer nor a great landed aristocrat: he is born an American. There is poverty in New York as there is poverty in London. Let any man compare the two cities. Let him walk in the slums of the one city and then in the slums of the other, and he will find this characteristic difference: in London they are going down the hill, in New York they are climbing up. There is a submerged "tenth" in London, there is an emerging "tenth" in New York. Almost every man you meet in any one of our great cities has either a hope in the future for himself or a hope in the future for his children. Why? Because the doors are open; his child may become whatever he has the power to become; and the father either clearly knows or dimly perceives it. I do not say we have equal justice to all men in America, but I say there are fewer obstacles and more opportunities for all men than in any other country on the globe.

HORATIO ALGERNESS OF AMERICA.

Along with this free field and a fair chance, there is in this country a more systematic, a more thorough, and a more richly endowed provision for the education of all the people than in any other country. Our public-school system is far from perfect. We lament (and rightly) because there are to-day thousands of children roaming the streets of Brooklyn and the streets of New York, for

EDUCATIONAL SYSTEM

whom we have no school room; but these thousands of children are the exceptions, and in other countries they have been for the most part the rule. I do not forget the public school system of Germany, nor that of Great Britain, lately developed; nor that of Switzerland, whose public-school system perhaps equals our own, perhaps is superior to it — I do not know. Nevertheless, I venture the affirmation that there is no nation under the sun which has made so thorough, so systematic an endeavor by taxing itself to provide education for the poor, the ignorant, those who could not educate themselves, broadening that system out until it is a comprehensive system of self-education, beginning at the kindergarten and not ending until the student is graduated from the university. . . .

This country, with its broad acres, its great wealth, its free institutions, its free field, its public-school system, its untrammeled religious life, we have not kept for ourselves; we have invited other peoples of the earth to come and share it with us. I do not think there is any other nation that has thrown as wide open its gates, and sent out so urgent invitations; that has said to the foreigner in other lands: Come; we have a good thing; come and share it with us. And they have come. Irish and German and Pole and Hungarian and Italian, they have come until we hardly know whether we are an Anglo-Saxon people or not. We have not only invited them to come, but we have invited them to come and share in all that we have. We have said: Our churches are for you, our public schools are for you, our privileges and our liberties are for you. More than that, we have asked them to share with us in the responsibilities of our country. We have invited them to partnership. Some of us have thought this was too audacious; some of us have thought the period before naturalization ought to be longer. Whether it has been wise or unwise, right or wrong, this is what the country has done, and no other country has done it — no other. It has been a distinguishing characteristic of the American people that it has said: We have such faith in men that we will ask them to come, and, provided the man has been here long enough, to make clear that he wants to stay, and gives evidence that he is a man of good moral character, we let him share with us in the government; he shall help to elect our presidents and senators, our mayors and judges; he shall not only govern himself, he shall help to govern us. Wise, perhaps; foolish, possibly — no matter, it is a distinguishing feature of our life. What I am trying to do this morning is to show what are the distinguishing characteristics of American civilization; and one of them is a faith in humanity that is almost if not absolutely audacious, certainly unparalleled, in the world's history.

That is not all. We had millions of acres of land. We could have held to them until they rose in value and sold them and helped to pay our taxes with them. What did we do? Gave them away. We said to men in Norway, in Sweden, in Ireland, in Germany, Come: you are welcome; our doors are open: come, you shall share with us in our government; you shall go into our public schools; you shall enter into our churches; and if you will come we will give you a part of our wealth. We made a law, and we have carried it out until now nearly all our land is gone — that any man who will settle down on a farm and cultivate it may have it for nothing. There has been nothing like it in the history of the world. You may say it is a wise policy — I think it has been; you may say it has enriched the nation — I think it has; you may agree with me that one strong industrious household is worth more than one hundred and sixty acres of land to a nation — I think it is. I think it has been a wise, shrewd national policy. But it has been wise because it has been a generous, a liberal one — a policy of giving away; and you may search the annals of history for a parallel to it.

GIVEN LAND

Not drunkenness — which is bad; nor corruption — which is bad; nor lawlessness — which is bad (all of which are to be seen in other nations and in other peoples) — not these are the distinguishing characteristics of America; but a faith in righteousness and a reason able to determine questions between communities as between man and man; a faith in conscience as a power that will itself enforce righteous laws; a faith in humanity that declares every man shall have a fair chance; a kindness and a mercy that offers to every man a fair education; a generosity that offers these not merely to the citizens of our own nation, but to the citizens of all others; a faith in them so transcendentally audacious that we ask them to help govern and to rule us; and this faith accompanied with a generosity which gives to them a part of our national domain for the asking and the using — these are the distinguishing characteristics of the American people.

And the one great civil war we have had, the one terrible exception to our peaceful settlements of differences, is unlike any other civil war in human history. Not that it was longer — it was not so long as some; not that it was more terrible; in proportion to the people engaged perhaps not so terrible, certainly not so wasting; but in this: It is the one civil war in history fought by one people to emancipate another people. Not in the wars of the Roses, not in the war of the French Revolution, not in the wasting wars of Germany, not in the civil wars of Marius and Scylla, was there

*FREEING THE
SLAVES.*

FIGHTING ITS OWN PEOPLE!

anything comparable to this — a great war fought through four years by one people to set another people free. I know that men now, looking back, say it was not to set the slave free, but not the men who lived in that time say that. We who did live then know there would have been no gun aimed at Fort Sumpter unless first the people of the North had said there shall be no more extension of slavery; and we who lived then know that there would have been no gun fired on Fort Sumpter, if before that gun was fired Lincoln and the Republican party and the North had said to the South: You may carry your slaves into the Territories and may bring them as property into the Northern States. It was because we would not have the responsibility of slavery that we fought four years to cleanse our land of it.

I have spoken more than once on this platform of our national vices and our national sins, and I shall not hesitate, I hope, to do so again. But when I try to understand what God means by the epoch on which we are entering, and have looked back on the history of the past to see what sort of nation He has built up here, what I see as distinguishing it is this: A nation that seeks the glory of peace, not of war; a nation that trusts in the conscience of men to enforce righteous enactment; a nation that means to give a fair chance to every man; a nation that means to give him more than a fair chance, something like adequate education; a nation that means that religion shall be the free will offering of men, and that every man shall be free to offer what he will and every man free to refuse all offering if he will; a nation that offers all its advantages to every people of the earth on the same terms and conditions which it takes for itself; and a nation whose one great civil war was a real act of self-sacrifice for another and ignorant and oppressed people.

And now, suddenly, we have entered on a new epoch in our national history. A boy grows up to his teens and gets pretty nearly to the point when he is coming out of them, and be begins to feel within himself the dormant and unfledged capabilities of manly action. He begins to feel like taking on new responsibilities. He is eager to get into business; he is eager to take part in political problems; and his sagacious father holds him back and his better instructed judgment holds him back; and he waits. At last, some sudden event throws him into life; his father dies and the whole responsibility of the household falls upon his shoulders; a great political campaign confronts him, and he feels he must take some part in it; some single act of injustice is done before his eyes, and he pledges himself to set it right. The next morning he awakes a man. He was a boy; now he is a man. Instantly has he blossomed out. He was but a child yesterday; now behold him a man, taking his place among the men of the village, among the men of the city. Something like that, I think, has happened to these United States. Not more than three or four months ago I was saying: We do not want to meddle with the other nations of the earth; we have got all the problems we can attend to ourselves; we want no others. I say so no more. Suddenly this nation has been thrust out to take its place among the nations of the earth. There are no more hemispheres; there is only one great sphere, and we are all on it. We have awakened to find ourselves on this globe with Turkey and Russia and England, whether we would or no. We have passed our teens and have entered our manhood. The crudities, the imperfections, the audaciousness of our youth still cling to us; we have yet a great deal to learn; none the less we have entered on our national manhood. We are to carry into this new phase of our national development the qualities and characteristics of our national history in the past. God grant that we may leave back of us the persecutings, the corruption, the lawlessness, the lynch law, but may carry into the future the love of liberty, the confidence in men, the belief in conscience, the determination that all men shall have an equal chance, the desire to give to all men an equal education, the resolve that religion shall be free from persecuting domination on the one side and from every kind of coercion on the other.

The issue seems to me to be the old issue in a new form. I do not wish to take this day and this platform to glorify my country on the one hand, nor would I take it to villify Spain on the other. I have no hate for Spain. I hope for her long life and national prosperity. I hope yet to see her take her place among the nations of the earth, where she ought to take it, marching with the nations of the earth toward a larger liberty and a nobler life. I would not villify Spain; but still, when I consider what the issue is and put these two nations side by side and see what in their history, in their constitution, in their laws, they stand for, this seems to me very clear: On one side self-government, and on the other side a despotism, still maintained, though under forms of constitutional law; on one side a public-school system providing education for all the people, though not yet adequately, and on the other side, I believe, the greatest illiteracy of any state in Europe; on one side progress, the nineteenth century, marching by quick step into the twentieth, and on the other side the sixteenth century with scarcely

1) LIST U.S. "CHARACTS."
2) EMERGENCE OF U.S.
CHARACTER AT TURNING
POINT.

a flower of the nineteenth blooming on it; on one side the doctrine that religion and irreligion are absolutely free, and on the other a persecuting church still in control. I hope these reporters will not misreport me; you will not misunderstand me, I know. The Church of Rome is not the persecuting church I mean. I believe to-day that religious liberty would be as free in the hands of the American Catholic as in the hands of the American Protestant, in the hands of Cardinal Gibbons and Archbishop Ireland as in the hands of any minister in the land. But the Church of Spain is a persecuting church still, and the Church of America, Catholic and Protestant, is a church that loves liberty and stands for liberty.

This issue — liberty — despotism, equal chance — caste, public-school system — ignorance, nineteenth century — sixteenth century, freedom of religion — religious persecution — is the same issue that was fought between Drake and the Armada, the same issue that was fought between William of Orange and the Duke of Alva, in a new form.

I must hasten to my close. In this issue we cannot halt nor turn back. I do not discuss the question whether we have entered into this battle in the most dignified manner possible; I think we did not. I do not discuss the question whether we could have avoided the conflict by diplomacy; I do not believe we could have avoided it by diplomacy. I do not debate the question whether it ought not to have been settled by arbitration; questions of right ought to be settled by arbitration; questions of duty no. Whether we were under obligation to stand still while cruelty and rapine and starvation did their work just across the border was a question for the American to settle for himself, not to be settled for himself by any other man or body of men on the globe. But I do not discuss these questions. We are in the war, and we are in this war with liberty on one side and despotism on the other. What then? It is to be pushed forward with all vigor, nor any halt, nor any step backward till the end is reached. I believe in peace, but I do not believe in peaceful war. And when there is war, then the more vigor, the more strength, the more expedition, the more terrible fire put into it, the more mercy, for the quicker the end.

We did not mean to free the Philippine Islands, but we have done it, and the responsibility of the Philippine Islands is upon us, whether we like it or no. The responsibility of Cuba and Porto Rico will soon be upon us, whether we like it or no. We must accept the responsibility with all that which it involves; nor, I think, should we sheathe the sword nor stop a gun until the Spanish flag is hauled down from every foot of territory <u>on this side of the globe</u>. Nor can we give back a foot of territory on the other side of the globe which has been taken from under her power. To do it would be for St. George to give back the maiden to the dragon after the maiden had been captured from him.

In this campaign we are to be stirred to a higher sense of our own national duty within our own borders. The new problem which God has given to us abroad, is to quicken us to attend better to our problems at home. It would be monstrously inconsistent of us if we set ourselves against corruption, against despotism, against ignorance, and against narrowness in another nation and leave them to flourish in our own. Our first duty is to fight the foes at home. And our worst foes are not the Spanish spies who are investigating our fortifications and sending reports abroad, they are the men who are endeavoring to bring into this land the same corruption, the same ignorance and the same stagnation which have sealed the doom of Spain. There is not a mother who cannot have her part in this great campaign, if I read it rightly; . . . it is a campaign between ignorance and intelligence, between liberty and despotism, between a free religion and a persecuting religion.

We can be a recluse no more. We can no longer say we will live on this side of the sphere and other nations shall live on the other side of the sphere. We have taken our place among the nations of the earth. <u>God has, as it were, taken us by the shoulders and thrust us into it</u>. We shall need new equipment for foreign policy. We shall need educated consuls; we shall need educated ambassadors; <u>we shall need to recognize that we are a nation, and that the foreign policy inaugurated by one administration is not to be disregarded and disavowed by its successor</u>. <u>We shall need to recognize the fact that the nation has a continuity of history to be maintained in dealing with foreign nations</u>.

We may need a larger army, we may need a larger navy, but not chiefly there. We have built this nation up on the faith that there is a conscience in humanity, and we can appeal to it. We can build international amity up on the same faith. There is a conscience in other nations, and we can appeal to it. Have you not read, have you not considered the fact that every foreign journal that speaks the popular sentiment speaks for America, and every journal that speaks the aristocratic sentiment speaks for Spain. We will appeal from kings and thrones and aristocracies to the plain people; and there is intelligence and conscience enough in France, in Germany, in England — in the great nations of the world, to answer that appeal. There is an unknown power in conscience that never yet has been evoked nor its power essayed. It is not enough for us to say that we have not entered on this war for aggression; that we do not wish to secure territory; that we are not a body of bandits trying to rob a nation; we have entered on this campaign, if it be a righteous one at all, as a guardian for liberty; and as we have stood among our own people and in our own land for these great principles of self-government, of an equal chance of mercy and consideration, of free religion, so in our national policy we must stand for the same.

I do not advocate annexation; I do not advocate acquisition; I do not advocate a protectorate; I do not discuss on this platform or on this day the methods to be pursued; but I do say this: Wherever our flag floats, wherever our responsibility begins, there we are to stand for the principles that are wrought into the very structure of our nation — self-government, peace, an equal chance for every man, justice; and if this requires a colonial policy, or a protectorate, or even annexation, we are to accept the inevitable. We are responsible for the lands we free and we cannot evade that responsibility.

And in this campaign that reaches far into the history we have found an ally where, two years ago, we thought we had an enemy. Our institutions have been borrowed from England. She is our mother land. We have gone beyond her in some respects. She can learn some things from us; we can learn some things from her. But we are of the same race, with the same institutions, inspired by the same great spirit. I know it is said that this is not an Anglo-Saxon nation. What determines a nation? The men who make its laws, the men who shape its thoughts, the men who inspire its action, the men who guide its destiny, and frame the institutions which it possesses; and these in the United States are Anglo-Saxon. Look at our list of presidents, at our list of generals, our list of senators, our list of educators, our list of writers and authors: the great men of this nation who have shaped and directed it have been, with very few exceptions, Anglo-Saxon men. And our kin across the sea is of Anglo-Saxon race; and England and America joining hands together, not for self-aggrandizement, not for acquisition of territory, not for glory by war, but joining hands together for the kingdom of conscience, the kingdom of justice, the kingdom of equal chance, the kingdom of universal education, the kingdom of free religion, in one word, the kingdom of God on the earth, may lead if they will the procession of the nations down the future time till the end shall come.

Six centuries before Christ, when Israel was a captive in Babylon, there was a prophet, who, with an audacious faith, looking at
Israel a prisoner in Babylon, said: "Arise, shine, thy light is come,"
though the nation was in the dungeon, and saw but a glimmer of
light shining on it through prison walls. To this American nation,
whose light of intelligence, of liberty, of humanity has been the
distinguishing characteristic of its life, though blurred and dimmed
by many a vice and many a folly; there comes to-day from the
guns of Dewey's fleet across the sea this prophetic call: "Arise, shine,
for thy light has come, and nations shall come to thy light, and
bring to the lightness of thy rising."

11

THE ACQUISITION OF OVERSEAS LANDS

The politician and biographer, Albert J. Beveridge (1862–1927), was possibly the most eloquent proponent of expansionism in the land. Elected to the Senate at the age of thirty-seven in 1899, he served as one of the great spokesmen in that exclusive club for twelve years. His reputation in American politics rests in the main upon his role as a Republican insurgent in the progressive upheaval which, in 1912, divided the G.O.P. and elected Woodrow Wilson. Practically every liberal issue from trust reform to the protection of child labor received Beveridge's enthusiastic endorsement.

Basing much of his thinking on a first-hand investigation of the Philippines situation after those islands were won from Spain, he proudly defended expansionism in strident terms. "The March of the Flag," a speech he delivered in 1898, forms the classic statement for the acquisition of overseas territory by the United States. Later, Beveridge lent stout support to the spirited and expansionist diplomacy of his idol, Theodore Roosevelt. It was Beveridge who chaired the Chicago Bull Moose Convention of 1912 which nominated ex-President Roosevelt. After his retirement from the Senate in 1911, Beveridge won fame for his incomparable biographies of John Marshall (a Pulitzer Prize winner) and Abraham Lincoln.

THE MARCH OF THE FLAG

Albert J. Beveridge

FELLOW CITIZENS:

It is a noble land that God has given us; a land that can feed and clothe the world; a land whose coast lines would enclose half the countries of Europe; a land set like a sentinel between the two imperial oceans of the globe, a greater England with a nobler destiny. It is a mighty people that He has planted on this soil; a people sprung from the most masterful blood of history; a people perpetually revitalized by the virile, man-producing working folk of all the earth; a people imperial by virtue of their power, by right of their institutions, by authority of their heaven-directed purposes — the propagandists and not the misers of liberty. It is a glorious history our God has bestowed upon His chosen people; a history whose keynote was struck by Liberty Bell; a history heroic with faith in our mission and our future; a history of statesmen who flung the boundaries of the republic out into unexplored lands and savage wildernesses; a history of soldiers who carried the flag across the blazing deserts and through the ranks of hostile mountains, even to the gates of sunset; a history of a multiplying people who overran a continent in half a century; a history of prophets who saw the consequences of evils inherited from the past, and of martyrs who died to save us from them; a history divinely logical, in the process of whose tremendous reasoning we find ourselves to-day.

Therefore, in this campaign, the question is larger than a party question. It is an American question. It is a world question. Shall the American people continue their resistless march toward the commercial supremacy of the world? Shall free institutions broaden their blessed reign as the children of liberty wax in strength, until the empire of our principles is established over the hearts of all mankind?

Have we no mission to perform, no duty to discharge to our fellow man? Has the Almighty Father endowed us with gifts beyond our deserts and marked us as the people of His peculiar favor, merely to rot in our own selfishness, as men and nations must who take cowardice for their companion and self for their deity — as China has, as India has, as Egypt has?

Shall we be as the man who had one talent and hid it, or as he who had ten talents and used them until they grew to riches?

FROM *Modern Eloquence*, XI (Philadelphia, 1903), pp. 224–43.

And shall we reap the reward that waits on our discharge of our high duty as the sovereign power of earth; shall we occupy new markets for what our farmers raise, new markets for what our factories make, new markets for what our merchants sell — aye, and, please God, new markets for what our ships shall carry?

Shall we avail ourselves of new sources of supply of what we do not raise or make, so that what are luxuries to-day will be necessities to-morrow? Shall our commerce be encouraged until, with Oceanica, the Orient, and the world, American trade shall be the imperial trade of the entire globe?

Shall we conduct the mightiest commerce of history with the best money known to man, or shall we use the pauper money of Mexico, of China, and of the Chicago platform?

What are the great facts of this administration? Not a failure of revenue; not a perpetual battle between the executive and legislative departments of government; not a rescue from dishonor by European syndicates at the price of tens of millions in cash and national humiliation unspeakable. These have not marked the past two years — the past two years, which have blossomed into four splendid months of glory.

But a war has marked it, the most holy ever waged by one nation against another — a war for civilization, a war for a permanent peace, a war which, under God, although we knew it not, swung open to the republic the portals of the commerce of the world. And the first question you must answer with your vote is, whether you indorse that war? We are told that all citizens and every platform indorse the war, and I admit, with the joy of patriotism, that this is true. But that is only among ourselves, and we are of and to ourselves no longer. This election takes place on the stage of the world, with all earth's nations for our auditors. If the administration is defeated at the polls, will England believe that we accept the results of the war?

Will Germany, that sleepless searcher for new markets for her factories and fields, and therefore the effective meddler in all international complications — will Germany be discouraged from interfering with our settlement of the war, if the administration is defeated at the polls?

Germany a meddler, U.S. not.

Will Russia, that weaver of the webs of commerce, into which province after province and people after people falls, regard us as a steadfast people if the administration is defeated at the polls?

The world is observing us to-day. Not a foreign office in Europe that is not studying the American republic and watching the American elections of 1898 as it never watched an American election before.

Are the American people the chameleon of the nations? "If so, we can easily handle them," say the diplomats of the world.

Which result, say you, will have the best effect for us upon the great powers who watch us with the jealousy strength always inspires — a defeat, at the hand of the American people, of the administration which has conducted our foreign war to a world-embracing success, and which has in hand the most important foreign problems since the Revolution; or such an indorsement of the administration by the American people as will swell to a national acclaim? . . .

God bless the soldiers of 1898, children of the heroes of 1861, descendants of the heroes of 1776! In the halls of history they will stand side by side with those elder sons of glory, and the opposition to the government at Washington shall not deny them.

No! they shall not be robbed of the honor due them, nor shall the republic be robbed of what they won for their country. For William McKinley is continuing the policy that Jefferson began, Monroe continued, Seward advanced, Grant promoted, Harrison championed, and the growth of the republic has demanded. Hawaii is ours; Porto Rico is to be ours; at the prayer of the people Cuba will finally be ours; in the islands of the East, even to the gates of Asia, coaling stations are to be ours; at the very least the flag of a liberal government is to float over the Philippines, and I pray God it may be the banner that Taylor unfurled in Texas and Fremont carried to the coast — the stars and stripes of glory.

And the burning question of this campaign is, whether the American people will accept the gifts of events; whether they will rise as lifts their soaring destiny; whether they will proceed upon the lines of national development surveyed by the statesmen of our past; or whether, for the first time, the American people doubt their mission, question fate, prove apostate to the spirit of their race, and halt the ceaseless march of free institutions.

The opposition tells us that we ought not to govern a people without their consent. I answer: The rule of liberty, that all just government derives its authority from the consent of the governed, applies only to those who are capable of self-government. I answer: We govern the Indians without their consent, we govern our territories without their consent, we govern our children without their consent. I answer: How do you assume that our government would be without their consent? Would not the people of the Philippines prefer the just, humane, civilizing government of this republic to the savage, bloody rule of pillage and extortion from which we have rescued them?

Do not the blazing fires of joy and the ringing bells of gladness in Porto Rico prove the welcome of our flag?

And, regardless of this formula of words, made only for enlightened, self-governing peoples, do we owe no duty to the world? Shall we turn these people back to the reeking hands from which we have taken them? Shall we abandon them to their fate, with the wolves of conquest all about them — with Germany, Russia, France, even Japan, hungering for them? Shall we save them from those nations, to give them a self-rule of tragedy? It would be like giving a razor to a babe and telling it to shave itself. It would be like giving a typewriter to an Eskimo and telling him to publish one of the great dailies of the world. This proposition of the opposition makes the Declaration of Independence preposterous, as the reading of Job's lamentations would be at a wedding or an Altgeld speech on the Fourth of July.

NO ACKNOWLEDGEMENT OF CULTURE.

They ask us how we will govern these new possessions. I answer: Out of local conditions and the necessities of the case methods of government will grow. If England can govern foreign lands, so can America. If Germany can govern foreign lands, so can America. If they can supervise protectorates, so can America. Why is it more difficult to administer Hawaii than New Mexico or California? Both had a savage and an alien population; both were more remote from the seat of government when they came under our dominion than Hawaii is to-day.

Will you say by your vote that American ability to govern has decayed; that a century's experience in self-rule has failed of a result? Will you affirm by your vote that you are an infidel to American vigor and power and practical sense? Or, that we are of the ruling race of the world; that ours is the blood of government; ours the heart of dominion; ours the brain and genius of administration? Will you remember that we do but what our fathers did — we but pitch the tents of liberty farther westward, farther southward — we only continue the march of the flag. . . .

Distance and oceans are no arguments. The fact that all the territory our fathers bought and seized is contiguous, is no argument. In 1819 Florida was farther from New York than Porto Rico is from Chicago to-day; Texas, farther from Washington in 1845 than Hawaii is from Boston in 1898; California, more inaccessible in 1847 than the Philippines are now. Gibraltar is farther from London than Havana is from Washington; Melbourne is farther from Liverpool than Manila is from San Francisco. The ocean does not separate us from lands of our duty and desire — the oceans join us, a river never to be dredged, a canal never to be repaired.

#2 ANTI-IMP.

Steam joins us; electricity joins us — the very elements are in
league with our destiny. Cuba not contiguous! Porto Rico not contiguous! Hawaii and the Philippines not contiguous! Our navy will
make them contiguous. Dewey and Sampson and Schley have made
them contiguous, and American speed, American guns, American
heart and brain and nerve will keep them contiguous forever.

But the opposition is right — there is a difference. We did not
need the western Mississippi valley when we acquired it, nor Florida,
nor Texas, nor California, nor the royal provinces of the far North-
west. We had no emigrants to people this imperial wilderness, no
money to develop it, even no highways to cover it. No trade awaited
us in its savage fastnesses. Our productions were not greater than
our trade. There was not one reason for the land-lust of our statesmen
from Jefferson to Grant, other than the prophet and the Saxon within
them.

But to-day we are raising more than we can consume. To-day
we are making more than we can use. To-day our industrial society
is congested; there are more workers than there is work; there is
more capital than there is investment. We do not need more
money — we need more circulation, more employment. Therefore
we must find new markets for our produce, new occupation for
our capital, new work for our labor. And so, while we did not need
the territory taken during the past century at the time it was required,
we do need what we have taken in 1898, and we need it now.

Think of the thousands of Americans who will pour into Hawaii
and Porto Rico when the republic's laws cover those islands with
justice and safety! Think of the tens of thousands of Americans
who will invade mine and field and forest in the Philippines when
a liberal government, protected and controlled by this republic, if
not the government of the republic itself, shall establish order and
equity there! Think of the hundreds of thousands of Americans who
will build a soap-and-water, common-school civilization of energy
and industry in Cuba, when a government of law replaces the double
reign of anarchy and tyranny. Think of the prosperous millions that
empress of islands will support when, obedient to the law of political
gravitation, her people ask for the highest honor liberty can bestow,
the sacred Order of the Stars and Stripes, the citizenship of the
Great Republic!

What does all this mean for every one of us? It means opportunity for all the glorious young manhood of the republic — the most
virile, ambitious, impatient, militant manhood the world has ever
seen. It means that the resources and the commerce of these immensely rich dominions will be increased as much as American energy

is greater than Spanish sloth; for Americans henceforth will monopolize those resources and that commerce.

In Cuba alone there are 15,000,000 acres of forest unacquainted with the ax. There are exhaustless mines of iron. There are priceless deposits of manganese, millions of dollars of which we must buy to-day from the Black Sea districts. There are millions of acres yet unexplored.

The resources of Porto Rico have only been trifled with. The riches of the Philippines have hardly been touched by the finger-tips of modern methods. And they produce what we cannot, and they consume what we produce — the very predestination of reciprocity — a reciprocity "not made with hands, eternal in the heavens." They sell hemp, silk, sugar, cocoanuts, coffee, fruits of the tropics, timber of price like mahogany; they buy flour, clothing, tools, implements, machinery, and all that we can raise and make. And William McKinley intends that their trade shall be ours.

Do you indorse that policy with your vote? It means creative investment for every dollar of idle capital in the land — an opportunity for the rich man to do something with his money besides hoarding it or lending it. It means occupation for every workingman in the country at wages which the development of new resources, the launching of new enterprises, the monopoly of new markets always brings.

Cuba is as large as Pennsylvania, and is the richest spot on all the globe. Hawaii is as large as New Jersey; Porto Rico half as large as Hawaii; the Philippines larger than all New England, New York, New Jersey, and Delaware. All these are larger than the British Isles, larger than France, larger than Germany, larger than Japan. The trade of these islands, developed as we will develop it by developing their resources, monopolized as we will monopolize it, will set every reaper in this republic singing, every spindle whirling, every furnace spouting the flames of industry.

I ask each one of you this personal question: Do you believe that these resources will be better developed and that commerce best secured; do you believe that all these priceless advantages will be better availed of for the benefit of this republic by Bryan, Bailey, Bland, and Blackburn and the opposition; or by William McKinley and a House and Senate that will help and not hinder him?

Which do you think will get the most good for you and the American people out of the opportunities which Providence has given us — the government at Washington, or the opposition in Nebraska, Texas, Kentucky, and Missouri?

Which side will you belong to — those who pull forward in

*NATURAL
PROGRESSION*

the traces of national prosperity and destiny, or those who pull back
in those traces, balk at every step of advancement, and bray at every
mile-post of progress . . .

Why not accept the gifts of nature and events — events which
have made the oceans our servants, the trade-winds our allies, and
the stars in their courses our champions?

Nature, which has thrown the wealth of Klondike, the new-
found gold of the Philippines, the unsuspected and exhaustless mines
of Colorado and the Cape into the crucible of financial agitation,
and thus dissolved the last excuse for war upon the gold standard
of civilization — the excuse that the gold supply is insufficient and
is failing.

Now, when new rivers of gold are pouring through the fields
of business, the foundations of all silver-standard arguments are
swept away. Why mumble the meaningless phrases of a tale that
is told, when the golden future is before us, the world calls us,
its wealth awaits us, and God's command is upon us?

Why stand in the fatal stupor of financial fallacies muttering
old sophistries that time has exploded, when opportunity beckons
you all over the world — in Cuba, Hawaii, the Philippines, on the
waters of commerce, in every market of the Occident and the Orient,
and in your factories and stores and fields, here in our own beloved
country, holy America, land of God's promise and home of God's
providence?

There are so many real things to be done — canals to be dug,
railways to be laid, forests to be felled, cities to be builded, unviolated
fields to be tilled, priceless markets to be won, ships to be launched,
peoples to be saved, civilization to be proclaimed, and the flag of
liberty flung to the eager air of every sea. Is this an hour to waste
upon triflers with nature's laws? Is this a season to give our destiny
over to word-mongers and prosperity wreckers? Is this a day to think
of office-seekers, to be cajoled by the politician's smile, or seduced
by the hand-shake of hypocrisy? No! No! my fellow citizens!

It is an hour to remember your duty to the home. It is a moment
to realize the opportunities fate has opened to this favored people
and to you. It is a time to bethink you of the conquering march
of the flag. It is a time to bethink you of your nation and its sovereignty of the seas. It is a time to remember that the God of our
fathers is our God, and that the gifts and the duties He gave to
them, enriched and multiplied, He renews to us, their children.

And so it is an hour for us to stand by the government at
Washington, now confronting the enemy in diplomacy, as our loyal

hearts on land and sea stood to their guns and stood by the flag when they faced the enemy in war. It is a time to strengthen and sustain that devoted man, servant of the people and of the most high God, who patiently, silently, safely is guiding the republic out into the ocean of world interests and possibilities infinite. It is a time to cheer the beloved President of God's chosen people, till the whole world is vocal with American loyalty to the American government.

Fellow Americans, we are God's chosen people. Yonder at Bunker Hill and Yorktown His providence was above us. At New Orleans and on ensanguined seas His hand sustained us. Abraham Lincoln was His minister, and His was the Altar of Freedom the boys in blue set on a hundred battle-fields. His power directed Dewey in the East, and delivered the Spanish fleet into our hands on the eve of Liberty's natal day, as He delivered the elder armada into the hands of our English sires two centuries ago. His great purposes are revealed in the progress of the flag, which surpasses the intentions of congresses and cabinets, and leads us like a holier pillar of cloud by day and pillar of fire by night into situations unforeseen by finite wisdom, and duties unexpected by the unprophetic heart of selfishness. The American people cannot use a dishonest medium of exchange; it is ours to set the world its example of right and honor. We cannot fly from our world duties; it is ours to execute the purpose of a fate that has driven us to be greater than our small intentions. We cannot retreat from any soil where Providence has unfurled our banner; it is ours to save that soil for liberty and civilization. For liberty and civilization and God's promise fulfilled, the flag must henceforth be the symbol and the sign to all mankind — the flag! — . . . .

12

EXPANSION JUSTIFIED IN TERMS OF SOCIAL DARWINISM

Harry Huntington Powers (1859–1936), educator and author, taught various social sciences at schools such as Smith College and Stanford and Cornell Universities. A world traveler of note, Powers wrote extensively on Italian and Greek art and the beauties of sightseeing in foreign lands. His published works include *America Among the Nations* (1917), *America and Britain* (1918), *The Great Peace* (1918), and *The American Era* (1920). Powers held that the world was still largely misguided and quarrelsome. In the essay here presented, Powers argues heatedly the notion of the day, resting upon Social Darwinism, that strong civilizations must and will overpower weaker ones.

THE ETHICS OF EXPANSION

Harry H. Powers

The discussion of the ethics of the new expansion policy of the United States seems to have suffered much from uncertainty in its fundamental assumptions. By what criterion are we to judge the ethics of larger human relations? Some quote Scripture or other venerable authority, only to be met by a counter-quotation, and the effort to determine who has wrested the Scripture to his own destruction brings back the original question. Others apply the rules governing individual relations and construe the commands against killing and theft into prohibitions of war and conquest. But are the cases really analogous? This is the original question in another form. As usual, we make no progress by elaborating primary equivocations. Very much recent argument seems to have been of this character. This is my excuse for calling brief attention to certain primary truths which are generally accepted as principles and regularly ignored in their practical applications.

Wherever there is life there is growth, and wherever there is growth there must sooner or later be competition. Inevitably the stronger forms of life displace the weaker and progress is the result. Progress is nothing else, can be nothing else in nature, than the substitution of the more efficient for the less efficient forms of life. This process, too, is one in which we have no choice but to acquiesce. Inefficiency can neither long maintain itself nor be long maintained against efficiency. This law is as universal as it is inexorable, and all other vital principles are its servants, never its rivals.

It is as useless to speculate about the ethics of this universal competition as to speculate about the ethics of gravitation. So far as we can see, the process is non-ethical, altogether transcending the limits of moral obligation. But ethical or not, it is absolutely universal. The notion that other laws are opposed to this and tend to displace it, is utterly unfounded. They are but refinements of it, and exist and develop solely on condition that they increase its efficiency. Ethical phenomena, therefore, like all other special phenomena, are resolvable into more fundamental elements, which are non-ethical or super-ethical. . . .

What is the ethical character of international relations? No answer can be given that is wholly comprehensive, but the general

FROM *International Journal of Ethics*, X (April 1900), pp. 288–306.

truth is clear. The relation between groups formed for competitive efficiency is primarily a competitive relation. There is no such dependence between them as exists between individuals within the group, nor does forbearance tend in any such degree to promote collective efficiency. The struggle for race supremacy is but a phase of that deeper conflict which we have seen to be universal in nature, and it cannot be condemned without condemning the whole process of nature. In this struggle, coöperation and all its attendant instincts are but incidents, strategic moves, dictated by considerations of expediency.

Like every phase of the struggle for existence, race competition is constructive. It develops not only increasingly hardy and efficient groups, but a progressive consolidation of groups looking towards an ultimate synthesis. With this tendency the higher social instincts are in universal accord. All look forward to a "parliament of man, a federation of the world." But it is urged that this synthesis should be voluntary and not coerced, that it should be accomplished by federation rather than conquest. That means that we should wait till the social instincts of men are sufficiently developed to draw us all together. But this is impossible under the existing conditions of social progress. The social instincts do not precede social experience, they proceed from it. Individuals unite from necessity and only after long adaptation does necessity pass over into choice. Whatever may be true of the future, federation is as yet merely a by-product of war. How soon would the Swiss cantons, the German States or the American colonies have united in pursuit of peaceful advantage? Even if the nations of mankind should at last effect a peaceable union, it could be little else than a potential conquest, an intelligent forecast of the inevitable outcome. Such a forecast implies a long experience in vast societies with world-wide interests, and these must be the product of conquest. It is impossible to believe that even the highest races have the intelligence to recognize the ascendencies and elect the affinities which must govern the future. Still less can we believe that the uncivilized races will develop that intelligence within any calculable period. Must we wait their time and leave them in festering disorganization in the midst of an organized humanity? It should not and it will not be.

We are confronted, therefore, with an ultimate synthesis of humanity, perhaps not far remote as such things go, the main lines of which we can already trace. Like every adjustment effected by nature, it will be based, not upon the equality but upon the inequality of its component parts. Some race, more virile and constructive than the rest, will get the ascendency. Other races, though nominally independent, will take their cue from this, recognizing at first by vehement denials and then by sullen acquiescence a hegemony which will at last pass over into automatic and even enthusiastic allegiance as time brings its inevitable adaptations. In attaining this result the weak races of the temperate zones seem destined to extinction, those races of the temperate zones seem destined to extension, those of the tropics to subjection. What else should or can be the fate of inferiority?

I know there is a feeling in some quarters that all this should somehow be prevented, that venerable civilizations should be preserved and vanishing races artificially protected. There is undoubtedly an element of tragedy in it all. The successive wane of Moorish, Spanish and Romance civilization has its pathetic aspect to which the most relentless rival cannot be insensible. But dying races suffer little and dead races suffer naught. To bewail the process is to misconceive its import and to squander sympathies which spent elsewhere would minister unto life. For happiness, however dependent for the moment on tottering institutions and obsolete adjustments, is ultimately synonymous with adaptation and health. What if Boer or Maori or Castillian be eliminated or lost to view! Will there be less of life where they have been, or that life be less worthy or less human? Is it a loss that the pterodactyle has vanished and that "Nature brings not back the mastodon"? Only those who conceive of the earth as intended for an ethnological museum can regret the progressive displacement of the lower by the higher races of mankind. If it be said that we can educate these races up to our level the reply is that it will not be done, because it is not the economical thing to do. It is vastly easier to displace a feeble stock than to assimilate it upward by education, and if we invest our vital capital in a losing process, a thriftier race will disposses both our protégés and us.

EVIL

It is clear that the organization of mankind will be as little hampered in the future as it has been in the past by such considerations as inalienable rights and the consent of the governed. Weakness has everywhere yielded to strength, sullenly and resistingly but inevitably. Yet out of these stern coercions have grown some of the stablest and most efficient governments on earth. It was not with their consent that the Danes passed under the rule of Alfred, or the Welsh under that of Edward. It was not with alacrity that the Southern States renewed their allegiance to the government at Washington. But these governments are stable, efficient and prosperous. They have followed the universal law of social evolution. Coerced into union, that union has become indissoluble through adaptations of structure and feeling effected by experience. Such governments may not be just (I confess I never did know what that word meant) but they rally all sympathies about them and are enduring monuments of social achievement. Voluntary unions may have some sacerdotal superiority, but it is one not easily translated into terms of efficiency or happiness. Even the union of which we are so proud knew no stability till the compact was ratified by the sword.

If my reasoning is correct the process with which we have here to do, coercive consolidation and the establishment of universal order, is inherently normal and wholesome. Should the United States participate or hold aloof?

It should be apparent from the foregoing pages that the question is primarily one of expediency. We are not estopped by any moral consideration from extending our territory at the expense of Spain or any other power. It is inherently as admissible to subjugate the Philippines with the sword as it is to subjugate France by industrial superiority. The subjugation is not more real or more painful. The question of ways and means is merely one of tactical advantage.

But while we are not restrained by any sweeping moral prohibition, moral factors enter largely into the question of expediency. The first of these factors is the one already referred to, the confusion of moral judgment, the tendency to interpret all relations by the analogy of those more intimate relations with which experience makes us familiar. It is evident that whatever of error is involved in these judgments can only be in the direction of exaggeration, since the less intimate relation is interpreted by the more intimate one. The right of Spain to Cuba is very different from the right of a Spaniard to his Cuban estate, but the tender conscience is at first inclined to assign it equal validity. Our "century of dishonor" in connection with the Indian race is merely a continuous attempt to reconcile sub-ethical relations with full ethical standards. The discovery that these judgments are erroneous does not obviate the necessity of showing deference to the instincts involved, for they are at best scarcely sufficient for the task legitimately required of them, and the least discouragement may have disastrous consequences. The ability to justify necessary action to these somewhat undiscriminating monitors is an indispensable condition of that union of inner forbearance and outward aggressiveness which makes nations great.

Fortunately, the American people is quite equal to all such emergencies. Its readiness to emancipate Cuba from oppression and to confer the blessing of American institutions on the benighted Philippines, and its ability to take such arguments seriously, fully convinced that they are the real ground of its action, are an admirable example of this necessary reconciliation of seemingly incompatible functions. It is idle to object that such devices are disingenuous and illogical. The whole social fabric is a tissue of beneficent fictions, of contradictory instincts specialized for divergent functions and harmonized by pseudo-logic. The veriest tyro in the study of society should know better than to take its logic seriously.

In one respect the moral sense of the American people is peculiarly adapted to this *role* of constructive aggression. Our whole experience has accustomed us to honor dynamic rather than static rights. Our territory has been appropriated, our wealth created and our authority established by our strong arm. When Spain, resting back upon centuries of undisputed possession, passionately declared, "Cuba is ours," she obeyed an impulse born of centuries of status and decay. America challenged this title with characteristic vigor and conviction. No title was valid which did not rest upon power to hold and use in the interests of humanity. And we said it in all conscience, for such is our only title to all we possess. This moral temper which is thus adjusted to the necessities of constructive aggression in a degree peculiarly fits us for the great struggle.

One further moral factor of the greatest importance remains to be considered. I have said that the relation between nations is primarily competitive rather than coöperative, but it is not exclusively so. Relations of forbearance and dependence recognized by each party do exist in varying degrees between nations. I confess that in the great majority of cases these international relations which may be called ethical seem to me extremely rudimentary. No greater tactical blunder could be made than to place serious reliance upon the most of these in practical affairs. If it be argued that with sufficient deference these feelings will grow to the degree necessary to meet all requirements, I reply that this is neither probable nor certainly desirable. It is in the highest degree unlikely that a peaceful organization of existing human elements into a world society on the basis of the present status, would be either possible or desirable. War, aggression, constructive conquest have not yet done their work. It is scarcely too much to say that a peaceful federation of mankind at the present juncture would be a misfortune, over-burdening the delicate selective agencies working within organized society with

COMPETITIVE VS.
COOPERATIVE
NATIONS.

the gross, heavy work which should be done by the powerful en-
ginery of race conflict. And as long as that work is not done we
must not lose the power or the will to do it. Woe to the nation
that unlearns war too soon while as yet cruder and hardier peoples
have not done with its schooling and have not learned the scruples
that paralyze its rival's arm. The great majority of these incipient
moral relations between races are destined to collapse before the
stress of race conflict, and, as the feebler contestants are eliminated
by incorporation or extinction, the budding sentiments of international comity will blast, which were not destined to bear fruit. There
is reason to believe that there will be exceptions to this rule, that
some existing international relations will develop into strictly social
relations, merging the nations in question in a common social life.
Where inner development has proceeded far enough to make such
a union stable and efficient, the ethics of such international relations
are not open to dispute.

The moral factors that complicate the problem of expediency
are thus of a varied character, requiring sometimes restraint, sometimes encouragement, and always tactful management. We can
hardly close our inquiry, however, without considering briefly some
of the more exclusively prudential factors which enter into the problem. Is our proposed move good strategy?

Three classes of objections are raised. The first have to do with
our constitution and its alleged limitations. These questions I shall
not discuss, both because a lay opinion is of little value and because
I do not imagine the obstacle to be very serious. If the move we
are contemplating is important the constitution is not likely to stand
in its way. If we cannot amend it we can "interpret" it, which is
quite as effectual and a far more normal method of adaptation. The
task now imposed upon our Supreme Court is certainly easy as
compared with former tasks, no matter which way the decision must
eventually go.

A more serious objection is that based upon the nature of our
government and its supposed ideals. We have founded a democracy
the essence of which is the participation of all citizens in the duties
and privileges of government. The advantages claimed for such a
system are two-fold. It prevents tyranny, or the exploitation of society
in the interest of a governing class, and it develops the individual
by the constant exercise of faculties of a high order. It is interesting
to note the *role* played by these arguments.

A century ago the first was considered the sufficient as it was
virtually the only argument for democracy. Hatred of tyranny and

NEW
IDEAS
EMERGIN'

sublime confidence in the power of the people, clothed with political rights, to avert that dread enemy of mankind is strangely prominent in the writings of our statesmen. The reason is, of course, to be found in contemporary experience. But from the time of John Stuart Mill much less attention has been given to this argument, while the educational function of democracy has risen to unwonted honor. Mill declares it to be more important that a government should educate than that it should maintain order. The same sentiment is vigorously expressed by a well-known writer in the assertion that the best government is not that which governs best but that which produces the best men.

It is hardly too much to say that this shifting in the line of defense is also due to political experience. The first century of democracy has been disappointing. I do not claim that democracy has failed in the United States, though its achievements have been finite, but certainly none of our imitators have even passably succeeded. Even France has probably achieved no substantial amelioration of her social conditions by adopting a popular government. This comparative failure of American democracy is tacitly confessed by one of its ablest defenders in a recent article, in which he argues that we have not yet given it a fair trial and must not throw it overboard.

Under such circumstances we can understand the emphasis upon the other argument. Democracy is a very congenial idea to certain temperaments and it is not likely to be readily abandoned. But whatever its merits, the argument now urged in its defense must be received with caution. Democracy, like any other social institution, educates men in that it adapts them to its own requirements. The assertion that it makes men or that it educates men implies that it fits men for requirements in general. But however near the truth this may happen to be, it is in principle false. All such education is special rather than general. Exercise in politics fits a man for politics, but not necessarily for other functions. The value of this education will depend primarily upon the necessity of these functions. If democracy is to be the government of the future, then to educate men for it is worth some blundering, but if not, then men had better be educated for what is actually in store for them. I am not disparaging democracy, as I shall presently make clear, but I much prefer to drive with the horse before the cart. To urge that a government be retained which does not govern well on the ground that it is an educator, is to overlook the fact that by the inexorable law of functional adaptation such a government must become a miseducator. To plead for the retention of democracy on the ground that it makes good citizens is like pleading for war on the ground that it makes good soldiers. All social functions and activities tend to fit men for their exercise, and in this respect democracy can have no preëminence. To say that the best government is the one that makes the best men is merely reasoning in a circle, since the best men are merely those that are the best adapted to the conditions, political and social, of their existence.

The criterion of government is the same as that of all other things, adaptation to the conditions of existence. That arrangement is best, here as everywhere, which is most workable, most efficient, best able to resist destroying forces, and those men are best who are best adapted to these arrangements. To assign to one government the function of establishing order and to another that of educating men is quite beyond our power. The function of government is determined by the necessities of human society, necessities to which it owes its being and which are sufficiently known to us to put that function beyond doubt. Government must maintain that equilibrium between liberty and control which will conduce to the highest social efficiency. It must not sacrifice efficiency in the interest of man-making any more than in the interest of machine-making, and the one is as possible as the other. The test of government is, first, last and always, its ability to govern, to perpetuate itself by perpetuating the society committed to its keeping.

We are told that either the Philippines must be admitted to full participation in our government (a proposal happily not widely entertained), or the whole theory of democracy falls. Apparently that would be about the extent of the damage. It is not plain why our government should not go on otherwise much as before. The exclusion from political rights is not of a kind to prove insidious, nor is the Anglo-Saxon inclined to carry out principles to their logical conclusion. Whatever works well in our institutions is likely to be retained. *— THE EXPEDIENCY OF THE ISLANDS AS RETAINED*

But it is urged that under the new conditions our institutions will not work well and we shall be forced in the interest of efficiency to adopt an "oligarchical" government like that of England, a necessity only to be averted by sticking to our proper function of making men. Anything so abhorrent to our instincts as an "oligarchy" should not be accepted without careful consideration. It may not be amiss, therefore, to inquire more closely into the nature of those institutions with which we are menaced.

In England as in America there is freedom of speech, freedom of the press and effective education of public opinion. In both there is substantially universal manhood suffrage, representative and re-

ANTI-IMPS. + IMPS. NEITHER WANT ISLANDS AS ACTUAL STATES

sponsible government and the amplest guarantee of civil rights. In some of these the advantage is certainly with England, in not one is it on our side. But in England the experts in charge of government are entrusted with a real power of initiative, a trust for which they are held hourly responsible, while in the United States that right of initiative is less centralized and less definite and is coupled with a correspondingly feeble and inefficient responsibility. The English Cabinet can make treaties or declare war on its own motion, while ours can do so only in consultation and with the approval of the Senate, a body with which it is in well-nigh constant feud. But while the former can be overturned in an hour if its action is not approved, the other can browbeat public opinion with impunity to the end of its allotted term. Both governments do, however, in practice, have regard for the popular will and execute its behests. Our own statesmen are notoriously deferential, too often mere fawning puppets of public opinion. On the other hand no government on earth is more effectively controlled by public opinion than that of England. The men who can alienate an Empire of their own volition, cannot build a torpedo-boat or appoint a postmaster without the consent of the people. They are untrammeled, but not irresponsible. Perhaps it would be too much to claim that a government whose every act is criticized, whose lease of power is but from hour to hour, which must answer interpellations in Parliament regarding every rumor of its intended action, a government that never concludes a treaty or conducts an important negotiation without defending itself in public addresses or issuing a blue-book to secure the fuller expression of popular opinion, — it would be too much, I say, to claim that such a government did anything in the way of educating or making men, because, forsooth, it is an oligarchy and as such must content itself with the ignoble function of schooling the world in peace and order and making glad its desolate places. However this may be, I suggest that if it be our fate to undergo the threatened transformation, there is a fair chance that our days may be long in the land by way of partial compensation. Nor does a worse fate seem to be demonstrably in store for us. It is largely in the settlement of such questions as this that the British government has become strong and efficient. If we cannot learn efficiency in the same school it will be because we are made of poorer stuff, and if so we shall finally show it, whether we expand or not.

I cannot but regard the assumption of these objectors as otherwise significant and far more serious than they admit. Can it be true that our government has not the capacity, present or potential, to deal efficiently with world problems? Are we unable to trust ourselves, or any whom we may designate from our number, with such discretionary power as that enjoyed by the English government in matters requiring promptness, decision and even occasional secrecy, without running the risk of caesarism and the subversion of our liberties? Have we no hope of a decent civil service, an efficient army organization and a respectable diplomacy? Must we stay at home because we are not fit to go abroad? Such is the too frequent implication of these arguments. If such be our plight, which I, for one, do not believe, is there not need of something rather more radical than "minding our own business"? Are the nations that have best minded their own business, in this gratuitous sense of the term, the ones that have progressed most rapidly toward the attainment of high ideals? It is true, we have problems enough already to tax our wisdom and our patriotism to the utmost, but these problems are not lightened by isolation. Abuses intrench themselves in the consciousness of security, and governments grow rotten and impotent in prosperity and peace. Every new burden laid upon our civil service increases the demand for its purification; every responsibility from without heals a dissension within; and closer contact with foreign powers and foreign problems cannot but favor that knowledge and adaptation, on the development of which the ultimate unity must depend.

The changes which our new responsibilities seem likely to effect in our democracy are precisely those which our present conditions require. Efficiency requires that initiative and direction be in the hands of the few and that they be untrammeled; safety requires that these few be held strictly responsible. Government, to be successful under any form, must be by the will of the many and by the wisdom of the few. The advantage of democracy is that it better reconciles the will of the many with the wisdom of the few than any other form. Its danger lies in confusing the two *roles*, in failing to recognize the few who are competent to direct or in failing to retain their services. Then its representatives become puppets, not directing but waiting for directions, and by shirking initiative contriving to shirk responsibility.

If the policy of participation in world affairs involves dangers of conflict and disaster, no less does the policy of isolation. Our advantageous position between two seas offers no guarantee against ultimate aggression. A nation with a world commerce such as we certainly covet and expect, has interests as wide as the planet, and no one will effectually guard or adequately respect those interests if we are supine and impotent. To guard these interests we may not need war, but we shall certainly need readiness for it, readiness in arsenal and fleet, but above all readiness in the national temper. "They have rights who dare maintain them."

But the protection of our commerce is not the only interest which enjoins upon us the maintenance of a certain military efficiency. European nations have not recognized the Monroe Doctrine or guaranteed the independence of any portion of the American continent. Some of them confidently expect to get a foothold upon it. A single well-equipped nation established in South America in a favorable latitude and with a rapidly-multiplying population would soon control the whole. What that would mean to us it is not difficult to see. We may smile at such projects, and fancy that Europe will stand in awe of us, but nobody stands in awe of bigness. The time will come when we must choose between a more vigorous assertion and a complete abandonment of that policy upon which our much-prized isolation depends.

To those who are content with the forecast of a decade or a generation the following considerations will have little interest. But it is not for such that I write. Larger forecasts are necessary if we are in any degree to wisely modify the course of human events.

The balance of power in Europe, never more than a temporary expedient, is tottering to its fall. Half the countries that once composed it have sunk into insignificance, while dual and triple alliances are becoming more frequent and permanent, foreshadowing an inevitable consolidation. Not that states will become conquered provinces governed by proconsuls from London, Berlin or St. Petersburg, but some one power will acquire an ascendency which will more and more influence and ultimately determine the action of the rest. Such ascendency will doubtless be fluctuating and intermittent, changing perhaps more than once its headquarters from one capital to another. But that which is of concern to us is the possibility of even a temporary unification of Europe or of the Continental powers. I will not say that such a combination would be certain to injure us, but it is certain that it might do so, not necessarily by armed invasion but by checkmating us in matters of vital policy, as, for instance, in getting a foothold on this continent. How long is it since Mexico was occupied by such a coalition, and who will say that under other and perfectly possible circumstances, the occupation might not have been permanent? Anything like a stable unification of Europe, involving as it would the whole of the Old World, would eventually dictate terms to us. This might not be the worst of evils, but it is plain that such a supremacy of any people would tend to make it the leader and determiner of the world's culture as well as of its government. The customs, manners, ideals, and language, — in a word, the civilization of such a directive centre, would have an enormous advantage over all others and would tend to become universal.

If we remain aloof, the world power can hardly fail to be a continental nation, presumably Russia, whose resources and capacity for growth will easily distance all competitors. Against Russian growth the other half of the Anglo-Saxon race will not permanently make headway, and the Saxon opposition, divided and ineffectual, will leave Russian civilization in the ascendant so far as political conditions can make it so. It may be said that this is no disaster, that eliminating our present feelings and habits from the problem, it is as well to have the world organized under Russian or even Mongolian ascendency as under that of the Anglo-Saxon. Perhaps so, but I see no occasion for eliminating those feelings of love and enthusiasm for our civilization which are the common birthright of all peoples and the measure of their virility. There is the less reason for so doing because I belong to the potentially dominant race; dominant beyond controversy, but upon one inexorable condi- ton. That race must pursue a common policy, a policy of cautious but energetic self-assertion, neglecting no advantage, granting no concession, casting the weight of its undivided influence into every scale into which the interests of the common civilization enter ever so little. Every strategic point, military, industrial and cultural, must be occupied, habitable territory must be peopled and controlled. The coal fields and mines that condition the industry of the future must be acquired. The order and freedom of intercourse necessary for the fullest internal development and the strongest cohesion must be unremittingly sought. This policy will require great patience, forbearance and sagacity, but not more, I am persuaded, than the intelligence of England and America can muster. Of all possible combinations looking toward world dominion, this is the only one likely to secure a bloodless supremacy. From beginning to end it is most nearly identical with universal interests, unless indeed the civilization itself prove deficient in capacity for growth and adaptation, and on this point we may take our chances.

It will be apparent how little such a course is compatible with a policy of isolation, and how far from final such objections as those based on the present accidents of our government must appear in the light of such a possibility and such a necessity as now confronts us. If it be urged that it is too early to talk about such things, the reply is that it is not too early to be determining them by our action

trying to make meaning out of nothing
(Anglo-Saxon/U.S. friendship
~ maintenance of value system)

in critical moments. They must be considered now, if consideration is to have any effect on their ultimate decision.

I have said that the struggle between nations is of the essence of that process which is deeper than all ethical relations, and that such relations inhere solely where there is association, dependence and trust. We are commissioned by the most supreme of all authorities, the inexorable necessity of nature, to participate in the struggle where expediency may dictate, having a care only for the moral sentiments which rightly or wrongly urge their claims, and for such of those incipient moral relations between nations as are likely to have permanent significance. In the case we have just been considering, these relations exist in the highest degree ever realized between independent powers. Not only are we bound to Great Britain by an extensive commerce and community of foreign interests, but we feel in the highest degree the sentiments that arise from conscious community of origin, speech, civilization, social and religious ideals. We have but to compare the friendship between England and America with that between Russia and France to appreciate how peculiar is the relation in question, and how heavy the moral obligation it involves. To prove recreant to that obligation would, as in moral relations between individuals, bring demoralization and disgrace. While the policy of expansion is primarily a question of expediency, it thus becomes in one most important connection a matter of sacred obligation.

Fortunately our policy in its essence is little determined by argument and deliberation. To the question, shall we hold aloof, we have yet to hear the most significant answer. *We cannot hold aloof.* The instincts which control the action of masses of men respond to appropriate stimuli with a regularity that suggests little dependence on argument and deliberation. The crisis came and we acted as our impulse dictated and then talked it over afterward. We have done so before and are likely to do so again. The consciousness of power as naturally expresses itself in self-assertion as the consciousness of weakness does in submission. Reason has vast influence in determining the details of the struggle, but scarce any in determining its essence. When the slumbering instincts of race unity and action are aroused, they brush aside the petty barriers of logic and pseudo-obligation without apology or hesitation. It behooves us who are compelled to recognize the supremacy of these instincts to remember that in the course of social evolution the instinct of dominion has been as constructive as that of moral obligation, and that the preservation of society and of moral relations themselves requires that this instinct should not become extinct.

13
A NEGATIVE VIEW OF EXPANSION

Every schoolboy knows Andrew Carnegie (1835–1919) as one of the giants of the American business world. Born in Scotland, he rose from bobbin-boy in a cotton factory to become the creator of the American steel industry. In 1901 he retired, selling his steel empire to J. P. Morgan. Carnegie's concept of the duty of the rich was described in his notable *The Gospel of Wealth.* He argued that the millionaire is only the trustee of his fortune which should be devoted to the welfare and benefit of the masses. Carnegie's name is equated in history with large-scale philanthropy for he established countless libraries and endowed foundations to search for the elusive path to world peace.

Always a sincere Anglophile, Carnegie nevertheless championed the supremacy of democratic American institutions over England's outworn monarchial tradition. The Pittsburgh steel magnate supported Secretary of State James G. Blaine's ambitious Latin American diplomacy, receiving as his reward an appointment as a delegate to the abortive 1881 Pan American Conference. Carnegie's earlier expansionism emphasized the protective role of the United States toward Latin America. In the 1890s, Carnegie changed his mind and the article cited here reflects his emotional feeling toward American expansion: that the acquisition of "distant possessions" was unhealthy for a republic and would impede the nation's development.

DISTANT POSSESSIONS— THE PARTING OF THE WAYS

Andrew Carnegie

Twice only have the American people been called upon to decide a question of such vital import as that now before them.

Is the Republic, the apostle of Triumphant Democracy, of the rule of the people, to abandon her political creed and endeavor to establish in other lands the rule of the foreigner over the people, Triumphant Despotism?

Is the Republic to remain one homogeneous whole, one united people, or to become a scattered and disjointed aggregate of widely separated and alien races?

Is she to continue the task of developing her vast continent until it holds a population as great as that of Europe, all Americans, or to abandon that destiny to annex, and to attempt to govern, other far distant parts of the world as outlying possessions, which can never be integral parts of the Republic?

Is she to exchange internal growth and advancement for the development of external possessions which can never be really hers in any fuller sense than India is British or Cochin-China French? Such is the portentous question of the day. Two equally important questions the American people have decided wisely, and their flag now waves over the greater portion of the English-speaking race; their country is the richest of all countries, first in manufactures, in mining and in commerce (home and foreign), first this year also in exports. But, better than this, the average condition of its people in education and in living is the best. The luxuries of the masses in other lands are the necessaries of life for ours. The schoolhouse and the church are nowhere so widely distributed. Progress in the arts and sciences is surprising. In international affairs her influence grows so fast and foreshadows so much, that one of the foremost statesmen has recently warned Europe that it must combine against her if it is to hold its own in the industrial world. The Republic remains one solid whole, its estate enclosed in a ring fence, united, impregnable, triumphant; clearly destined to become the foremost power of the world, if she continue to follow the true path. Such

FROM *North American Review*, CLXVII (August, 1898), pp. 239–48.

are the fruits of wise judgment in deciding the two great issues of the past, Independence and The Union.

In considering the issue now before us, the agitator, the demagogue, has no part. Not feeling, not passion, but deliberate judgment alone should have place. The question should be calmly weighed; it is not a matter of party, nor of class; for the fundamental interest of every citizen is a common interest, that which is best for the poorest being best for the richest. Let us, therefore, reason together and be well assured, before we change our position, that we are making no plunge into an abyss. Happily, we have the experience of others to guide us, the most instructive being that of our own race in Great Britain.

There are two kinds of national possessions, one colonies, the other dependencies. In the former we establish and reproduce our own race. Thus Britain has peopled Canada and Australia with English-speaking people, who have naturally adopted our ideas of self-government. That the world has benefited thereby goes without saying; that Britain has done a great work as the mother of nations is becoming more and more appreciated the more the student learns of worldwide affairs. No nation that ever existed has done so much for the progress of the world as the little islands in the North Sea, known as Britain.

With "dependencies" it is otherwise. The most grievous burden which Britain has upon her shoulders is that of India, for there it is impossible for our race to grow. The child of English-speaking parents must be removed and reared in Britain. The British Indian official must have long respites in his native land. India means death to our race. The characteristic feature of a "dependency" is that the acquiring power cannot reproduce its own race there.

Inasmuch as the territories outside our own continent which our country may be tempted to annex cannot be "colonies," but only "dependencies," we need not dwell particularly upon the advantages or disadvantages of the former, although the writer is in thorough accord with Disraeli, who said even of colonies: "Our colonies are millstones round the neck of Britain; they lean upon us while they are weak, and leave us when they become strong." This is just what our Republic did with Britain.

There was something to be said for colonies from the point of view of pecuniary gain in the olden days, when they were treated as the legitimate spoil of the conqueror. It is Spain's fatal mistake that she has never realized that it is impossible to follow this policy in our day. Britain is the only country which has realized this truth.

British colonies have complete self-government; they even tax the products of their own motherland. That Britain "possesses" her colonies is a mere figure of speech; that her colonies "possess" her is nearer the truth. "Our Colonial Empire" seems a big phrase, but, as far as material benefits are concerned, the balance is the other way. Thus, even loyal Canada trades more with us than with Britain. She buys her Union Jacks in New York. Trade does not follow the flag in our day; it scents the lowest price current. There is no patriotism in exchanges.

Some of the organs of manufacturing interests, we observe, favor foreign possessions as necessary or helpful markets for our products. But the exports of the United States this year are greater than those of any other nation in the world. Even Britain's exports are less, yet Britain "possesses," it is said, a hundred "colonies" and "dependencies" scattered all over the world. The fact that the United States has none does not prevent her products and manufactures from invading Japan, China, Australia, New Zealand, Canada, and all parts of the world in competition with those of Britain. "Possession" of colonies or dependencies is not necessary for trade reasons. What her colonies are valued for, and justly so, by Britain, is the happiness and pride which the mother feels in her children. The instinct of motherhood is gratified, and no one living places a higher estimate upon the sentiment than I do. Britain is the kindest of mothers, and well deserves the devotion of her children.

If we could establish colonies of Americans, and grow Americans in any part of the world now unpopulated and unclaimed by any of the great powers, and thus follow the example of Britain, heart and mind might tell us that we should have to think twice, yea, thrice, before deciding adversely. Even then our decision should be adverse; but there is at present no such question before us. What we have to face is the question whether we should embark upon the difficult and dangerous policy of undertaking the government of alien races in lands where it is impossible for our own race to be produced.

As long as we remain free from distant possessions we are impregnable against serious attack; yet, it is true, we have to consider what obligations may fall upon us of an international character requiring us to send our forces to points beyond our own territory. Up to this time we have disclaimed all intention to interfere with affairs beyond our own continent, and only claimed the right to watch over American interests according to the Monroe Doctrine, which is now firmly established. This carries with it serious responsibilities, no doubt, which we cannot escape. European nations must consult us upon territorial questions pertaining to our Continent, but this makes no tremendous demand upon our military or naval forces. We are at home, as it were, near our base, and sure of the support of the power in whose behalf and on whose request we may act. If it be found essential to possess a coaling station at Porto Rico for future possible, though not probable, contingencies, there is no insuperable objection. Neither would the control of the West Indies be alarming, if pressed upon us by Britain, since the islands are small and the populations must remain insignificant and without national aspirations. Besides, they are upon our own shores, American in every sense. Their defense by us would be easy. No protest need be entered against such legitimate and peaceful expansion in our own hemisphere, should events work in that direction. I am no "Little" American, afraid of growth, either in population or territory, provided always that the new territory be American and that it will produce Americans, and not foreign races bound in time to be false to the Republic in order to be true to themselves.

As I write, the cable announces the annexation of Hawaii, which is more serious, but the argument for this has been the necessity for holding the only coaling station in the Pacific so situated as to be essential to any power desirous of successfully attacking our Pacific coast. Until the Nicaragua Canal is made, it is impossible to deny the cogency of this contention. We need not consider it a measure of offense or aggression, but as strictly defensive. The population of the islands is so small that national aspirations are not to be encountered, which is a great matter, nor is it obtained by conquest. It is ours by a vote of its people, which robs its acquisition of many dangers. Let us hope that our far outlying possessions may end with Hawaii.

To reduce it to the concrete, the question is: Shall we attempt to establish ourselves as a power in the Far East and possess the Philippines for glory? The glory we already have, in Dewey's victory overcoming the power of Spain in a manner which adds one more to the many laurels of the American navy, which, from its infancy till now, has divided the laurels with Britain upon the sea. The Philippines have about seven and a half millions of people, composed of races bitterly hostile to one another, alien races, ignorant of our language and institutions. Americans cannot be grown there. The islands have been exploited for the benefit of Spain, against whom they have twice rebelled, like the Cubans; but even Spain has received little pecuniary benefit from them. The estimated revenue

of the Philippines in 1894–95 was £2,715,980, the expenditure being
£2,656,026, leaving a net result of about $300,000. The United States
could obtain even this trifling sum from the inhabitants only by
oppressing them as Spain has done. But, if we take the Philippines,
we shall be forced to govern them as generously as Britain governs
her dependencies, which means that they will yield us nothing, and
probably be a source of annual expense. Certainly, they will be a
grievous drain upon revenue if we consider the enormous army and
navy which we shall be forced to maintain upon their account.

There are many objections to our undertaking the government
of dependencies; one I venture to submit as being peculiar to ourselves. We should be placed in a wrong position. Consider Great
Britain in India to-day. She has established schools and taught the
people our language. In the Philippines, we may assume that we
should do the same, and with similar results? To travel through
India as an American is a point of great advantage if one wishes
to know the people of India and their aspirations. They unfold to
Americans their inmost thoughts, which they very naturally withhold
from their masters, the British. When in India, I talked with many
who had received an English education in the British schools; and
found that they had read and pondered most upon Cromwell and
Hampden, Wallace and Bruce, and Tell; upon Washington and
Franklin. The Briton is sowing the seed of rebellion with one hand
in his schools — for education makes rebels — while with the other
he is oppressing patriots who desire the independence of their
country. The national patriotism upon which a Briton plumes himself
he must repress in India. It is only a matter of time when India,
the so-called gem of the British crown, is to glitter red again. British
control of India is rendered possible to-day only by the division
of races, or rather of religions there. The Hindoos and Moham-
medans still mistrust each other more than they do the British, but
caste is rapidly passing away, and religious prejudices are softening.
Whenever this distrust disappears, Britain is liable to be expelled,
at a loss of life and treasure which cannot be computed. The aspirations of a people for independent existence are seldom repressed,
nor, according to American ideas hitherto, should they be. If it be
a noble aspiration for the Indian or the Cuban, as it was for the
citizen of the United States himself, and for the various South American republics once under Spain, to have a country to live and, if
necessary, to die for, why is not the revolt noble which the man
of the Philippines has been making against Spain? Is it possible
that the Republic is to be placed in the position of the suppressor

of the Philippine struggle for independence? Surely, that is impossible. With what face shall we hang in the school houses of the Philippines the Declaration of our own Independence, and yet deny independence to them? What response will the heart of the Philippine Islander make, as he reads of Lincoln's Emancipation Proclamation? Are we to practise independence and preach subordination, to teach rebellion in our books, yet to stamp it out with our swords, to sow the seed of revolt and expect the harvest of loyalty? President McKinley's call for volunteers to fight for Cuban independence against the cruel dominion of Spain meets with prompt response, but who would answer the call of the President of an "imperial" republic for free citizens to fight the Washington and slaughter the patriots of some distant dependency which struggles for independence?

It has hitherto been the glorious mission of the Republic to establish upon secure foundations Trimphant Democracy, and the world now understands government of the people for the people and by the people. Tires the Republic so soon of its mission that it must, perforce, discard it to undertake the impossible task of establishing Triumphant Despotism, the rule of the foreigner over the people, and must the millions of the Philippines who have been asserting their God-given right to govern themselves, be the first victims of Americans, whose proudest boast is that they conquered independence for themselves?

Let another phase of the question be carefully weighed. Europe is to-day an armed camp, not chiefly because the home territories of its various nations are threatened, but because of fear of aggressive action upon the part of other nations touching outlying "possessions." France resents British control of Egypt and is fearful of its West African possessions; Russia seeks Chinese territory, with a view of expansion to the Pacific; Germany also seeks distant possessions; Britain, who has acquired so many dependencies, is so fearful of an attack upon them that this year she is spending nearly eighty millions of dollars upon additional warships, and Russia, Germany and France follow suit. Japan is a new element of anxiety; and by the end of the year it is computed she will have 67 formidable ships of war. The naval powers of Europe, and Japan also, are apparently determined to be prepared for a terrific struggle for possessions in the Far East, close to the Philippines — and why not for these islands themselves? Into this vortex the Republic is cordially invited to enter by those powers who expect her policy to be of benefit to them, but her action is jealously watched by those who fear that her power might be used against them.

It has never been considered the part of wisdom to thrust one's hand into the hornet's nest, and it does seem as if the United States must lose all claim to ordinary prudence and good sense if she enter this arena, and become involved in the intrigues and threats of war which make Europe an armed camp.

It is the parting of the ways. We have a continent to populate and develop; there are only 23 persons to the square mile in the United States. England has 370, Belgium 571, Germany 250. A tithe of the cost of maintaining our sway over the Philippines would improve our internal waterways; deepen our harbors; build the Nicaraguan Canal; construct a waterway to the ocean from the Great Lakes; an inland canal along the Atlantic seaboard; a canal across Florida, saving 800 miles distance between New York and New Orleans; connect Lake Michigan with the Mississippi; deepen all the harbors upon the lakes; build a canal from Lake Erie to the Allegheny River; slackwater through movable dams the entire length of the Ohio River to Cairo; thoroughly improve the Lower and Upper Mississippi, and all our seaboard harbors. All these enterprises would be as nothing in cost in comparison to the sums required for the experiment of possessing the Philippine Islands, 7,000 miles from our shores. If the object be to render our Republic powerful among nations, can there be any doubt as to which policy is the better? To be more powerful at home is the surest way to be more powerful abroad. To-day the Republic stands the friend of all nations, the ally of none; she has no ambitious designs upon the territory of any power upon another continent; she crosses none of their ambitious designs, evokes no jealousy of the bitter sort, inspires no fears; she is not one of them, scrambling for "possessions;" she stands apart, pursuing her own great mission, and teaching all nations by example. Let her become a power annexing foreign territory, and all is changed in a moment.

If we are to compete with other nations for foreign possessions we must have a navy like theirs. It should be superior to any other navy, or we play a second part. It is not enough to have a navy equal to that of Russia or of France, for Russia and France may combine against us just as they may against Britain. We at once enter the field as a rival of Britain, the chief possessor of foreign possessions, and who can guarantee that we shall not even have to measure our power against her?

What it means to enter the list of military and naval powers having foreign possessions may be gathered from the following considerations. First, look at our future navy. If it is only to equal that of France it means 51 battleships; if of Russia, 40 battleships. If we cannot play the game without being at least the equal of any of our rivals, then 80 battleships is the number Britain possesses. We now have only 4, with 5 building. Cruisers, armed and unarmed, swell the number threefold, Britain having 273 ships of the line built or ordered, with 308 torpedo boats in addition; France having 134 ships of the line and 269 torpedo boats. All these nations are adding ships rapidly. Every armor and gun making plant in the world is busy night and day. Ships are indispensable, but recent experience shows that soldiers are equally so. While the immense armies of Europe need not be duplicated, yet we shall certainly be too weak unless our army is at least twenty times what is has been — say 500,000 men. Even then we shall be powerless as against three of our rivals. Germany's army on a peace footing numbers 562,352 men; on a war footing, 3,000,000; France's army on a peace footing, 615,413; on a war footing, 2,500,000; Russia's on a peace footing, 750,944; on a war footing, 2,512,143. Even Spain has an army, as we are discovering in Cuba. It foots up on a peace footing 128,000; on a war footing, 1,083,000 men. All Spaniards, like all Frenchmen, and Germans, over 19 years of age, are subject to military service. They are in fact first soldiers, then citizens.

This drain upon the resources of these countries has become a necessity from their respective positions, largely as graspers for foreign possessions. The United States, happily, to-day has no such necessity, her neighbors being powerless against her, since her possessions are concentrated and her power is one solid mass.

To-day two great powers in the world are compact, developing themselves in peace throughout vast coterminous territories. When war threatens they have no outlying "possessions" which can never be really "possessed," but which they are called upon to defend. They fight upon the exposed edge only of their own soil in case of attack, and are not only invulnerable, but they could not be more than inconvenienced by the world in arms against them. These powers are Russia and the United States. The attempt of Britain to check Russia, if the wild counsels of Mr. Chamberlain were followed, could end in nothing but failure. With the irresistible force of the glacier, Russia moves upon the plains below. Well for Russia, and well for the world, is her advance over pagan China, better even for Britain from the standpoint of business, for every Russian to-day trades as much with Britain as do nine Chinamen. Britain, France, Germany, Belgium, Spain, are all vulnerable, having departed from the sagacious policy of keeping possessions and power concentrated. Should the United States depart from this policy, she also must be so weakened in consequence as never to be able to play the commanding part in the world, disjointed, that she can play whenever she desires if she remain compact.

Whether the United States maintain its present unique position of safety or forfeit it through acquiring foreign possessions, is to be decided by its action in regard to the Philippines; for, fortunately, the independence of Cuba is assured, for this the Republic has proclaimed to the world that she has drawn the sword. But why should the less than two millions of Cuba receive national existence and the seven and a half millions of the Philippines be denied it? The United States, thus far in their history, have no page reciting self-sacrifice made for others; all their gains have been for themselves. This void is now to be grandly filled. The page which recites the resolve of the Republic to rid her neighbor Cuba from the foreign "possessor" will grow brighter with the passing centuries, which may dim many pages now deemed illustrious. Should the coming American be able to point to Cuba and the Philippines rescued from foreign domination and enjoying independence won for them by his country and given to them without money and without price, he will find no citizen of any other land able to claim for his country services so disinterested and so noble.

We repeat there is no power in the world that could do more than inconvenience the United States by attacking its fringe, which is all that the world combined could do, so long as our country is not compelled to send its forces beyond its own compact shores to defend worthless "possessions." If our country were blockaded by the united powers of the world for years, she would emerge from the embargo richer and stronger, and with her own resources more completely developed. We have little to fear from external attack. No thorough blockade of our enormous seaboard is possible; but even if it were, the few indispensable articles not produced by ourselves (if there were any such) would reach us by way of Mexico or Canada at slightly increased cost.

From every point of view we are forced to the conclusion that the past policy of the Republic is her true policy for the future; for safety, for peace, for happiness, for progress, for wealth, for power — for all that makes a nation blessed.

Not till the war drum is silent and the day of calm peace returns, can the issue be soberly considered.

Twice have the American people met crucial issues wisely, and in the third they are not to fail.

14
A POLITICIAN OPPOSES WAR

 Carl Schurz (1829–1906), who was born in Prussia, fled the revolutionary torment of his native land in the wake of the 1848 upheavals. In America he championed Abraham Lincoln's election among German voters, became a Union general, a post-war journalist, and a United States senator from his adopted state of Missouri. While serving on Capitol Hill, he led the "Liberal Republican" revolt against the G.O.P. Old Guard, attempting to deny Ulysses S. Grant a second term in the White House. Under President Hayes, Schurz served as Secretary of the Interior (1877–1881) and later was closely associated with the 1884 Mugwump reformers in his party. As Secretary of the Interior, Schurz was instrumental in pioneering civil service reform for his Department and from 1892 to 1901, he served as President of the National Civil Service Reform League.

In 1898, Schurz ended his association with *Harper's Weekly* because he refused to support the war against Spain which that periodical sanctioned. As an elder statesman of his party, Schurz delivered a convocation address at the University of Chicago in 1899 in which he developed with characteristic thoroughness his criticism of the expansionist policy of the day.

AMERICAN IMPERIALISM

Carl Schurz

... It is proposed to embark this republic in a course of imperialistic policy by permanently annexing to it certain islands taken, or partly taken, from Spain in the late war. The matter is near its decision, but not yet decided. The peace treaty made at Paris is not yet ratified by the Senate; but even if it were, the question whether those islands, although ceded by Spain, shall be permanently incorporated in the territory of the United States would still be open for final determination by Congress. As an open question therefore I shall discuss it.

If ever, it behooves the American people to think and act with calm deliberation, for the character and future of the republic and the welfare of its people now living and yet to be born are in unprecedented jeopardy. To form a candid judgment of what this republic has been, what it may become, and what it ought to be, let us first recall to our minds its condition before the recent Spanish War.

Our government was, in the words of Abraham Lincoln, "the government of the people, by the people, and for the people." It was the noblest ambition of all true Americans to carry this democratic government to the highest degree of perfection and justice, in probity, in assured peace, in the security of human rights, in progressive civilization; to solve the problem of popular self-government on the grandest scale, and thus to make this republic the example and guiding star of mankind.

We had invited the oppressed of all nations to find shelter here, and to enjoy with us the blessings of free institutions. They came by the millions. Some were not so welcome as others, but under the assimilating force of American life in our temperate climate, which stimulates the working energies, nurses the spirit of orderly freedom, and thus favors the growth of democracies, they became good Americans, most in the first, all in the following generations. And so with all the blood-crossings caused by the motley immigration, we became a substantially homogeneous people, united by common political beliefs and ideals, by common interests, laws, and aspirations — in one word, a nation. Indeed, we were not without our difficulties and embarrassments, but only one of them, the race

FROM "American Imperialism," the convocation address delivered on the occasion of the twenty-seventh convocation of the University of Chicago, January 4, 1899 (Chicago, 1899).

antagonism between the negroes and the whites, especially where the negroes live in mass, presents a problem which so far has baffled all efforts at practical solution in harmony with the spirit of our free institutions, and thus threatens complications of a grave charac- ter.

We gloried in the marvellous growth of our population, wealth, power, and civilization, and in the incalculable richness of the re- sources of our country, capable of harboring three times our present population, and of immeasurable further material development. Our commerce with the world abroad, although we had no colonies, and but a small navy, spread with unprecedented rapidity, capturing one foreign market after another, not only for the products of our farms, but also for many of those of our manufacturing industries, with prospect of indefinite extension.

Peace reigned within our borders, and there was not the faintest shadow of danger of foreign attack. Our voice, whenever we chose to speak in the councils of nations, was listened to with respect, even the mightiest sea-power on occasion yielding to us a deference far beyond its habit in its intercourse with others. We were consid- ered ultimately invincible, if not invulnerable, in our continental stronghold. It was our boast, not that we possessed great and costly armies and navies, but that we did not need any. This exceptional blessing was our pride, as it was the envy of the world. We looked down with pitying sympathy on other nations which submissively groaned under the burden of constantly increasing armaments, and we praised our good fortune for having saved us from so wretched a fate.

Such was our condition, such our beliefs and ideals, such our ambition and our pride, but a short year ago. Had the famous peace message of the Czar of Russia, with its protest against growing militarism and its plea for disarmament, reached us then, it would have been hailed with enthusiasm by every American as a triumph of our example. We might have claimed only that to our republic, and not to the Russian monarch, belonged the place of leadership in so great an onward step in the progress of civilization.

Then came the Spanish War. A few vigorous blows laid the feeble enemy helpless at our feet. The whole scene seemed to have suddenly changed. According to the solemn proclamation of our government, the war had been undertaken solely for the liberation of Cuba, as a war of humanity and not of conquest. But our easy victories had put conquest within our reach, and when our arms occupied foreign territory, a loud demand arose that, pledge or no pledge to the contrary, the conquests should be kept, even the Philippines on the other side of the globe, and that as to Cuba herself, independence would only be a provisional formality. Why not? was the cry. . . .

Compare now with our old acquisitions as to all these important points those at present in view.

They are not continental, not contiguous to our present domain, but beyond seas, the Philippines many thousand miles distant from our coast. They are all situated in the tropics, where people of the northern races, such as Anglo-Saxons, or, generally speaking, people of Germanic blood, have never migrated in mass to stay; and they are more or less densely populated, parts of them as densely as Massachusetts — their populations consisting almost exclusively of races to whom the tropical climate is congenial — Spanish creoles mixed with negroes in the West Indies, and Malays, Tagals, Filipinos, Chinese, Japanese, Negritos, and various more or less barbarous tribes in the Philippines.

When the question is asked whether we may hope to adapt those countries and populations to our system of government, the advocates of annexation answer cheerily, that when they belong to us, we shall soon "Americanize" them. This may mean that Americans in sufficiently large numbers will migrate there to determine the character of those populations so as to assimilate them to our own.

This is a delusion of the first magnitude. We shall, indeed, be able, if we go honestly about it, to accomplish several salutary things in those countries. But one thing we cannot do. We cannot strip the tropical climate of those qualities which have at all times deterred men of the northern races, to which we belong, from migrating to such countries in mass, and to make their homes there, as they have migrated and are still migrating to countries in the temperate zone. This is not a mere theory, but a fact of universal experience.

It is true, you will find in tropical regions a sprinkling of persons of Anglo-Saxon or other northern origin — merchants, railroad builders, speculators, professional men, miners, and mechanics; also here and there an agriculturist. But their number is small, and most of them expect to go home again as soon as their money-making purpose is more or less accomplished.

Thus we observe now that business men with plenty of means are casting their eyes upon our "new possessions" to establish mercantile houses there, or manufactories to be worked with native labor;

and moneyed syndicates and "improvement companies" to exploit the resources of those countries, and speculators and promotors to take advantage of what may turn up — the franchise grabber, as reported, is already there — many having perfectly legitimate ends in view, others ends not so legitimate, and all expecting to be more or less favored by the power of our government; in short, *the capitalist* is thinking of going there, or to send his agents, his enterprises in most cases to be directed from these more congenial shores. But you will find that laboring men of the northern races, as they have never done so before, will not now go there in mass to do the work of the country, agricultural or industrial, and to found there permanent homes; and this is not merely because the rate of wages in such countries is, owing to native competition, usually low, but because they cannot thrive there under the climatic conditions.

But it is the working-masses, those laboring in agriculture and the industries, that everywhere form the bulk of the population; and they are the true constituency of democratic government. And as the northern races cannot do the work of the tropical zone, they cannot furnish such constituencies. It is an incontestable and very significant fact that the British, the best colonizers in history, have, indeed, established in tropical regions governments and rather absolute ones, but they have never succeeded in establishing there democratic commonwealths of the Anglo-Saxon type, like those in America or Australia.

The scheme of Americanizing our "new possessions" in that sense is therefore absolutely hopeless. The immutable forces of nature are against it. Whatever we may do for their improvement, the people of the Spanish Antilles will remain in overwhelming numerical predominance, Spanish creoles and negroes, and the people of the Philippines, Filipinos, Malays, Tagals, and so on — some of them quite clever in their way, but the vast majority utterly alien to us, not only in origin and language, but in habits, traditions, ways of thinking, principles, ambitions — in short, in most things that are of the greatest importance in human intercourse and especially in political cooperation. And under the influences of their tropical climate they will prove incapable of becoming assimilated to the Anglo-Saxon. They would, therefore, remain in the population of this republic a hopelessly heterogeneous element — in some respects more hopeless even than the colored people now living among us.

What, then, shall we do with such populations? Shall we, according, not indeed to the letter, but to the evident spirit of our constitution, organize those countries as territories with a view to their eventual admission as states? If they become states on an equal footing with the other states they will not only be permitted to govern themselves as to their home concerns, but they will take part in governing the whole republic, in governing us, by sending senators and representatives into our Congress to help make our laws, and by voting for president and vice-president to give our national government its executive. The prospect of the consequences which would follow the admission of the Spanish creoles and the negroes of West India islands and of the Malays and Tagals of the Philippines to participation in the conduct of our government is so alarming that you instinctively pause before taking the step.

But this may be avoided, it is said, by governing the new possessions as mere dependencies, or subject provinces. I will waive the constitutional question and merely point out that this would be a most serious departure from the rule that governed our former acquisitions, which are so frequently quoted as precedents. It is useless to speak of the District of Columbia and Alaska as proof that we have done such things before and can do them again. Every candid mind will at once admit the vast difference between those cases and the *permanent* establishment of substantially arbitrary government over large territories with many millions of inhabitants, and with a prospect of there being many more of the same kind, if we once launch out on a career of conquest. The question is not merely whether we *can* do such things, but whether, having the public good at heart, we *should* do them.

If we do adopt such a system, then we shall, for the first time since the abolition of slavery, again have two kinds of Americans: Americans of the first class, who enjoy the privilege of taking part in the government in accordance with our old constitutional principles, and Americans of the second class, who are to be ruled in a substantially arbitrary fashion by the Americans of the first class, through congressional legislation and the action of the national executive — not to speak of individual "masters" arrogating to themselves powers beyond the law,

This will be a difference no better — nay, rather somewhat worse — than that which a century and a quarter ago still existed between Englishmen of the first and Englishmen of the second class, the first represented by King George and the British Parliament, and the second by the American colonists. This difference called forth that great paean of human liberty, the American Declaration of Independence — a document which, I regret to say, seems, owing to the intoxication of conquest, to have lost much of its charm among some of our fellow citizens. Its fundamental principle was that "governments derive their just powers from the consent of the governed." We are now told that we have never fully lived up to that principle, and that, therefore, in our new policy we may cast it aside altogether. But I say to you that, if we are true believers in democratic government, it is our duty to move in the direction towards the full realization of that principle and not in the direction away from it. If you tell me that we cannot govern the people of those new possessions in accordance with that principle, then I answer that this is a good reason why this democracy should not attempt to govern them at all.

If we do, we shall transform the government of the people, for the people, and by the people, for which Abraham Lincoln lived, into a government of one part of the people, the strong, over another part, the weak. Such an abandonment of a fundamental principle as a permanent policy may at first seem to bear only upon more or less distant dependencies, but it can hardly fail in its ultimate effects to disturb the rule of the same principle in the conduct of democratic government at home. And I warn the American people that democracy cannot so deny its faith as to the vital conditions of its being — it cannot long play the king over subject populations without creating within itself ways of thinking and habits of action most dangerous to its own vitality — most dangerous especially to those classes of society which are the least powerful in the assertion, and the most helpless in the defense of their rights. Let the poor and the men who earn their bread by the labor of their hands pause and consider well before they give their assent to a policy so deliberately forgetful of the equality of rights.

I do not mean to say, however, that all of our new acquisitions would be ruled as subject provinces. Some of them, the Philippines, would probably remain such, but some others would doubtless become states. In Porto Rico, for instance, politicians of lively ambition are already clamoring for the speedy organization of that island as a regular territory, soon to be admitted as a state of the Union. You may say that they will have long to wait. Be not so sure of that. Consult your own experience. Has not more than one territory, hardly fitted for statehood, been precipitated into the Union as a state when the majority party in Congress thought that, by doing so, its party strength could be augmented in the senate and in the house and in the electoral college? Have our parties become so unselfishly virtuous that this may not happen again? So we may see Porto Rico admitted before we have had time to rub our eyes.

You may say that little Porto Rico would not matter much. But can any clear thinking man believe that, when we are once fairly started in the course of indiscriminate expansion, we shall stop there? Will not the same reasons which induced us to take Porto Rico also be used to show that the two islands of San Domingo with Hayti, and of Cuba, which separate Porto Rico from our coast, would, if they were in foreign hands, be a danger to us, and that we *must* take them? Nothing could be more plausible. Why, the necessity of annexing San Domingo is already freely discussed, and agencies to bring this about are actually at work. And as to Cuba, every expansionist will tell you that it is only a matter of time. And does any one believe that those islands, if annexed, will not become states of this Union? That would give us at least three, perhaps four, new states, with about 3,500,000 inhabitants, Spanish and French Creoles and negroes, with six or eight senators, and from fifteen to twenty representatives in Congress and a corresponding number of votes in the electoral college.

Nor are we likely to stop there. If we build and own the Nicaragua Canal, instead of neutralizing it, we shall easily persuade ourselves that our control of that canal will not be safe unless we own all the country down to it, so that it be not separated from our borders by any foreign, and possibly hostile power. Is this too adventurous an idea to become true? Why, it is not half as adventurous and extravagant as the idea of uniting to this republic the Philippines, 9,000 miles away. It is already proposed to acquire in some way strips of territory several miles wide on each side of that canal for its military protection. But that will certainly be found insufficient if foreign countries lie between. We must, therefore, have those countries. That means Mexico and various small Central American republics, with a population in all of about 14,000,000, mostly Spanish-Indian mixture — making at least fifteen states, entitled to thirty senators and scores of representatives and presidential electors. . . .

The American people began their career as one of the colonial offshoots of the English stock. They found a great continent to occupy and to fill with democratic commonwealths. Our country is large enough for several times our present population. Our home resources are enormous, in great part not yet touched. We need not fear to be starved by the completest blockade of our coasts, for we have enough of everything and to spare. On the contrary such a blockade might rather result in starving others that need our products. We are to-day one of the greatest powers on earth, without having the most powerful fleet, and without stepping beyond our continent.

We are sure to be by far the greatest power of all, as our homogeneous, intelligent, and patriotic population multiplies, and our resources are developed, without firing a gun or sacrificing a life for the sake of conquest — far more powerful than the British Empire with all its Hindoos, and than the Russian Empire with all its Mongols. We can exercise the most beneficent influences upon mankind, not by forcing our rule or our goods upon others that are weak at the point of the bayonet, but through the moral power of our example, in proving how the greatest as well as the smallest nation can carry on the government of the people, by the people, and for the people in justice, liberty, order, and peace without large armies and navies.

Let this republic and Great Britain each follow the course which its conditions and its history have assigned to it, and their ambitions will not clash, and their friendships can be maintained for the good of all. And if our British cousins should ever get into serious stress, American friendship may stand behind them; but then Britain would depend on our friendship, which, as an American, I should prefer, and not America on British friendship, as our British friends who so impatiently urge us to take the Philippines, would have it. But if we do take the Philippines, and thus entangle ourselves in the rivalries of Asiatic affairs, the future will be, as Lord Salisbury predicted, one of wars and rumors of wars, and the time will be forever past when we could look down with condescending pity on the nations of the old world groaning under militarism with all its burdens.

We are already told that we shall need a regular army of at least 100,000 men, three-fourths of whom are to serve in our "new possessions." The question is whether this necessity is only to be temporary or permanent. Look at the cost. Last year the support of the army proper required about $23,000,000. It is computed that, taking the increased costliness of the service in the tropics into account, the army under the new dispensation will require about $150,000,000; that is, $127,000,000 a year more. It is also officially admitted that the possession of the Philippines would render indispensable a much larger increase of the navy than would otherwise be necessary, costing untold millions for the building and equipment of ships, and untold millions every year for their maintenance and for the increased number of officers and men. What we shall have to spend for fortifications and the like cannot now be computed. But there is a burden upon us which in like weight no other nation has to bear. To-day, thirty-three years after the Civil War, we have a pension roll of very nearly one million names. And still they come. We paid to pensioners over $145,000,000 last year, a sum larger than the annual cost of the whole military peace establishment of the German Empire, including its pension roll. Our recent Spanish War will, according to a moderate estimate, add at least $20,000,000 to our annual pension payments. But if we send troops to the tropics and keep them there, we must look for a steady stream of pensioners from that quarter, for in the tropics soldiers are "used up" very fast, even if they have no campaigning to do.

But all such estimates are futile. There may, and probably will be, much campaigning to do to keep our new subjects in obedience, or even in conflicts with other powers. And what military and naval expeditions will then cost, with our extravagant habits, and how the pension roll then will grow, we know to be incalculable. Moreover, we shall then be in the situation of those European powers, the extent of whose armaments are determined, not by their own wishes, but by the armaments of their rivals. We, too, shall nervously watch reports from abroad telling us that this power is augmenting the number of its warships, or that another is increasing its battalions, or strengthening its colonial garrisons in the neighborhood of our far-away possessions; and we shall have to follow suit. Not we ourselves, but our rivals and possible enemies will decide how large our armies and navies must be, and how much money we must spend for them. And all that money will have to come out of the pockets of our people, the poor as well as the rich. Our tax-paying capacity and willingness are indeed very great. But set your policy of imperialism in full swing, as the acquisition of the Philippines will do, and the time will come, and come quickly, when every American farmer and workingman, when going to his toil, will, like his European brother, have "to carry a fully armed soldier on his back." . . .

I ask in all candor, taking President McKinley at his word: Will the forcible annexation of the Philippines by our code of morals not be criminal aggression — a self-confessed crime? I ask further, if the Cubans, as Congress declared, are *and of right ought to be* free and independent, can anybody tell me why the Porto Ricans and the Filipinos ought not *of right* to be free and independent? Can you sincerely recognize the right of freedom and independence of one and refuse the same right to another in the same situation, and then take his land? Would not that be double-dealing of the most shameless sort?

We hear much of the respect of mankind for us having been greatly raised by our victories. Indeed, the valor of our soldiers and the brilliant achievements of our navy have won deserved admiration. But do not deceive yourselves about the respect of mankind. Recently I found in the papers an account of the public opinion of Europe, written by a prominent English journalist. This is what he says: "The friends of America wring their hands in unaffected grief over the fall of the United States under the temptation of the lust of territorial expansion. Her enemies shoot out the lip and shriek in derision over what they regard as the unmistakable demonstration which the demand for the Philippines affords of American cupidity, American bad faith and American ambition. 'We told you so,' they exclaim. That is what the unctuous rectitude of the Anglo-Saxon always ends in. He always begins by calling heaven to witness his unselfish desire to help his neighbor, but he always ends by stealing his spoons!"

Atrocious, is it not? And yet this is substantially what the true friends of America, and what her enemies in Europe, think — I mean those friends who had faith in the nobility of the American people, who loved our republican government, and who hoped that the example set by our great democracy, would be an inspiration to those struggling for liberty the world over; and I mean those enemies who hate republican government and who long to see the American people disgraced and humiliated. So they think: I know it from my own correspondence. Nothing has in our times discredited the name of republic in the civilized world as much as the Dreyfus outrage in France and our conquest furor in America; and our conquest furor more, because from us the world hoped more.

No, do not deceive yourselves. If we turn that war which was so solemnly commended to the favor of mankind as a generous war of liberation and humanity into a victory for conquest and self-aggrandizement, we shall have thoroughly forfeited our moral credit with the world. Professions of unselfish virtue and benevolence, proclamations of noble humanitarian purposes coming from us will never, never be trusted again. Is this the position in which this great republic of ours should stand among the family of nations? Our American self-respect should rise in indignant protest against it.

And now compare this picture of the state of things which threatens us, with the picture I drew of our condition existing before the expansion fever seized us. Which will you choose?

What can there be to justify a change of policy fraught with such direful consequences? Let us pass the arguments of the advocates of such imperialism candidly in review.

The cry suddenly raised that this great country has become

too small for us is too ridiculous to demand an answer, in view of the fact that our present population may be tripled and still have ample elbow-room, with resources to support many more. But we are told that our industries are gasping for breath; that we are suffering from over-production; that our products must have new outlets, and that we need colonies and dependencies the world over to give us more markets. More markets? Certainly. But do we, civilized beings, indulge in the absurd and barbarous notion that we must own the countries with which we wish to trade? Here are our official reports before us, telling us that of late years our export trade has grown enormously, not only of farm products, but of the products of our manufacturing industries; in fact, that "our sales of manufactured goods have continued to extend with a facility and promptitude of results which have excited the serious concern of countries that, for generations, had not only controlled their home markets, but had practically monopolized certain lines of trade in other lands." . . .

"But the Pacific Ocean," we are mysteriously told, "will be the great commercial battlefield of the future, and we must quickly use the present opportunity to secure our position on it. The visible presence of great power is necessary for us to get our share of the trade of China. Therefore, we must have the Philippines." Well, the China trade is worth having, although for a time out of sight the Atlantic Ocean will be an infinitely more important battlefield of commerce than the Pacific, and one European customer is worth more than twenty or thirty Asiatics. But does the trade of China really require that we should have the Philippines and make a great display of power to get our share? Read the consular reports, and you will find that in many places in China our trade is rapidly gaining, while in some British trade is declining, and this while Great Britain had on hand the greatest display of power imaginable and we had none. And in order to increase our trade there, our consuls advise us to improve our commercial methods, saying nothing of the necessity of establishing a base of naval operations, and of our appearing there with war ships and heavy guns. Trade is developed, not by the best guns, but by the best merchants. But why do other nations prepare to fight for the Chinese trade? Other nations have done many foolish things which we have been, and I hope will remain, wise enough not to imitate. If it should come to fighting for Chinese customers, the powers engaged in that fight are not unlikely to find out that they pay too high a price for what can be gained, and that at last the peaceful and active NEUTRAL will have the best bargain. At any rate, to launch into all the embroilments of an imperialistic policy by annexing the Philippines in order to snatch something more of the Chinese trade would be for us the foolishest game of all.

Generally speaking, nothing could be more irrational than all the talk about our losing commercial or other opportunities which "will never come back if we fail to grasp them now." Why, we are so rapidly growing in all the elements of power ahead of all other nations that, not many decades hence, unless we demoralize ourselves by a reckless policy of adventure, not one of them will be able to resist our will if we choose to enforce it. This the world knows, and is alarmed at the prospect. Those who are most alarmed may wish that we should give them now, by some rash enterprise, an occasion for dealing us a damaging blow while we are less irresistible.

"But we must have coaling stations for our navy!" Well, can we not get as many coaling stations as we need without owning populous countries behind them that would entangle us in dangerous political responsibilities and complications? Must Great Britain own the whole of Spain in order to hold Gibraltar?

"But we must civilize those poor people!" Are we not ingenious and charitable enough to do much for their civilization without subjugating and ruling them by criminal aggression?

The rest of the pleas for imperialism consist mostly of those high-sounding catch-words of which a free people when about to decide a great question should be especially suspicious. We are admonished that it is time for us to become a "world power." Well, we *are* a world power now, and have been for many years. What is a world power? A power strong enough to make its voice listened to with deference by the world whenever it chooses to speak. Is it necessary for a world power, in order to be such, to have its finger in every pie? Must we have the Philippines in order to become a world power? To ask the question is to answer it.

The American flag, we are told, whenever once raised, must never be hauled down. Certainly, every patriotic citizen will always be ready, if need be, to fight and to die under his flag wherever it may wave in justice and for the best interests of the country. But I say to you, woe to the republic if it should ever be without citizens patriotic and brave enough to defy the demagogues' cry and to haul down the flag wherever it may be raised not in justice and not for the best interests of the country. Such a republic would not last long. . . .

We are told that, having grown so great and strong, we must at last cast off our childish reverence for the teachings of Washington's farewell address — those "nursery rhymes that were sung around the cradle of the republic." I apprehend that many of those who now so flippantly scoff at the heritage the Father of his Country left us in his last words of admonition, have never read that venerable document. I challenge those who have, to show me a single sentence of general import in it that would not as a wise rule of national conduct apply to the circumstances of to-day! What is it that has given to Washington's farewell address an authority that was revered by all until our recent victories made so many of us drunk with wild ambitions? Not only the prestige of Washington's name, great as that was and should ever remain. No, it was the fact that under a respectful observance of those teachings this republic has grown from the most modest beginnings into a Union spanning this vast continent; our people have multiplied from a handful to 75 millions; we have risen from poverty to a wealth the sum of which the imagination can hardly grasp; this American nation has become one of the greatest and most powerful on earth, and, continuing in the same course, will surely become the greatest and most powerful of all. Not Washington's name alone gave his teachings their dignity and weight. It was the practical results of his policy that secured to it, until now, the intelligent approbation of the American people. And unless we have completely lost our senses, we shall never despise and reject as mere "nursery rhymes" the words of wisdom left us by the greatest of Americans, following which the American people have achieved a splendor of development without parallel in the history of mankind. . . .

If this democracy, after all the intoxication of triumph in war, conscientiously remembers its professions and pledges, and soberly reflects on its duties to itself and others, and then deliberately resists the temptation of conquest, it will achieve the grandest triumph of the democratic idea that history knows of. It will give the government of, for, and by the people a prestige it never before possessed. It will render the cause of civilization throughout the world a service without parallel. It will put its detractors to shame, and its voice will be heard in the council of nations with more sincere respect and more deference than ever. The American people, having given proof of their strength and also of their honesty and wisdom, will stand infinitely mightier before the world than any number of subjugated vassals could make them. Are not here our best interests, both moral and material? Is not this genuine glory? Is not this true patriotism?

I call upon all who so believe never to lose heart in the struggle for this great cause, whatever odds may seem to be against us. Let there be no pusillanimous yielding while the final decision is still in the balance. Let us relax no effort in this, the greatest crisis the republic has ever seen. Let us never cease to invoke the good sense, the honesty, and the patriotic pride of the people. Let us raise high the flag of our country — not as an emblem of reckless adventure and greedy conquest, of betrayed professions and broken pledges, of criminal aggressions and arbitrary rule over subject populations — but the old, the true flag, the flag of George Washington and Abraham Lincoln, the flag of the government of, for, and by the people; the flag of national faith held sacred and of national honor unsullied; the flag of human rights and of good example to all nations; the flag of true civilization, peace, and goodwill to all men. Under it let us stand to the last, whatever betide.

15

A PROFESSOR ARGUES AGAINST OVERCOMMITMENT

William Graham Sumner (1840–1910), a leading educator, economist, and sociologist, taught many generations of students at Yale University. A thoroughgoing disciple of Charles Darwin and Herbert Spencer, Sumner applied evolutionary principles to societies and nations. Like John Fiske, Sumner believed in the gradual development of a perfected society and deplored as actually harmful any governmental interference or violation of the policy of laissez-faire. Thus, he opposed social and economic reforms such as the income tax, the regulation of monopolies, bimetallism and the free coinage of silver, and even tariffs.

Sumner was widely criticized during the Spanish-American War for his unflinching stand against imperialism. In the article that appears below, he reveals himself characteristically as a realist who opposed expansion on the ground that the United States could not afford to overcommit its power.

THE CONQUEST OF THE UNITED STATES BY SPAIN

William G. Sumner

During the last year the public has been familiarized with descriptions of Spain and of Spanish methods of doing things until the name of Spain has become a symbol for a certain well-defined set of notions and policies. On the other hand, the name of the United States has always been, for all of us, a symbol for a state of things, a set of ideas and traditions, a group of views about social and political affairs. Spain was the first, for a long time the greatest, of the modern imperialistic States. The United States, by its historical origin, its traditions and its principles, is the chief representative of the revolt and reaction against that kind of a state. I intend to show that, by the line of action now proposed to us, which we call expansion and imperialism, we are throwing away some of the most important elements of the American symbol, and are adopting some of the most important elements of the Spanish symbol. We have beaten Spain in a military conflict, but we are submitting to be conquered by her on the field of ideas and policies. . . .

There is . . . [an] observation . . . about the war which is of far greater importance; that is, that it was a gross violation of self-government. We boast that we are a self-governing people, and in this respect, particularly, we compare ourselves with pride with older nations. What is the difference after all? The Russians, whom we always think of as standing at the opposite pole of political institutions, have self-government, if you mean by it acquiescence in what a little group of people at the head of the government agree to do. The war with Spain was precipitated upon us headlong, without reflection or deliberation, and without any due formulation of public opinion. Whenever a voice was raised in behalf of deliberation and the recognized maxims of statesmanship, it was howled down in a storm of vituperation and cant. Everything was done to make us throw away sobriety of thought and calmness of judgment, and to inflate all expressions with sensational epithets and turgid phrases. It cannot be denied that everything in regard to the war has been treated in an exalted strain of sentiment and rhetoric very unfavorable

[handwritten margin note: ASSUMES THAT PUBLIC OPINION SHOULD BE CONSULTED.]

FROM *Yale Law Journal*, VIII (January, 1899), pp. 168–93.

to the truth. At present the whole periodical press of the country seems to be occupied in tickling the national vanity to the utmost by representations about the war which are extravagant and fantastic. There will be a penalty to be paid for all this. Nervous and sensational newspapers are just as corrupting, especially to young people, as nervous and sensational novels. The habit of expecting that all mental pabulum shall be highly spiced, and the corresponding loathing for whatever is soberly truthful, undermines character as much as any other vice. Patriotism is being prostituted into a nervous intoxication which is fatal to an apprehension of truth. It builds around us a fool's paradise, and it will lead us into errors about our position and relations just like those which we have been ridiculing in the case of Spain. . . .

INFLATED IMAGE OF U.S.

There is not a civilized nation which does not talk about its civilizing mission just as grandly as we do. The English, who really have more to boast of in this respect than any body else, talk least about it, but the Phariseeism with which they correct and instruct other people has made them hated all over the globe. The French believe themselves the guardians of the highest and purest culture, and that the eyes of all mankind are fixed on Paris, from whence they expect oracles of thought and taste. The Germans regard themselves as charged with a mission, especially to us Americans, to save us from egoism and materialism. The Russians, in their books and newspapers, talk about the civilizing mission of Russia, in language that might be translated from some of the finest paragraphs in our imperialistic newspapers. The first principle of Mohammedanism is that we Christians are dogs and infidels, fit only to be enslaved or butchered by Moslems. It is a corollary that wherever Mohammedanism extends, it carries, in the belief of its votaries, the highest blessings, and that the whole human race would be enormously elevated if Mohammedanism should supplant Christianity everywhere. To come last to Spain, the Spaniards have, for centuries, considered themselves the most zealous and self-sacrificing Christians, especially charged by the Almighty, on this account, to spread true religion and civilization over the globe. They think themselves free and noble, leaders in refinement and the sentiments of personal honor, and they despise us as sordid money-grabbers and heretics. I could bring you passages from peninsular authors of the first rank about the grand role of Spain and Portugal in spreading freedom and truth. Now each nation laughs at all the others when it observes these manifestations of national vanity. You may rely upon it that they are all ridiculous by virtue of these

EACH NATION IS IN ITS OWN RECOGNIZABLE SPHERE.

pretensions, including ourselves. The point is that each of them repudiates the standards of the others, and the outlying nations, which are to be civilized, hate all the standards of civilized men. We assume that what we like and practice, and what we think better, must come as a welcome blessing to Spanish-Americans and Philippinos. This is grossly and obviously untrue. They hate our ways. They are hostile to our ideas. Our religion, language, institutions and manners offend them. They like their own ways, and if we appear amongst them as rulers, there will be social discord on all the great departments of social interest. The most important thing which we shall inherit from the Spaniards will be the task of suppressing rebellions. If the United States takes out of the hands of Spain her mission, on the ground that Spain is not executing it well, and if this nation in its turn, attempts to be school-mistress to others, it will shrivel up into the same vanity and self-conceit of which Spain now presents an example. To read our current literature one would think that we were already well on the way to it. Now, the great reason why all these enterprises which begin by saying to somebody else: We know what is good for you, better than you know yourself, and we are going to make you do it — are false and wrong, is that they violate liberty; or, to turn the same statement into other words: the reason why liberty, of which we Americans talk so much, is a good thing, is that it means leaving people to live out their own lives in their own way, while we do the same. If we believe in liberty, as an American principle, why do we not stand by it? Why are we going to throw it away to enter upon a Spanish policy of dominion and regulation?

The United States cannot be a colonizing nation for a long time yet. We have only 23 persons to the square mile in the United States without Alaska. The country can multiply its population by 13, that is, the population could rise above a billion, before the whole country would be as densely populated as Rhode Island is now. There is, therefore, no pressure of population, which is the first condition of rational expansion, unless we could buy another territory like the Mississippi Valley with no civilized population in it. If we could do that it would postpone the day of over-population still further, and make easier conditions for our people in the next generations. In the second place, the islands which we have taken from Spain never can be the residence of American families, removing and settling to make their homes there. The climatic conditions forbid it. Although Spaniards have established themselves in Spanish America, even in the tropics, the evils of Spanish rule have largely arisen from the fact that Spaniards have gone to the colonies as adventurers, eager to make fortunes as quickly as possible, that they might return to Spain to enjoy them. . . .

The Americans have been committed from the outset to the doctrine that all men are equal. We have elevated it into an absolute doctrine as a part of the theory of our social and political fabric. It has always been a domestic dogma in spite of its absolute form, and as a domestic dogma it has always stood in glaring contradiction to the facts about Indians and negroes, and to our legislation about Chinamen. In its absolute form it must, of course, apply to Kanakas, Malays, Tagals and Chinese just as much as to Yankees, Germans and Irish. It is an astonishing event that we have lived to see American arms carry this domestic dogma out where it must be tested in its application to uncivilized and half-civilized peoples. At the first touch of the test we throw the doctrine away and adopt the Spanish doctrine. We are told by all the imperialists that these people are not fit for liberty and self-government; that it is rebellion for them to resist our beneficence; that we must send fleets and armies to kill them if they do it; that we must devise a government for them and administer it ourselves; that we may buy them or sell them as we please, and dispose of their "trade" for our own advantage. What is that but the policy of Spain to her dependencies? What can we expect as a consequence of it? Nothing but that it will bring us where Spain is now.

But, then, if it is not right for us to hold these islands as dependencies, you may ask me whether I think that we ought to take them into our Union, at least some of them, and let them help to govern us. Certainly not. If *that* question is raised, then the question whether they are, in our judgment, fit for self-government or not is in order. The American people, since the civil war, have to a great extent lost sight of the fact that this state of ours, the United States of America, is a confederated state of a very peculiar and artificial form. It is not a state like the states of Europe, with the exception of Switzerland. The field for dogmatism in our day is not theology; it is political philosophy. "Sovereignty" is the most abstract and metaphysical term in political philosophy. Nobody can define it. For this reason it exactly suits the purposes of the curbstone statesman. He puts into it whatever he wants to get out of it again, and he has set to work lately to spin out a proof that the United States is a great imperialistic state, although the Constitution, which tells us just what it is, and what it is not, is there to prove contrary. . . .

It follows,..., that it is unwisdom to take into a state like
this any foreign element which is not congenial to it. Any such
element will act as a solvent upon it. Consequently we are brought
by our new conquests face to face with this dilemma: we must either
hold them as inferior possessions, to be ruled and exploited by us
after the fashion of the old colonial system, or we must take them
in on an equality with ourselves, where they will help to govern
us and to corrupt a political system which they do not understand,
and in which they cannot participate. From that dilemma there is
no escape except to give them independence and to let them work
out their own salvation or go without it. Hayti has been independent
for a century, and has been a theatre of revolution, tyranny and
bloodshed all the time. There is not a Spanish-American state which
has proved its capacity for self-government as yet. It is a fair question
whether any one of them would have been worse off than it is to-day
if Spanish rule had been maintained in it. The chief exception is
Mexico. Mr. Lummis, an American, has recently published a book
on Mexico, in which he tells us that we would do well to go to
school to Mexico for a number of important public interests, but
Mexico has been, for 10 or 15 years, under a dictator, and the
republican forms have been in abeyance. What will happen there
when the dictator dies nobody knows. The doctrine that we are
to take away from other nations any possessions of theirs which
we think that we could manage better than they are managing them,
or that we are to take in hand any countries which we do not think
capable of self-government, is one which will lead us very far. With
that doctrine in the background, our politicians will have no trouble
to find a war ready for us the next time that they come around
to the point where they think that it is time for us to have another.
We are told that we must have a big army hereafter. What for;
unless we propose to do again bye-and-bye what we have just done?
In that case our neighbors have reason to ask themselves who we
will attack next. They must begin to arm, too, and by our act the
whole western world is plunged into the distress under which the
eastern world is groaning. Here is another point in regard to which
the conservative elements in the country are making a great mistake
to allow all this militarism and imperialism to go on without protest.
It will be established as a rule that, whenever political ascendancy
is threatened, it can be established again by a little war, filling the
minds of the people with glory and diverting their attention from
their own interests. Hardheaded old Benjamin Franklin hit the point
when, referring back to the days of Marlborough, he talked about

the "pest of glory." The thirst for glory is an epidemic which robs a people of their judgment, seduces their vanity, cheats them of their interests, and corrupts their consciences. . . .

If we treat the dependencies as inside the national system, we must have absolute free trade with them. Then, if, on the policy of the "open door," we allow all others to go to them on the same terms as ourselves, the dependencies will have free trade with all the world, while we are under the restrictive system ourselves. Then, too, the dependencies can obtain no revenues by import duties.

If we take the other branch of the dilemma and treat the dependencies as outside of our national policy, then we must shut out their products from our market by taxes. If we do this on the policy of the "open door," then any taxes which the islands lay upon imports from elsewhere, they must also lay upon imports from us. Then they and we will be taxing each other. If we go upon the protectionist policy, we shall determine our taxes against them, and theirs against other nations, and we shall let them lay none against us. That is exactly the Spanish system. Under it the colonies will be crushed between the upper and the nether mill-stone. They will revolt against us for just the same reason for which they revolted against Spain.

I have watched the newspapers with great interest for six months, to see what indications were presented of the probable currents of opinion on the dilemma which I have described. There have been but few. A few extreme protectionist newspapers have truculently declared that our protective system was to be extended around our possessions, and that everybody else was to be excluded from them. From a number of interviews and letters, by private individuals, I select the following as expressing well what is sure to be the view of the unregenerate man, especially if he has an interest to be protected as this writer had:

"I am opposed to the 'open door' policy, as I understand it. To open the ports of our new territories free to the world would have the effect of cheapening or destroying many of the benefits of territorial acquisition, which has cost us blood and money. As a nation we are well qualified to develop and handle the trade of our new possessions, and by permitting others to come in and divide the advantages and profits of this trade we not only wrong our own citizens, who should be given preference, but exhibit a weakness that ill becomes a nation of our prominence."

This is exactly the view which was held in Spain, France, Holland and England, in the 18th century, and upon which the navigation system, against which our fathers revolted, was founded.

If we adopt this view we may count upon it that we shall be embroiled in constant wars with other nations, which will not consent that we should shut them out of parts of the earth's surface until we prove that we can do it by force. Then we shall be parties to a renewal of all the 18th century wars for colonies, for supremacy on the sea, for "trade," as the term is used, for world supremacy, and for all the rest of the heavy follies from which our fathers fought to free themselves. That is the policy of Russia and France at the present time, and we have before our eyes proofs of its effect on the peace and welfare of mankind.

Our modern protectionists have always told us that the object of their policy is to secure the home market. They have pushed their system to an extravagant excess. The free traders used to tell them that they were constructing a Chinese wall. They answered that they wished we were separated from other nations by a gulf of fire. Now it is they who are crying out that they are shut in by a Chinese wall. When we have shut all the world out, we find that we have shut ourselves in. The protective system is applied especially to certain selected lines of production. Of course these are stimulated out of proportion to the requirements of the community, and so are exposed to sharp fluctuations of high profits and over-production. At great expense and loss we have carried out the policy of the home market, and now we are called upon at great expense and loss to go out and conquer territory in order to widen the market. In order to have trade with another community the first condition is that we must produce what they want, and they must produce what we want. That is the economic condition. The second condition is that there must be peace and security, and freedom from arbitrary obstacles interposed by government. This is the political condition. If these conditions are fulfilled, there will be trade, no matter whether the two communities are in one body politic or not. If these conditions are not fulfilled, there will be no trade, no matter what flag floats. If we want more trade we can get it any day by a reciprocity treaty with Canada, and it will be larger and more profitable than that of all the Spanish possessions. It will cost us nothing to get it. Yet while we were fighting for Porto Rico and Manilla, and spending three or four hundred millions to get them, negotiations with Canada failed through the narrow-mindedness and bigotry which we brought to the negotiation. Conquest can do nothing for trade except to remove the political obstacles which the conquered could not, or would not, remove. From this it follows that the only justification for territorial extension is the extension of free and enlightened policies in regard to commerce.

Even then extension is an irksome necessity. The question always is, whether you are taking an asset or a liability. Land grabbing means properly taking territory and shutting all the rest of the world out of it, so as to exploit it ourselves. It is not land grabbing to take it and police it and throw it open to all. This is the policy of the "open door." Our external commercial policy is, in all its principles, the same as that of Spain. We had no justification, on that ground, in taking anything away from her. If we now seek to justify ourselves, it must be by going over to the free policy, but, as I have shown, that forces to a crisis the contradiction between our domestic and our external policy as to trade. It is very probable, indeed, that the destruction of our restrictive system will be the first good result of expansion, but my object here has been to show what a network of difficulties environ us in the attempt to establish a commercial policy for these dependencies. We have certainly to go through years of turmoil and political bitterness, with all the consequent chances of internal dissension, before these difficulties can be overcome. . . .

The point which I have tried to make in this lecture is that expansion and imperialism are at war with the best traditions, principles and interests of the American people, and that they will plunge us into a network of difficult problems and political perils, which we might have avoided, while they offer us no corresponding advantage in return.

Of course "principles," phrases and catchwords are always invented to bolster up any policy which anybody wants to recommend. So in this case. The people who have led us on to shut ourselves in, and who now want us to break out, warn us against the terrors of "isolation." Our ancestors all came here to isolate themselves from the social burdens and inherited errors of the old world. When the others are all over ears in trouble, who would not be isolated in freedom from care? When the others are crushed under the burden of militarism, who would not be isolated in peace and industry? When the others are all struggling under debt and taxes, who would not be isolated in the enjoyment of his own earnings for the benefit of his own family? When the rest are all in a quiver of anxiety lest at a day's notice they may be involved in a social cataclysm, who would not be isolated out of reach of the disaster? What we are doing is that we are abandoning this blessed isolation to run after a share in the trouble.

The expansionists answer our remonstrances on behalf of the great American principles by saying that times have changed, and that we have outlived the fathers of the republic and their doctrines.

As far as the authority of the great men is concerned, that may well be sacrificed without regret. Authority of persons and names is a dangerous thing. Let us get at the truth and the right. I, for my part, am also afraid of the great principles, and I would make no fight on their behalf. In the ten years before the Revolution our ancestors invented a fine lot of "principles" which they thought would help their case. They repudiated many of them as soon as they got their independence, and the rest of them have since made us a great deal of trouble. I have examined them all critically, and there is not one of them which I consider sound, as it is popularly understood. I have been denounced as a heretic on this account by people who now repudiate them all in a sentence. But this only clears the ground for the real point. There is a consistency of character for a nation as well as for a man. A man who changes his principles from week to week is destitute of character and deserves no confidence. The great men of this nation were such because they embodied and expressed the opinion and sentiments of the nation in their time. Their names are something more than clubs with which to knock an opponent down when it suits one's purpose, but to be thrown away with contempt when they happen to be on the other side. So of the great principles; whether some of us are skeptical about their entire validity, and want to define and limit them somewhat, is of little importance. If the nation has accepted them, sworn by them, founded its legislation on them, imbedded them in the decisions of its courts, and then if it throws them away at six months' warning, you may depend upon it that that nation will suffer in its moral and political rectitude a shock of the severest kind. Three years ago we were ready to fight Great Britain to make her arbitrate a quarrel which she had with Venezuela. The question about the Maine was the fittest subject for arbitration that ever arose between two nations, and we refused to listen to such a proposition. Three years ago, if you had said that any proposition put forth by anybody was "English," he might have been mobbed in the streets. Now the English are our beloved friends, and we are going to try to imitate them and adopt their way of doing things. They are encouraging us to go into difficulties, first because our hands will be full and we will be unable to interfere elsewhere, and secondly, because if we are in difficulties we shall need allies, and they think that they will be our first choice as such. Some of our public journals have been pouring out sentimental drivel for years about arbitration, but last summer they turned around and began to pour out sentimental drivel about the benefits of war. We congratulate ourselves all the time on the increased means of producing wealth, and then we take the opposite fit and commit some great folly in order to prove that there is something grander than the pursuit of wealth. Three years ago we were on the verge of a law to keep immigrants out who were not good enough to be in with us. Now we are going to take in 8,000,000 barbarians and semi-barbarians, and we are paying $20,000,000 to get them. For thirty years the negro has been in fashion. He has had political value and has been petted. Now we have made friends with the Southerners. They and we are hugging each other. We are all united. The negro's day is over. He is out of fashion. We cannot treat him one way and the Malays, Tagals and Kanakas another way. A Southern senator two or three days ago thanked an expansionist senator from Connecticut for enunciating doctrines which proved that, for the last thirty years, the Southerners have been right all the time, and his inference was incontrovertible. So the "great principles" change all the time, or, what is far more important, the phrases change. Some go out of fashion; others come in, but the phrase-makers are with us all the time. So when our friends the expansionists tell us that times have changed, what it means is that they have a whole set of new phrases which they want to force into the place of the old ones. The new ones are certainly no more valid than the old ones. All the validity that the great principles ever had they have now. Anybody who ever candidly studied them and accepted them for no more than they were really worth can stand by them now as well as ever. The time when a maxim or principle is worth something is when you are tempted to violate it.

Another answer which the imperialists make is that Americans can do anything. They say that they do not shrink from responsibilities. They are willing to run into a hole, trusting to luck and cleverness to get out. There are some things that Americans cannot do. Americans cannot make 2 and 2 = 5. You may answer that that is an arithmetical impossibility and is not in the range of our subject. Very well: Americans cannot collect $2 a gallon tax on whisky. They tried it for many years and failed. That is an economic or political impossibility, the roots of which are in human nature. It is as absolute an impossibility on this domain as the former on the domain of mathematics. So far as yet appears, Americans cannot govern a city of 100,000 inhabitants so as to get comfort and convenience in it at a low cost and without jobbery. The fire department of this city is now demoralized by political jobbery. Spain and all her possessions are not worth as much to you and me as the efficiency of the fire department of New Haven. The Americans in Connecticut cannot abolish the rotten borough system. The English abolished their rotten borough system seventy years ago, in spite of nobles and landlords. We cannot abolish ours in spite of the small towns. Americans cannot reform the pension list. Its abuses are rooted in the methods of democratic self-government, and no one dares to touch them. It is very doubtful indeed if Americans can keep up an army of 100,000 men in time of peace. Where can 100,000 men be found in this country who are willing to spend their lives as soldiers? or, if they are found, what pay will it require to induce them to take this career? Americans cannot disentangle their currency from the confusion into which it was thrown by the civil war, and they cannot put their currency on a simple, sure and sound basis which would give stability to the business of the country. This is a political impossibility. Americans cannot assure the suffrage to negroes throughout the United States. They have tried it for thirty years, and now, contemporaneously with this war with Spain, it has been finally demonstrated that it is a failure. Inasmuch as the negro is now out of fashion no further attempt to accomplish this purpose will be made. It is an impossibility on account of the complexity of our system of State and federal government. If I had time to do so, I could go back over the history of negro suffrage and show you how curbstone arguments, exactly analogous to the arguments about expansion, were used to favor it, and how objections were thrust aside in this same blustering and senseless manner in which objections to imperialism are met. The ballot, we were told, was an educator and would solve all difficulties in its own path as by magic. Worse still: Americans cannot assure life, liberty and the pursuit of happiness to negroes inside of the United States. When the negro postmaster's house was set on fire in the night in South Carolina, and not only he, but his wife and children, were murdered as they came out, and when, moreover, this incident passed without legal investigation or punishment, it was a bad omen for the extension of liberty, etc., etc., to Malays and Tagals by simply setting over them the American flag. Upon a little serious examination the off-hand disposal of an important question of policy by the declaration that Americans can do anything proves to be only a silly piece of bombast, and upon a little reflection, we find that our hands are quite full at home of problems, by the solution of which the peace and happiness of the American people could be greatly increased. The laws of nature and of human nature are just as valid for Americans as for anybody else, and if we commit acts, we shall have to take consequences, just like other people. Therefore prudence demands that we look ahead to see what we are about to do, and that we gauge the means at our disposal, if we do not want to bring calamity on ourselves and our children. We see that the peculiarities of our system of government set limitations on us. We cannot do things which a great centralized monarchy could do. The very blessings and special advantages which we enjoy, as compared with others, bring disabilities with them. That is the great fundamental cause of what I have tried to show throughout this lecture, that we cannot govern dependencies consistently with our political system, and that, if we try it, the state which our fathers founded will suffer a reaction which will transform it into another empire just after the fashion of all the old ones. That is what imperialism means. That is what it will be, and the democratic republic, which has been, will stand in history as a mere transition form like the colonial organization of earlier days.

And yet this scheme of a republic which our fathers formed was a glorious dream which demands more than a word of respect and affection before it passes away. Indeed, it is not fair to call it a dream or even an ideal. It was a possibility which was within our reach if we had been wise enough to grasp and hold it. It was favored by our comparative isolation, or, at least, by our distance from other strong states. The men who came here were able to throw off all the trammels of tradition and established doctrine. They went out into a wilderness, it is true, but they took with them all the art, science and literature which, up to that time, civilization had produced. They could not it is true, strip their minds of the ideas which they had inherited, but, in time, as they lived on in the New World, they sifted and selected these ideas, retaining what they chose. Of the old world institutions also they selected and adopted what they chose and threw aside the rest. It was a grand opportunity to be thus able to strip off all the follies and errors which they had inherited, so far as they chose to do so. They had unlimited land with no feudal restrictions to hinder them in the use of it. Their idea was that they would never allow any of the social and political abuses of the old world to grow up here. There should be no manors, no barons, no ranks, no prelates, no idle classes, no paupers, no disinherited ones except the vicious. There were to be no armies except a militia, which would have no functions but those of police. They would have no court and no pomp; no orders, or ribbons, or decorations, or titles. They would have no public debt. They repudiated with scorn the notion that a public debt is a public blessing. If debt was incurred in war it was to be paid in peace and not entailed on posterity. There was to be no grand diplomacy, because they intended to mind their own business, and not be involved in any of the intrigues to which European statesmen were accustomed. There was to be no balance of power and no "reason of state" to cost the life and happiness of citizens. The only part of the Monroe doctrine which is valid was their determination that the social and political systems of Europe should not be extended over any part of the American Continent, lest people who were weaker than we should lose the opportunity which the new continent gave them to escape from those systems if they wanted to. Our fathers would have an economical government, even if grand people called it a parsimonious one, and taxes should be no greater than were absolutely necessary to pay for such a government. The citizen was to keep all the rest of his earnings, and use them as he thought best for the happiness of himself and his family. The citizen was, above all, to be insured peace and quiet while he pursued his honest industry and obeyed the laws. No adventurous policies of conquest or ambition, such as, in their belief, kings and nobles had forced, for their own advantage, on European states, would ever be undertaken by a free democratic republic. Therefore the citizen here would never be forced to leave his family, or to give his sons to shed blood for glory and to leave widows and orphans in misery for nothing. Justice and law were to reign in the midst of simplicity, and a government which had little to do was to offer little field for ambition. In a society where industry, frugality and prudence were honored, it was believed that the vices of wealth would never flourish.

We know that these beliefs, hopes and intentions have been only partially fulfilled. We know that, as time has gone on, and we have grown numerous and rich, some of these things have proved impossible ideals, incompatible with a large and flourishing society, but it is by virtue of this conception of a commonwealth that the United States has stood for something unique and grand in the history of mankind, and that its people have been happy. It is by virtue of these ideals that we have been "isolated," isolated in a position which the other nations of the earth have observed in silent envy, and yet there are people who are boasting of their patriotism, because they say that we have taken our place now amongst the nations of the earth by virtue of this war. My patriotism is of the kind which is outraged by the notion that the United States never was a great nation until in a petty three months campaign it knocked to pieces a poor, decrepit bankrupt old state like Spain. To hold such an opinion as that is to abandon all American standards, to put shame and scorn on all that our ancestors tried to build up here, and to go over to the standards of which Spain is a representative.

PART III

THE PERILS OF POWER
1900–1914

16

ECONOMIC COOPERA-
TION URGED

 William McKinley (1843–1901), long identified with the championship of high tariff rates, came to national attention while in the House of Representatives (1876–1891) where he sponsored in 1890 the protectionist bill that bears his name. Raising duties beyond previous levels, the McKinley Tariff aroused great controversy and had tremendous diplomatic implications, especially in regard to our relationships with such sugar producers as Hawaii, Puerto Rico, and Cuba. Defeated for reelection to the House, McKinley became Governor of Ohio, and in 1897 was inaugurated as the twenty-fifth President of the United States.

Given McKinley's record on the tariff issue, it is interesting that in his last speech, delivered in Buffalo on September 5, 1901 at the Pan American Exposition, he revealed a refreshing flexibility with regard to the need for lowering international tariff barriers. McKinley held that "the period of exclusiveness is past," mirroring a change of mind resulting from the consequences of the Spanish-American War. This change of heart, however, came too late, for the President was not fated to implement what might possibly have been a forerunner of the New Deal policy of tariff reciprocity. Shot the very next day by an anarchist, Leon Czolgosz, McKinley died within a week leaving to future Presidents the political hot potato of tariff revision.

PRESIDENT McKINLEY'S LAST PUBLIC UTTERANCE TO THE PEOPLE

William McKinley

Link-Leary

I am glad to be again in the city of Buffalo and exchange greetings with her people, to whose generous hospitality I am not a stranger, and with whose good will I have been repeatedly and signally honored. To-day I have additional satisfaction in meeting and giving welcome to the foreign representatives assembled here, whose presence and participation in this exposition have contributed in so marked a degree to its interest and success. To the commissioners of the Dominion of Canada and the British colonies, the French colonies, the republics of Mexico and of Central and South America, and the commissioners of Cuba and Porto Rico, who share with us in this undertaking, we give the hand of fellowship and felicitate with them upon the triumphs of art, science, education, and manufacture, which the old has bequeathed to the new century.

Expositions are the timekeepers of progress. They record the world's advancement. They stimulate the energy, enterprise and intellect of the people, and quicken human genius. They go into the home. They broaden and brighten the daily life of the people. They open mighty storehouses of information to the student. Every exposition, great or small, has helped to some onward step. Comparison of ideas is always educational; and as such instructs the brain and hand of man.

Friendly rivalry follows, which is the spur to industrial improvement, the inspiration to useful invention and to high endeavor in all departments of human activity. It exacts the study of the wants, comforts, and even the whims of the people, and recognizes the efficacy of high quality and new prices to win their favor. The quest for trade is an incentive to men of business to devise, invent, improve, and economize in the cost of production. Business life, whether among ourselves, or with other people, is ever a sharp struggle for success. It will be none the less so in the future. Without competition we would be clinging to the clumsy and antiquated processes of farming and manufacture and the methods of business of long ago, and the twentieth would be no further advanced than the eighteenth

FROM *A Compilation of the Messages and Papers of the Presidents,* James D. Richardson, ed., (New York, 1905), vol. XV, pp. 6618–22.

century. But though commercial competitors we are, commercial enemies we must not be.

The Pan-American Exposition has done its work thoroughly, presenting in its exhibits evidence of the highest skill and illustrating the progress of the human family in the Western Hemisphere. This portion of the earth has no cause for humiliation for the part it has performed in the march of civilization. It has not accomplished everything; far from it. It has simply done its best, and, without vanity or boastfulness, and recognizing the manifold achievements of others, it invites the friendly rivalry of all the powers in the peaceful pursuits of trade and commerce, and will co-operate with all in advancing the highest and best interests of humanity. The wisdom and energy of all the nations are none too great for the world's work. The success of art, science, industry, and invention is an international asset and a common glory.

After all, how near one to the other is every part of the world! Modern inventions have brought into close relation widely separated peoples and made them better acquainted. Geographic and political divisions will continue to exist, but distances have been effaced. Swift ships and fast trains are becoming cosmopolitan. They invade fields which a few years ago were impenetrable. The world's products are exchanged as never before, and with increasing transportation facilities come increasing knowledge and larger trade. Prices are fixed with mathematical precision by supply and demand. The world's selling prices are regulated by market and crop reports. We travel greater distances in a shorter space of time and with more ease than was ever dreamed of by the fathers. Isolation is no longer possible or desirable. The same important news is read, though in different languages, the same day in all Christendom. The telegraph keeps us advised of what is occurring everywhere, and the press foreshadows, with more or less accuracy, the plans and purposes of the nations. Market prices of products and of securities are hourly known in every commercial mart, and the investments of the people extend beyond their own national boundaries into the remotest parts of the earth.

Vast transactions are conducted and international exchanges are made by the tick of the cable. Every event of interest is immediately bulletined. The quick gathering and transmission of news, like rapid transit, are of recent origin, and are only made possible by the genius of the inventor and the courage of the investor. It took a special messenger of the government, with every facility known at the time for rapid travel, nineteen days to go from the city of

Washington to New Orleans with a message to General Jackson that the war with England had ceased, and that a treaty of peace had been signed. How different now.

We reached General Miles in Porto Rico by cable, and he was able through the military telegraph to stop his army on the firing line with the message that the United States and Spain had signed a protocol suspending hostilities. We knew almost instantly of the first shots fired at Santiago, and the subsequent surrender of the Spanish forces was known at Washington within less than an hour of its consummation. The first ship of Cervera's fleet had hardly emerged from that historic harbor when the fact was flashed to our capital, and the swift destruction that followed was announced immediately through the wonderful medium of telegraphy.

So accustomed are we to safe and easy communication with distant lands, that its temporary interruption, even in ordinary times, results in loss and inconvenience. We shall never forget the days of anxious waiting and awful suspense when no information was permitted to be sent from Peking, and the diplomatic representatives of the nations in China, cut off from all communication, inside and outside the walled capital, were surrounded by an angry and misguided mob that threatened their lives; nor the joy that thrilled the world when a single message from the Government of the United States brought, through our Minister, the first news of the safety of the besieged diplomats.

At the beginning of the nineteenth century there was not a mile of steam railroad on the globe. Now there are enough miles to make its circuit many times. Then there was not a line of electric telegraph; now we have a vast mileage traversing all lands and all seas.

God and man have linked the nations together. No nation can longer be indifferent to any other. And as we are brought more and more in touch with each other, the less occasion is there for misunderstandings and the stronger the disposition, when we have differences, to adjust them in the court of arbitration, which is the noblest forum for the settlement of international disputes.

My fellow citizens, trade statistics indicate that this country is in a state of unexampled prosperity. The figures are almost appalling. They show that we are utilizing our fields and forests and mines and that we are furnishing profitable employment to the millions of workingmen throughout the United States, bringing comfort and happiness to their homes, and making it possible to lay by savings for old age and disability. That all the people are participating in this great prosperity is seen in every American community, and shown by the enormous and unprecedented deposits in our savings banks. Our duty is the care and security of these deposits, and their safe investment demands the highest integrity and the best business capacity of those in charge of these depositories of the people's earnings.

We have a vast and intricate business, built up through years of toil and struggle, in which every part of the country has its stake, which will not permit of either neglect, or of undue selfishness. No narrow, sordid policy will subserve it. The greatest skill and wisdom on the part of the manufacturers and producers will be required to hold and increase it. Our industrial enterprises which have grown to such great proportions affect the homes and occupations of the people and the welfare of the country. Our capacity to produce has developed so enormously, and our products have so multiplied that the problem of more markets requires our urgent and immediate attention. Only a broad and enlightened policy will keep what we have. No other policy will get more. In these times of marvelous business energy and gain we ought to be looking to the future, strengthening the weak places in our industrial and commercial systems, that we may be ready for any storm or strain.

By sensible trade arrangements, which will not interrupt our home production, we shall extend the outlets for our increasing surplus. A system which provides a mutual exchange of commodities is manifestly essential to the continued and healthful growth of our export trade. We must not repose in fancied security that we can forever sell everything and buy little or nothing. If such a thing were possible, it would not be best for us or for those with whom we deal. We should take from our customers such of their products as we can use without harm to our industries and labor. Reciprocity is the natural outgrowth of our wonderful industrial development under the domestic policy now firmly established. What we produce beyond our domestic consumption must have a vent abroad. The excess must be relieved through a foreign outlet, and we should sell everywhere we can, and buy wherever the buying will enlarge our sales and production, and thereby make a greater demand for home labor.

The period of exclusiveness is past. The expansion of our trade and commerce is the pressing problem. Commercial wars are unprofitable. A policy of good will and friendly trade relations will prevent reprisals. Reciprocity treaties are in harmony with the spirit of the times; measures of retaliation are not.

If perchance some of our tariffs are no longer needed, for revenue or to encourage and protect our industries at home, why should they not be employed to extend and promote our markets abroad? Then, too, we have inadequate steamship service. New lines of steamers have already been put in commission between the Pacific ports of the United States and those on the western coast of Mexico and Central and South America. These should be followed up with direct steamship lines between the Eastern coast of the United States and South American ports. One of the needs of the times is direct commercial lines from our vast fields of production to the fields of consumption that we have but barely touched.

Next in advantage to having the thing to sell is to have the convenience to carry it to the buyer. We must encourage our merchant marine.

We must have more ships. They must be under the American flag, built and manned and owned by Americans. These will not only be profitable in a commercial sense; they will be messengers of peace and amity wherever they go. We must build the Isthmian Canal, which will unite the two oceans and give a straight line of water communication with the Western coasts of Central and South America and Mexico. The construction of a Pacific cable cannot longer be postponed.

In the furtherance of these objects of national interest and concern, you are performing an important part. This exposition would have touched the heart of that American statesman whose mind was ever alert and thought ever constant for a larger commerce and a truer fraternity of the republics of the new world. His broad American spirit is felt and manifested here. He needs no identification to an assemblage of Americans anywhere, for the name of Blaine is inseparably associated with the Pan-American movement which finds this practical and substantial expression, and which we all hope will be firmly advanced by the Pan-American Congress that assembles this autumn in the capital of Mexico. The good work will go on. It cannot be stopped. These buildings will disappear; this creation of art and beauty and industry will perish from sight, but their influence will remain to

> "Make it live beyond its too short living,
> With praises and thanksgiving."

Who can tell the new thoughts that have been awakened, the ambitions fired and the high achievements that will be wrought through this exposition? Gentlemen, let us ever remember that our interest is in concord, not conflict, and that our real eminence rests in the victories of peace, not those of war. We hope that all who are represented here may be moved to higher and nobler effort for their own and the world's good, and that out of this city may come, not only greater commerce and trade for us all, but, more essential than these, relations of mutual respect, confidence, and friendship which will deepen and endure.

Our earnest prayer is that God will graciously vouchsafe prosperity, happiness, and peace to all our neighbors, and like blessings to all the peoples and powers of the earth.

17

THE NAVY AND AMERICA'S NEW STATUS AS A WORLD POWER

Richmond Pearson Hobson (1870–1937), who graduated from the United States Naval Academy in 1889, seemed destined for a humdrum naval career. During the Spanish-American War he was taken prisoner, and after the war he served in the Far East (1899–1900). Hobson was also intimately involved in Theodore Roosevelt's plan for the construction of a strong navy. As a lecturer and author he advocated naval supremacy and a *pax Americana* resting on a strong navy. Hobson, while rising to the rank of Rear Admiral, constantly appealed for adequate defenses in the Pacific. He was one of the prime leaders of the Prohibition Movement, serving on the American Alcoholic Association and organizing a world conference on drug addiction. Hobson wrote widely on these evils, and was also the author of the fictional *Buck Jones at Annapolis* (1907).

In the article that follows, Hobson elaborates on the new Great Power status of the United States, not only defending this role, but also interpreting it as a harbinger of global good will and comity among nations.

AMERICA MISTRESS OF THE SEAS

Richmond P. Hobson

The two facts of the century just closed that portend most for the human race are the rise of Russia and the growth of the United States.

Within these two nations are gathering mighty factors of national power, mightier factors than have yet appeared in the history of the world, factors resembling in general nature but exceeding in magnitude those that brought forth the Empire of Rome and the British Empire — cumulative factors that mark Russia for a military empire destined to throw Rome into the shade, and the United States for a mighty Naval Power toward which the vast power of Great Britain is but a stepping-stone.

In the United States we find elements of power, numbers and vigor of population and material resources, without a parallel in history, together with conditions never yet equalled — maritime frontiers, vast material interests, and sacred principles — which demand the growth of power upon the sea.

In population, the United States is half again as large as Germany, nearly twice as large as the white population of the British Empire, nearly twice as large as Austria-Hungary, and more than twice as large as France. The population of the United States is increasing twice as rapidly as the population of Germany, and three times as rapidly as the population of Great Britain and the other nations of Europe, while it has from twelve to fifteen times the space to expand in, with a richness of soil that would enable the United States to support a population equal to the present population of the earth, without taxing the soil beyond the degree now existing in Europe; and every improvement in transportation and means of intercommunication will cause the United States to draw off more and more the hardy and vigorous people of Europe, and thus to make even a greater disparity in the rate of increase.

Moreover, the average American, man for man, is from two to five times as vigorous as the average European. The average American man is an inch taller than the average Englishman, who is the tallest man in Europe, and the average American eats about twice as much strong food as the average Englishman, who is the best fed man in Europe.

In the United States, furthermore, about two and a half times

FROM *North American Review,* CLXXV (October, 1902), pp. 544-57.

as much is spent *per capita* for education as is spent in England and Germany, which stand at the top of the list in Europe.

CHAPTER 17
The Navy and America's
New Status as a
World Power

193

The average American wheat-grower produces three times as much wheat as the average English wheat-grower, four times as much as the average French, five times as much as the average German. Similar averages are found in the output of manufactured articles. The output per man in American locomotive works is twice as large as the output in the English locomotive works, which stand first in Europe. The average American wields about 2,000 foot-tons of mechanical energy per day; the average Englishman about 1,500; the average Frenchman and German about 900; and the other averages in Europe are below 500.

There are in the United States nearly 100,000 more members of the international organization, the Young Men's Christian Association, than there are in all the rest of the world combined. If a famine occurs in Russia, or a cataclysm in the Islands of the Seas, the first relief ships sail from American shores. An American army besieging the City of Santiago feeds the women, children and old men, instead of starving these to reduce the city. America, concluding a war with a fallen foe, restrains its fleet and pays twenty millions of dollars, instead of ravaging the enemy's coast and exacting two hundred millions for war indemnity. America, after pouring out blood and treasure, gives Cuba its independence.

Every test goes to show that Americans, with a few generations of free life in a free continent, are already, physically, intellectually and spiritually, a race of giants.

For vigor in warfare, no such manifestations are found in history as were shown in the American Civil War. Though having but 16,000 men in the United States Army at the beginning, the war involved numbers twice as large as the hordes of Xerxes, the casualties alone being 200,000 more than there were soldiers altogether in the German armies that invaded France in the Franco-Prussian War. Campaigns in that war, for distances covered and obstacles overcome, have no parallel, except, perhaps, in Hannibal's invasion of Italy; while numberous battle-fields counted percentage losses from three to five times as great as the bloodiest on record, those of Napoleon and Frederick the Great. In the supreme test of individual fighting, as shown by regimental records, there were over five hundred cases in the Civil War where the losses of single regiments in single engagements exceeded the loss of the Light Brigade at Balaclava, and one hundred and twenty-five cases exceeding the record of the German Army in the war with France.

For vigor in naval warfare, no such record exists in the world as that of the American Navy. In the war of 1812, the British Navy was at the zenith of its glory, fresh from the victories of Nelson, having counted an almost unbroken record of 200 victories with European foes. The force sent against America was seven times as strong as the American Navy; eighteen battles were fought, and fifteen were won by the American ships, with losses less than one-sixth the British losses.

In the Spanish-American war, the American Navy simultaneously broke two world records, first with cruising vessels against cruising vessels at Manila, then with armored vessels against armored vessels at Santiago, achieving in both cases a mathematical maximum of fighting efficiency, compassing the total destruction of the enemy without any loss to the victor. The American Navy alone of all the navies of the earth, has never known defeat.

Together with its vast, vigorous population, the United States has unmeasured natural resources, a domain from sea to sea spanning the temperate zone, in richness of soil, the Earth's Garden Area, holding below the soil one-third of the known mineral deposits of the earth, having matchless waterways, the granary, butchery and workshop of the world.

Thus, with a heavy preponderance of numbers, great superiority of vigor, and matchless natural resources, the United States, compared with other Powers, has stupendous elements of world influence.

This world influence can rest only upon sea power. Our frontiers are all maritime. Though Canada is a hostage from the British Empire, our contact with that Empire, as with all the World Powers, is the sea. The conditions and mighty forces are wonderfully concurrent for bringing forth naval growth, sure, swift, irresistible.

We have in the United States, 17,000 miles of coast-line, and on this coast-line, and upon the harbors and great rivers leading up from the coast-line, we have built innumerable cities representing accumulations of more homes and property vulnerable from the sea than are found on all the coast-line, harbors and navigable rivers of the continent of Europe combined. Fortifications, mines and torpedoes have been, and still are, useful accessories in coast defence, but they never have arrested, and they cannot now effectually stop, a determined commander of a strong fleet.

The only accident policy, the only insurance, the only adequate guarantee of security, for all this property, for all these homes, upon which depends the happiness of so many millions of American citizens, is the Navy; and the prosperity of the inland population is inseparably bound up with the prosperity of the coastwise popula- tions. Moreover, without adequate protection, this exposed side of the nation would be a standing invitation for attack from nations jealous of our commercial ascendency.

Estimating legitimate naval requirements from coast-line ex- posure, the Navy of the United States should be the largest in the world.

Besides the largest amount of coast property, the United States has the largest amount of water-borne property exposed to attack from the sea, billions upon billions in coastwise, river and lake trade, and exports now the largest in the world, exceeding $1,500,000,000 annually. When we are at war, the Navy only can prevent blockade of our ports, and insure the departure of this property; the Navy only can give safe convoy or a clear road for passage. When Europe is at war, the Navy only can insure our rights as a neutral, and permit us to realize the security of our isolation, and render us, in fact as in word, independent of European turmoil.

Estimating legitimate naval requirements by the quantity of exposed water-borne property, the Navy of the United States, again, should be the largest in the world.

But the huge figures of $1,500,000,000 of American property now shipped annually over the seas, is only an introduction to the coming importance of over-sea markets. With the differentiation of labor and the increasing necessity for free exchange of products, the national importance of foreign markets is, in a general way, proportional to the productiveness of the nation, notwithstanding the importance of the home markets. With the United States now producing one-third of the world's foodstuffs, one-third of the world's mineral products, eight-tenths of the world's principal article of clothing, while she stands but on the threshold of her possibilities of production in these fields; with the United States now employing more mechanical energy than all Europe combined, and now produc- ing $12,500,000,000 annually of manufactured articles, more than the combined manufactured articles of Great Britain, Germany and France, while its rate of increase of manufactured articles is twice as great as the rate of increase in Europe; with the United States thus advancing by leaps and bounds, and already almost at the point where it will produce as much as all Europe combined, the matter of foreign markets, important for all the nations, is of supreme importance for us.

While the domestic markets of the other great Powers offer an inviting field, they are subject to embarrassment by local legislation. The markets of most importance for all the great nations are the new markets of undeveloped lands, where all may have an equal chance. These markets are of vital importance to a nation making such giant strides as the United States is making in industrial and commercial expansion. In the fierce and fiercer-growing competition of the great Powers for advantage in new markets over the seas, where the local people themselves can make but feeble show of power, the security of the nation's interests can rest only upon the nation's fleets.

To emphasize the far-reaching importance of this question, take the case of the new market of China. From long experience in the reconstruction of the gunboats raised at Manila and reconstructed at Hong-kong, I can testify that the industrial capacity of the Chinese is scarcely below that of Americans, while from careful investigation I should estimate the average wages of a hard-working man in China at less than six cents a day. These two facts have a momentous significance. China will be opened up. The disturbances which drew the attention of the world and which were the occasion of opening the eyes of the soldiers sent there as to conditions existing in the Orient — who, in turn, spread the knowledge broadcast over all parts of the world — will but accelerate a movement already rapid; and soon we shall see more than one-quarter of the human race double, then quadruple, then increase tenfold, then twentyfold its productiveness, demanding, as the standard of life rises with the rate of wages, double, quadruple, then tenfold, then twentyfold more products from the rest of the world. The history of the world does not record a parallel to the magnitude of the economic impulse that will be felt, an impulse overtopping that felt in the Renaissance and at the discovery of America.

In this coming market of China, the United States has an incontestible right to an equal chance. Moreover, lying, as she does, midway between Europe and Asia with the Atlantic and Gulf coastline and the Mississippi Valley to be brought by the Isthmian Canal, along with the Pacific Coast, face to face with the Orient, and being the pre-eminent producing nation with a natural elasticity and adaptability, she should with a fair chance and no favor hold control in the Chinese market.

Over this field, fraught with so much of vital interest, there is a danger line. China herself can offer no resistance to aggression. The European nations, which fought long and bloody wars for the American continents that offered only virgin resources, and for India with its slothful population, will strive for control in China, where, with unmeasured virgin resources, there is an ocean of wealth in the industrial population. Protestations and treaties to the contrary notwithstanding, the European nations will have a steady set toward the seizure of China.

CHAPTER 17
· The Navy and America's
New Status as a
World Power

197

History shows that the conquering nation invariably absorbs the commerce of the conquered. Promises of an open door will not suffice. Our recognized rights to an equal chance in China's markets can rest in security only upon a strong policy that will not permit the partition of China. For such a policy, the United States must rely on herself alone, and must maintain in the Far East a comparatively large fleet.

Similar conditions hold for the important coming market of South America, markets of the present and immediate future, and of the more distant though not overdistant future when European and American immigration will develop a second America.

Generally, similar conditions hold for all the other new markets of the world; and we may say broadly, for all over-sea markets, that the security of America's trade interests must depend upon the size of her fleets. Having interests great and wide-flung, and increasing more rapidly than those of any other nation, the United States should have the greatest navy in the world. Here again, our insurance against attempts to invade our rights, and thus for the security of our peace, will rest upon the size of our Navy.

Thus, from considerations of material interests far-reaching and vital to our country's welfare — considerations that involve the security of our coast, the protection of our water-borne commerce, the safeguarding of our rights in foreign markets and new markets, our interests in each of these cases being larger than those of any other nation — from each and every consideration of material interest upon which the legitimate size of a navy should be computed, the United States should maintain the greatest navy in the world; indeed, the size being proportioned to her needs, the Navy of the United States should be almost equal to the combined navies of the world.

But material interests are not the only considerations that should prompt the United States to maintain a great navy. We have sacred principles committed to our charge which can be upheld only by a great navy.

We have not receded one step from the Monroe Doctrine of our forefathers, yet South America is as far from us as it is from Europe. When the race for South-American markets becomes close, and when the growing European immigration to South America becomes stronger and more controlling, we can maintain the Monroe

Doctrine there, and be guaranteed against an assault upon it, only by being able to send to South America as large a fleet as Europe could send.

But Americans now living have a greater Monroe Doctrine to uphold. We may differ among ourselves in judgment as to methods adopted and to be adopted with the Philippine Islands; but no earnest American would willingly see his country stand aside and allow those 10,000,000 of helpless people, now committed to our charge, to pass under the yoke of a European monarchy. In other words, the Monroe Doctrine has already crossed the Pacific and to-day covers the Philippine Archipelago. Yet, the Philippine Islands are more than 8,000 miles away across the seas. How can we, a nation of action that means what it says, how can we fulfil our bounden duty of protection for the Filipinos except through a strong Navy?

But in principle the Monroe Doctrine should have wider extension, an extension limited only by our nation's opportunities and possibilities for world influence. The white race, in possession of the truths of science and the forces of nature, now controls the destinies of the yellow and black races, though these number nearly three times the entire white race. In the action of the great white nations, controlling the happiness of these hundreds of millions, the United States should have a strong and determining influence. Would it not be selfish and cowardly in us to stand off and see the destinies of these myriads of helpless people dominated by the harsh methods of European monarchies and despotisms?

No man liveth unto himself, neither does any nation; no individual enjoys a blessing without a concurrent responsibility to his fellows, neither does any nation. With nations as with men, Heaven requires works proportionate to talents and opportunities.

We are the only completely liberal nation of the earth. Europe has been evolved by series of conquests, the processes of which have left its society stratified, men and women living and dying where they are born, the vast bulk being born peasants. We have been evolved by free processes only, never ruling over others, and never being ruled over ourselves, producing in our body social and body politic a homogeneous medium, in which men and women rise and fall and seek their levels, according to their relative weights, according to individual force and usefulness, according to individual attainments and worth. Being the only completely liberal nation of the earth, we are constituted the champion of free institutions, and the advocate of human liberties for the whole earth.

It was no mere chance that planted the foot of America at the

CHAPTER 17
The Navy and America's
New Status as a
World Power

199

Gateway of the Orient, the habitat of the teeming millions. Our forefathers laid down the Monroe Doctrine when they numbered less than 10,000,000 of population, shortly after our shores had been invaded. Now, with more than 80,000,000 of population, having passed beyond the point where any nation or combination of nations could invade our shores and threaten the nation's life, with unparalleled elements of power and influence, I do not believe I overestimate our enlarged responsibilities, or over-estimate our possibilities of realizing practical world policies, when I say that Americans of to-day should extend the Monroe Doctrine to cover the Empire of China. We have a perfect right to say that China shall not be partitioned. In addition, I think we should say to the Powers of Europe, "We will join you in opening up China. It is best for China and for the world that life and property should be secure and Western methods have free course throughout that empire; but we propose that China shall be opened up as Japan was opened up, by the American method — not as India was opened up, and as Africa is being opened up, by the European monarchical method, that involves the conquest and subjugation of the peoples."

Further, without venturing to intermeddle with affairs of others, I believe we should extend the Monroe Doctrine into an American Doctrine that would exert influence and lend a helping hand to all the less happy peoples of the earth, creating and exerting powerful influence and for the oppressed of all lands, and for all the yellow and black peoples as they come under the dominion of the white race — a doctrine that would exalt the idea of responsibility and duty, making the best interests of these peoples the guiding purpose of the great nations.

In advancing such a doctrine, we should render a service not only to the belated races themselves, but to the white nations and the world at large, ourselves included, increasing the industrial productiveness and thereby the commerce of the world, and adding to the intellectual and spiritual progress of the races, which would be a moral asset for the world.

Further, we are the only innately peaceful nation of the great Powers. The European Powers are organized for invasion and for repelling of invasion, the nations constituting great military camps, where war and warfare, the military and militarism, permeate and mould the minds and character of the peoples. In America, the contrast is complete; with no wish for conquest, no dread of invasion, free from the military, Americans are engaged in and absorbed by the useful pursuits of peace. Indeed, the absorption of individual business is so complete and personal liberty is so secure, that the citizens forget public affairs — this forgetfulness constituting, in fact, an incidental weakness from which flows periodically bad government in the cities and slackness in our national purposes, especially our foreign policies, a weakness that should be reduced to a minimum by every thoughtful citizen making it a point, whether entering politics himself or not, to take an interest in public affairs.

Being the only fundamentally peaceful people of the world, we are constituted the advocate and champion of peace for the world.

Moreover, in championing peace as in championing free institutions, we should render a service to the world, including ourselves. War that would injure the British Empire, with which we have $800,000,000 annual commerce, would injure us in injuring our market; similarly, war that would injure France would injure us; war that would injure Germany would injure us; an injury to any part of the human race would be an injury to us and the whole race.

In addition, engaged in peaceful pursuits, we learn to appreciate and respect the rights of others, and are coming more and more to recognize the principle that advantage as well as right lies not in injuring one's neighbor, not in reducing his happiness, but actually in helping him and adding to his happiness — that an increase of happiness for any citizen is an asset for the community, that an advance in the welfare of any people is an asset for the world. With our wonderful system of government, too, where each unit retains control of the affairs of the unit and participates in the common affairs in the measure warranted by its interests involved, we are evolving the only system which can be extended indefinitely, and which can lead to a brotherhood of the nations in which they could live in peace with each other, each attending to its own affairs, having only its just weight in the common council, while endeavoring not to injure other nations, but actually to help them as much as possible.

As pointed out above, the world influence of our country must rest upon the Navy alone; it is only through a great Navy that we can extend our Monroe Doctrine to China, through it alone can we give effect to our general advocacy of free institutions, to our advocacy of peace and of the brotherhood of man. Our forefathers and fathers were nobly engaged and showed a splendid devotion when they colonized our country, won its independence, founded the government, perfected its institutions and perpetuated the nation. Our country has now graduated, and we of this generation are called upon to shape its course as it steps forth into the world to play

Restatement of Fiske.

*Federalist proposals —
whites get together
to rule the
world
peacefully —*

its part as a World Power, to inaugurate its career of world service. We should be unworthy of our inheritance, did we not lay out and seek for our country a mighty and beneficent role, to fill its majestic and glorious opportunities and possibilities for useful service to mankind.

CHAPTER 17
The Navy and America's
New Status as a
World Power

201

For this glorious rôle, that we should all covet for our country, for fulfilling our sacred duties as a nation, we must maintain a great navy.

To meet these demands of sacred principles that appeal to the conscience, as for those of material interests, the United States should have the largest navy in the world; indeed, the proportions would not be strained if the Navy of the United States equalled the combined navies of the earth.

Furthermore, conditions are such in the world, with the great European nations holding each other in check, one Power against another, one alliance against another, that the United States with a mighty navy can hold the balance of power for the world, and can cast the deciding vote in the councils of the nations where world policies are determined, where questions of war and peace are considered. It is hardly overstating the case to say that, with a dominating navy, the United States can dictate peace to the world and can wonderfully hasten the reign of beneficence in world policies.

Let all earnest men and women, who wish for the reign of peace and good-will on earth, realize the fact that, though Hague Conferences and International Peace Societies are useful, the real practical way to hasten this reign is to place control in the hands of the nation of peace, the nation of liberty, the nation of beneficent promptings; let them realize that the United States Navy, which alone can give control to the nation, is thus the bulwark of human liberty, the agent of peace, the instrument of brotherly love.

No one need have apprehension as to the effect on our institutions of having a great navy. No navy ever overthrew any government in the history of the world. With a navy equal to the combined navies of the earth, the numbers of citizens involved would be but a little handful out on the sea, and however strict in discipline and military methods they may be among themselves, the body of the nation would remain unaffected. There could not be the slightest tendency toward militarism; while the accompanying sense of power and of control would but deepen, in the minds and hearts of men engaged only in peaceful pursuits, the feeling of responsibility, quickening the nation's conscience, advancing the nation's moral development. Indeed, noble efforts for other nations and for the world would be a wholesome tonic for our nation. Breathing the purer air of such an exalted station would quicken the pulse of the nation and send a brighter, stronger current to eliminate morbid germs from all the tissues of the body politic, offsetting tendencies toward commercialism and materialism.

It is of momentous significance that naval power can go hand in hand with complete liberalism, the struggle for supremacy being simply a race for wealth. Here the liberal nations, in which productiveness is the prime incentive, where the population remains in productive pursuits, will hold the controlling advantage. It is naval power that ultimately will give control to the useful and the good, that will give the earth's inheritance to the meek; naval power is the agency for regenerating and redeeming the world.

The resources of the United States, as pointed out above, are so stupendous that if our Navy equalled the combined navies of the earth, the American tax-payer would not be conscious of even the slightest burden, and in the practical work of building ships and preparing them, and organizing a navy, there are no evidences that any nation has greater aptitude, and our shipyards have already the necessary capacity.

While there are thus paramount reasons why we should be the greatest of naval powers, we are to-day only the fourth power, having 550,000 tons of warship displacement. Great Britain has 1,800,000 tons; France has 715,000 tons; Russia has 20,000 tons more than we have; Germany is but little below us and has recently authorized a vast increase, equivalent to doubling and trebling her entire naval force. The other Powers have also undertaken large programmes of construction. At the session of Congress before the last, not a single new ship was authorized. I do not believe the people know this. I believe they wish and will demand, irrespective of party, that every session of Congress make adequate, sure, consecutive appropriation for increases in ships and personnel. . . .

If the European nations continue to build along their present lines, I estimate that we should overtake Great Britain about 1920, when, at the rate indicated, our naval appropriation for new ships would be $120,000,000. The probabilities are strong, however, that the Powers will accelerate even their present rates of increase, and we could scarcely expect to reach the top before 1930, when the annual appropriation would be $170,000,000 for new ships.

Pursuing this course, we should prevent Germany from passing us and should ultimately convince even Great Britain that she cannot remain in the race.

Of course, there is a chance that some Power or combination of Powers may endeavor to deal us a staggering blow before we have gathered full speed. For such a case, we should be prepared to accelerate to any required extent the momentary speed of increase. We cannot ignore in this light the gigantic efforts now being put forth by Germany. It is only a dictate of prudence for us not to let Germany pass us. It is possible, too, that our world interests and the principles we stand for may gradually cause Continental nations to make combinations for the purpose of checking us. We should be alive to any such movement and prepared to make efforts in proportion.

It may be remarked, however, that any present or future effort of a single nation or combination of nations to strike at America's naval growth would but hasten the day of America's naval supremacy. The conditions for supremacy now exist. Mighty forces are at work. The most potential nation in history, standing upon the strategic vantage-ground of the world, with unparalleled equipment, is being called upon by the strongest demands of interest and the most imperative appeals of duty. Like the cumulative processes of nature, the movement will be irresistible. It cannot be checked. The finger of fate is pointing forward. America will be the controlling World Power, holding the sceptre of the sea, reigning in mighty beneficence with the guiding principle of a maximum of world service. She will help all the nations of the earth. Europe will be saved by her young offspring grown to manhood. The race will work out its salvation through the rise of America. I believe this is the will of God.

CHAPTER 17
The Navy and America's
New Status as a
World Power

203

18

CHINA: SYMBOL OF AMERICA'S NEW FAR-FLUNG INTERESTS

William Woodville Rockhill (1854–1914) was one of America's most experienced China experts. An Orientalist of repute, he participated in two expeditions to Tibet and Mongolia under the auspices of the Smithsonian Institution, and studied the relationship of the China trade with lands adjacent to the Indian Ocean. In the diplomatic service his work was varied and effective, including such posts as Chief Clerk of the State Department, Assistant Secretary of State, service in the Balkans, Secretary to the American Legation at Peking, delegate to many international conferences, and Director of the International Bureau of American Republics. So knowledgeable was Rockhill that Secretary of State John Hay felt that he and Henry White were probably the country's two outstanding diplomats of their day.

While in China, Rockhill became friendly with the British diplomat, Alfred E. Hippisley, and under his influence came to emphasize the need for equality among the Great Powers toward China. Hippisley was alarmed at London's plans to use newly-leased territory as a base to smuggle imports into China without paying tariff duties. If the British did this in their own sphere of influence then, Hippisley reasoned, other nations would follow this precedent, thus endangering Chinese sovereignty.

Despite the British influence, a Russian ukase in August, 1899 stating that she had no intention of interfering with the Chinese customs duties and that no restriction on foreign trade would be made in her sphere of influence probably was the encouragement Secretary Hay needed to instruct Rockhill to prepare a memorandum on America's China policy. As a close adviser to Hay, Rockhill is credited with influencing him in formulating his celebrated policy of the Open Door to trade for all nations in China as well as the expressed concern of the United States for the integrity of Chinese sovereignty. The "breakup of China" in the 1890s led in part to the place China was assuming in the business thought of the United States. In a sense, therefore, the Open Door concept reflected both traditional American anti-colonialism and economic imperialism. Rockhill's article clearly reveals high hopes for the future of American-Chinese relations, hopes that seem so far from realization since the 1949 victory of the Chinese Communists.

THE UNITED STATES AND THE FUTURE OF CHINA

William W. Rockhill

When, in March, 1895, at Shimonoseki, Li Hung-Chang met the Japanese Plenipotentiaries in order to negotiate a treaty putting an end to the war then raging between the two countries, he urged upon Count Ito that they should establish an enduring peace, in order to prevent the yellow race of Asia from succumbing to the white race of Europe. Undoubtedly Japan had this object in view when she insisted, in Article 2 of the Treaty which she required China to accept, that the Liao-tung peninsula should be ceded to her in full sovereignty; for she must have realized that, without such cession, Russia, unable to secure a foothold in Eastern Korea, would make her advance to the sea through Manchuria, acquire the territory in question, and thus precipitate a disruption of China by Europe under pretext of maintaining the balance of power in the Far East.

The designs of Japan, however, were frustrated by Russia, supported by France and Germany, and also by the weakness and vacillation of the British Government, which refused to support Japan's demands. Under pressure from the governments mentioned, Japan was finally compelled to yield, and, in consideration of the payment of 30,000,000 taels, to evacuate and retrocede to China the territory she had claimed in Manchuria. Thus the door was left open for Russia.

But it was Germany who inaugurated in China the grab policy

FROM *Forum*, XXIX (May, 1900), pp. 324–31.

of to-day. In November, 1897, she seized the port of Kiao-chao, on the Shan-tung promontory, assigning as her reason for this action the desire to obtain satisfaction for the murder of certain German missionaries in the adjacent territory. A few months later this seizure was legalized through a treaty by which Kiao-chao and the adjacent territory were leased to Germany by China for a term of ninety-nine years (practically in perpetuity), with the right to land troops, construct fortifications, establish a naval station, build railroads, and open and operate mines, not only in the leased territory, but throughout the province of Shan-tung.

This aggressive move on the part of Germany gave Russia the opportunity she sought; and in December, 1897, she obtained permission for her squadron to winter at Port Arthur, in the Liao-tung peninsula, which Japan had been forced to relinquish. An agreement followed by which Port Arthur, Ta-lien Wan, and the adjacent territory were leased to Russia for a term of twenty-five years, the lease (or cession in usufruct as it was called) to be subsequently extended by mutual agreement — which practically amounted to cession. Alarmed at these portentous events, Great Britain secured from China the assurance that she would neither "mortgage, lease nor cede" to another power any portion of the Yang-tsze basin. Not content with this, the British Government insisted on occupying the port of Wei-hai-Wei, facing Port Arthur on the other side of the Gulf of Pechili. This strategic point had just been evacuated by Japan, who had held it since the conclusion of peace with China. The occupation of Wei-hai-Wei was demanded by Britain as a means of maintaining the balance of power in northern China.

While these events were taking place in the north, France, ostensibly as compensation for the murder of some of her missionaries, and as an offset for some concessions of a commercial nature just then made to Great Britain by China, secured from the latter a lease of a port near to her Tonking frontier, on the Kuang-chao Bay. Japan now became alarmed at these cessions of strategic points, and under the same stereotyped plea, to maintain the balance of power, she secured from China the promise that the latter would not alienate, except to Japan, any of her territory in the province of Fu-kien, which faces the island of Formosa.

But the end was not yet. The concessions made to France by helpless China were immediately followed by fresh demands on the part of Great Britain, who, for the purpose of strengthening the defences of her settlement at Hong Kong, insisted that a considerable strip of the mainland in the Chinese province of Kuang-tung should be leased to her. With this, for the time, the demands for territory ceased, though Italy, supported by Great Britain, endeavored to secure a naval base in the Bay of San-mun.

Not content with the possession of such valuable strategic points, and with the hope of winning from the mercantile classes at home an approval of their policy in the Far East, Germany, Great Britain, and France used every opportunity to wring from China concessions in favor of their respective nationals. Concessions for the building of railroads even were demanded by some of the Treaty Powers as a punitive measure for injuries received by their subjects, or for delay in complying with other demands; in fact, any pretext seemed a sufficient basis for a demand.

It would be easy to multiply instances of the unjust and senseless way in which, for the last few years, this battle for commercial privileges in China has been waged by European Powers; but enough has been said to serve my purpose. The true interests of China have never been considered; her ability to meet the obligations she was forced to incur have never been pondered; and the ultimate result on foreign trade has been ignored. It is hardly conceivable that those responsible for this hurtful policy should not have realized that the end to which they were rapidly pushing China was internal disruption, the overthrow of all constituted authority in the Empire, and the consequent temporary ruin of foreign trade.

The acquisition by European Powers of these various strips of territory along the coast of China has done more perhaps than anything else to intensify the anti-foreign and anti-missionary feeling of a conceited and ignorant people, who, from the fact that the seizures of Kiao-chao and of Kuang-chao Wan were made ostensibly as punishments for the murder, by bandits, of foreign missionaries, have conceived the idea that the missionaries are the prime cause of all their present troubles and humiliations. Furthermore, the prestige of the court of Peking has suffered in the eyes of the people, who have realized the utter inability of their rulers to resist foreign demands or to enforce authority, even when desirous of doing so.

Under the financial strain consequent upon the construction of railways, the organizing of a new army and navy and of expensive public works, to say nothing of the interest on its large, and newly incurred, foreign debt, every source of revenue known to the Chinese Government was taxed to its limit, and found insufficient to meet the demands made upon it. The Chinese Government was literally on the brink of bankruptcy, largely brought about by the insatiable greed and impolitic haste of some of the Treaty Powers. The Powers have permanently fastened on the country an internal tax called *likin*, against which, for thirty years and more, they had, one and all, fought tooth and nail, and which is recognized on all sides as highly prejudicial to the extension of foreign trade. Not only have they saddled foreign trade with this tax, but they have practically forced the Chinese Government to have recourse to additional taxation, to the further detriment of foreign trade, and to the increased misery and growing discontent of the people.

As a result of the ever-recurring demands of Peking for money, the provincial governments, forced to effect economies, reduced their armies till they were not sufficient to insure order. In consequence anti-foreign riots have become more frequent, bringing with them new demands by the Treaty Powers; and the prestige of the throne of Peking has begun to disappear under these repeated blows.

Naval bases and concessions were not, however, enough. For strategical purposes, as well as for securing for their nationals new fields for commercial activity within which these should have preferential rights, especially for railway building and mining, Russia, Germany, France, and Britain divided China among themselves, creating what are now called "areas of interest or influence." What these rights might eventually be claimed to include no one could or would tell; but it was evident that they might be extended to carry with them territorial jurisdiction and the imposition of differential dues, taxes, or rates, in ports or on railroads, and thus result in excluding the trade of all foreign competitors.

The mercantile classes of Europe and of the United States, as well as the foreign mercantile classes in China, claimed that the one essential to the healthy development of their trade was the untrammelled exercise of the rights insured them under treaties with China, or what we now call "the open door." But each one of the European Powers had conceded preferential rights to some other within certain areas, and could no longer insist, with any semblance of logic or hope of success, that the whole Empire be left open to all comers for purposes of trade.

It was reserved for the Government of the United States to obtain this much-desired end. Bound by no agreements with any of the Treaty Powers concerning respective commercial rights in China; with an increased influence in Eastern Asiatic affairs since the acquisition of the Philippines; with the purely commercial nature of its interests in China, and with its determination to maintain the rights of its citizens there under existing treaties with China recognized by all, it could do for the commerce of America, and for that of the whole world, what none of the other Powers could possibly accomplish.

In the latter part of last year, France, Germany, Great Britain, Italy, Russia, and Japan were informed by the Government of the United States that it sought a declaration from them concerning the commercial policy they proposed pursuing within their so-called "areas of interest," and a formal written expression of the oft-repeated oral assurances they had made to the United States, after each aggressive move on their part, of their determination to recognize the untrammelled exercise by all of the rights insured by existing treaties with China.

The Government of the United States proposed that this declaration should cover three points: 1, That the Powers claiming spheres of interest in China should in no way interfere with any port open by treaty with China to foreign trade which might happen to fall within the area of interest claimed by them, or be in any territory leased by them, or with the vested rights of any person not of their own nationality in any such port or territory; 2, that all ports they might open within such areas or leased territory should either be free ports (as are at present Kiao-chao and Ta-lien Wan), or that the only customs dues which should be collected at them should be those provided for by the treaties with China at the time in force, and that said duties should be collected by the Chinese Government; and, 3, that they would not levy any higher harbor dues on vessels of other nationalities frequenting such ports, or higher railroad charges on merchandise belonging to, or destined for, subjects of other Powers transported through their areas of interest than would be levied on their national vessels or charged for merchandise belonging to their own subjects.

These broad principles have now been accepted by all the Powers approached, and the commercial world has thereby been secured in the enjoyment of all its rights under treaties with China, the one and only security needed to insure the healthy development of trade.

The results of the negotiations of this Government are not, however, to be judged by their purely commercial side. They reach much farther; for, temporarily at least, they have put a stop to the grab policy which, as previously shown, has resulted so disastrously to China and to the real interests of foreigners and their enterprises in the Empire. They have also shown the Peking Government that the integrity of the country is not menaced, that the aim of the Powers henceforth is the peaceful development of the natural resources and vast trade of China, that they still look to China to maintain order and protect persons and property, and that they will now afford her an opportunity of working out her own regeneration.

By its action, therefore, the Government of the United States has not only served the cause of peace and civilization, but has rendered a vast service to China, of which it cannot be doubted she must ultimately show herself worthy. Immediate aggression on the part of any of the foreign powers in China is now for the time improbable, if the Chinese Government will but honestly perform the duty of maintaining order throughout the Empire and of protecting foreigners, especially missionaries and their converts, so long as they do not violate Chinese laws. If it fails in this, it may expect, and nothing can in fact prevent, further encroachments by Western nations, and a recurrence of the events of the last few years.

In 1896 this Government proposed that China, in pursuance of her immemorial custom concerning official responsibility, and as the best means of preventing anti-foreign riots, should "hold responsible and promptly punish not only all individuals or minor officials directly or remotely involved upon the occurrence of any riot whereby peaceful American citizens were affected in person or property, or injured in their just rights, but also the viceroy or governor of the province in which the outbreak had occurred, who is directly responsible to the throne for the acts and omissions of every one of his subordinates, although his only fault may be ignorance." If the Chinese Government would take this one step, anti-foreign riots would be a thing of the past.

Financial reform in China is urgently needed, if she is to maintain her independence and take the position she is entitled to among the great nations of the world. It is simply inconceivable that she should much longer delay taking some steps in that direction; and the united efforts of the Powers should now be turned to effect the change. One of the most serious sources of financial trouble in China is the system of inland taxation called *likin*. The revenues derived from it never reach the Imperial exchequer untouched, the larger part being embezzled by those charged with its collection. To this ill-advised tax may be traced in some way or other nearly every conflict which has arisen with foreign powers since it was first imposed.

The changing of this vicious system should be the first step taken in the way of reform. By organizing this service under foreign management like that of the Chinese Maritime Customs, the Imperial treasury would gain large sums, illegal taxes would be prevented, the people of the country would be benefited, and a source of constant irritation to foreign trade would be removed. Nothing would do so much to allay anti-foreign feeling in China, to raise the prestige of the Government in the eyes of the people, and to develop trade and local industries.

Will these two steps — the protection of foreigners and their treaty rights, and the reform of the system of internal taxation — be taken by the present Cabinet at Peking? Relieved of all outside pressure, it is safe to assert that it will not take a single step in the way of reform. China has never given and never will give any encouragement or additional facilities to foreigners, except under the strongest pressure. Each successive step made in the opening of China during the present century has been gained by coercion, or by threat of such, on the part of some one of the European Powers. The greatest strides made were after the wars with Great Britain, France, and Japan; and had these not occurred it is safe to affirm that trade would still be confined to the port of Canton.

The conclusion is that pressure from the Powers must continue; but that pressure must be steady, the same from all quarters, and tend to a common end. China must be made to realize that she must reorganize her administration, must make herself a factor in the development of her resources and the guardian of her own territorial integrity, and that, if she does not, partition and subjection to foreign rule are but questions of a little time.

The position taken by the United States in demanding of the great Powers the untrammelled exercise of our rights under treaties with China has suggested to some writers in this country that we should grant to these Powers at least, and practically to all foreign Powers, the same freedom of trade, the same "open door," in the Philippines, and considerable stress has been laid on this argument by a section of our press and by many political speakers. The two cases, however, have absolutely no analogy. In China we asked simply that commercial rights already secured to us by treaties with a sovereign nation, within territory over which no other Power claimed jurisdiction, should be respected. Should any portion, however, of the Chinese Empire be ceded in absolute sovereignty to any other Power, then our rights under previous treaties with China within such ceded territory would lapse. Chinese sovereignty in such territory being extinct, that of the country acquiring it would be substituted in its stead, and our treaties with the new sovereign Power would define our rights in its newly acquired territory.

It was thus in the case of the conquest of Madagascar by the French in 1896. Until the French Government informed us categorically that Madagascar had become French territory by conquest and absorption, and that Malagasy autonomy was completely wiped out of existence, we claimed the free exercise in Madagascar of our rights under the treaty concluded in 1881 with Queen Ranavalo. From the day the French Government made a categorical declaration of the extinction of Malagasy independence, the conventions between the United States and France became applicable.

The case of the Philippines is identical. By treaty with Spain they have been acquired in absolute sovereignty by this country, and treaties made by other Powers with Spain concerning them became thereby extinct, and those concluded by the same Powers with the United States were extended to them.

Briefly stated, the results of the recent negotiations by the United States are, that, notwithstanding the encroachments made on Chinese territory and sovereignty by European Powers, the commercial interests of our people have been preserved in their entirety, and that a temporary guarantee has been secured that these will not be interfered with in any way. Furthermore, by their declarations that they expect no exclusive rights for their citizens in their sphere of interest, the Powers claiming them have not only limited the extent of their future demands, but have practically expressed an intention not to interfere henceforth with China's sovereign rights. At the same time, China is clearly given to understand that she must satisfactorily discharge the duties she has assumed through treaties.

The events of the last four years must have shown China that if she fails in these duties she is destined to share the fate of all weak states. Serious breaches of faith on the part of China, dereliction in performing her international duties, must inevitably be followed by fresh demands for territory and guarantees, and if again begun no one can predict where these will end. No Power at the present time is desirous to see the spark ignited which will produce the final catastrophe. China, and China alone, can prevent it. All of her well-wishers can but pray that she may not let the opportunity now afforded her by the United States pass away unused.

19

THE PANAMA CANAL ROUTE VINDICATED

Willis Fletcher Johnson (1857–1931), a longstanding advocate of overseas expansion, reflected this interest in his writings which include *A Century of Expansion* (1903), *Four Centuries of the Panama Canal* (1906), and *America's Foreign Relations* (1916). Johnson's voluminous other works include popular biographies of American political leaders, and histories of Cuba, the Johnstown Flood, the Republican Party, the National Flag, the Sioux Indians, and New York University. An alumnus of that school, Johnson was made honorary Professor of American Foreign Relations. His literary career began as a journalist on the staff of the New York *Tribune* and later he wrote for many periodicals.

Johnson's article, "Justice and Equity in Panama," is an unequivocal defense of an American action that has been likened to rape on a diplomatic scale. Yet the author justified the Panamanian *coup* on grounds of domestic needs and moral obligation to the civilized world. Johnson hoped, and by inference predicted, that the benefits of the Panama Canal to the world would surpass those of the Suez venture. Thus he applauded American unselfishness and declared that the United States would be vindicated by the canal's benefit to mankind. This vindication would come, he predicted, with the perspective that history alone affords. Thus far, the prediction of this court historian has not been justified, for few authorities today uphold Theodore Roosevelt's precipitate action in hastening the digging of the Canal.

JUSTICE AND EQUITY IN PANAMA

Willis F.
Johnson

The question of our Government's policy in Panama is, as the term implies, a question of policy. It is not a question of executive details, because there were no such details concerning which, *per se,* any material question could be raised. There was no waging of war. There was no slaughter. There were no torturings nor imprisonments. There was no arbitrary overthrowing of an established government. All that was done was to exercise the moral influence of a definite and peaceful policy. . . .

. . . The question at issue is whether that policy was just and equitable.

1.   It was justified, and indeed made necessary, by domestic obligations. Congress had directed the President to construct a canal at Panama, rather than at any other point. We need not stop to consider why Panama was chosen. That was a matter of congressional enactment, not of administrative policy. The question of route had been discussed, with a wealth of investigation and detail, for many years. Whether wisely or not, and whether for adequate or inadequate reasons, Congress finally declared, explicitly and unequivocally, in favor of Panama. The President had to obey that mandate. There was no alternative, save in case of his inability to make satisfactory terms within a reasonable time. The President promptly proceeded to do the work prescribed by Congress. He made terms, which the Senate accepted as satisfactory, for the construction and control of the canal. He was himself the sole judge of what was a "reasonable time" in which to make such terms. That time proved to be something less than a year and a half, and it was approved as "reasonable" by the Senate. Thus far, then, the President scrupulously obeyed the law.

But it is said that the law directed him to make his terms with the Colombian Government, and that, instead, he made them with Panama. It is true that Congress mentioned the Colombian Government as the one with which he was to negotiate. Obviously, that was because it was at that time the sovereign of Panama. But it is equally obvious that Congress meant not that Government, *per*

FROM *Forum*, XXXVI (July, 1904), pp. 125-37.

se, but whatever lawful Government the President might find in possession of the Isthmus. That is because (*a*) the Congress of the United States could not guarantee that President Marroquin's or any special Colombian Government would remain in power at Panama, nor give the President any assurance of what Government he would find there when he made the treaty; and because (*b*) it did not say that if a change of government should occur upon the Isthmus before a treaty could be made, he should abandon Panama and go elsewhere. The prescription had reference to the place, rather than to the power. It was geographical rather than political. The President then made satisfactory terms, within a reasonable time, and he made them with the actual Government of the Isthmus of Panama. He obeyed the law of Congress in letter and in spirit. So far as domestic obligations were concerned, his policy was just and equitable.

2.   It was justified by our legal obligations to Colombia. Our Treaty of 1846 with New Granada guaranteed to New Granada (or Colombia) "the perfect neutrality" of the Isthmus of Panama, "with the view that the free transit from the one to the other sea may not be interrupted or embarrassed"; and also guaranteed "the rights of sovereignty and property which New Granada has and possesses over the said territory." It was perfectly understood, and was specifically and repeatedly declared, that this guarantee was solely against alien aggression, and was not to be interpreted as promising protection against domestic revolution or as assuring the perpetuity of the same domestic system of government that then existed. "The purpose of the stipulation," wrote Mr. Secretary Seward on November 9, 1865, "was to guarantee the Isthmus against seizure or invasion by a foreign Power only. It could not have been contemplated that we are to become a party to any civil war in that country by defending the Isthmus against another party." As a matter of fact, there were several revolutions in Colombia after the making of that treaty, to none of which was the United States a party, and none of which in any way affected the force of the treaty.

Thus we made the treaty with the Republic of New Granada, under the Constitution of 1843. A new Constitution was promulgated in 1853, under which the federal system was introduced. In 1855 the Constitution was amended so as to make Panama a sovereign State, connected with the rest of the Republic by only a federal relationship. That amendment specifically named the State of Panama as separate from, and in nearly all respects independent of, the State of New Granada. Practically, it renounced those "rights of sovereignty and property" which New Granada had over Panama at the time when the Treaty of 1846 was made. But the United States did not intervene to compel the maintenance of them, nor was it asked or expected to do so. On the contrary, if it had done so it would have been resisted, and would have been properly regarded as guilty of oppression. In that circumstance was a pretty plain proof of the fact that the guarantee of "rights and sovereignty" made in the treaty was a guarantee only against foreign interference or oppression, and not against domestic changes of sovereignty and ownership. In 1858 another new Constitution was adopted for the whole country, in which the federal system was confirmed "in perpetuity." In 1862 there was a forcible revolution, which led to the adoption in 1863 of another Constitution, under which Panama and the other states were declared to be sovereign, but confederated in perpetuity for exterior security and reciprocal aid. That Constitution could be amended only by the unanimous consent of the states. Finally, in 1885, another violent revolution occurred, and in 1886 the victorious party dictated a new Constitution, sweeping away that of 1863, abolishing without their consent the independent sovereignty of the states, and replacing the federal system with a strongly centralized government. To this latest Constitution the State of Panama never assented, but maintained an almost incessant revolt against it. In addition to these revolutions resulting in changes of the Constitution, there were others which resulted in mere changes of government. The latest of these was in 1900, when President Sanclemente was thrown into prison, where he died, and the Vice-President, Dr. Marroquin, was installed in his place through a *coup d'état.*

The United States held strictly aloof from all of these proceedings, so far as politics were concerned. The Treaty of 1846, however, gave this country the right to preserve peace and freedom of transit across the Isthmus, and was consistently interpreted and understood as giving us that right, even to the extent of intervening in local Colombian affairs and preventing either party in a domestic war from making belligerent use of the line of transit. Thus, to quote Mr. Seward again, while the United States would take no interest in any internal revolution in the State of Panama, it would hold itself ready "to protect the transit trade across the Isthmus against either foreign or domestic disturbance of the peace of the State of Panama." Note that it was not the sovereignty of the Bogota Government, but "the transit trade across the Isthmus," that the United States was ready to protect against domestic disturbance; leaving it to the people of Colombia and Panama to determine whether Panama should be governed at Panama or at Bogota.

Note also that the United States was to protect that transit trade "against domestic disturbance of the peace." How would it have been possible to do that if either of the domestic belligerents had been permitted to use the railroad as a base of military operations and thus to involve it in acts of war? The only effective fulfilment of the treaty was in protection of the road from attack, or even belligerent use, by either faction. Such protection was repeatedly given, to the extent of forbidding either the Colombian Government or the insurgents to use the railroad as an engine of war. That was what was done in November, 1903. The President protected the transit trade of the Isthmus against "domestic disturbance of the peace of the State of Panama," regardless of whether the menace of disturbance proceeded from Colon or from Bogota.

It cannot justly be charged that the United States, while insisting upon free transit across the Isthmus for itself, prevented Colombia from enjoying it. The United States never but once — and that was not in November, 1903 — forbade the Colombian Government to make nonbelligerent use of the railroad, and it did so only through a subordinate functionary, who was promptly overruled by the Washington Government. All that it did prohibit was such conversion of the railroad into an engine of war as would interrupt free transit across the Isthmus and subject the road itself to destruction. That the intention of the Treaty of 1846 was to exempt the road from such belligerent use seems obvious and indisputable.

Mr. Secretary Hay set forth this phase of the case with epigrammatic force when he described the treaty as a covenant which "ran with the land." The application of the treaty was geographical rather than political. The United States had no right to say what government there should be in Colombia, save that the domestic government should not be oppressed or overthrown by a foreign power. But it had the right to say that whatever government there was should fulfil its treaty obligations in the maintenance of free transit across the Isthmus. It had the right to say that such freedom of transit should not be interrupted by rebellion arising at Panama or Colon, and equally that it should not be interrupted by government coercion from Bogota. It had, finally, the right to say, as it did say, that after she had practically relinquished Panama to the control of its own people, and they had restored peace and established an orderly government of their own, Colombia should not reinvade that State for the purpose of waging war and interrupting commerce.

If it be said that this barred Colombia from using her sovereign power and resources for the performance of some of the supreme functions of government, to wit, the suppression of rebellion and the maintenance of national integrity, the answer is that she should have thought of that before she made the treaty. Unquestionably she did, in making that treaty, to a certain extent abrogate and relinquish her sovereignty over the Isthmus of Panama. She did so in return for a *quid pro quo,* which then seemed to her adequate, and which, in the event, proved for many years not only to be adequate, but to put the balance of advantage upon her side of the account. Having thus enjoyed the benefits of the treaty for half a century, it was not lawful for her to evade its obligations or to repudiate its penalties. The United States, having fulfilled its duties toward her, in protecting her from alien oppression, was amply justified, legally, in exacting from her its full privileges. That was what our Government did at the beginning of November, 1903.

The United States was right, of course, in rejecting the Colombian proposal, that it should, in return for a canal concession, suppress for Colombia the already successful revolution in Panama, and restore that State to Colombian authority. The United States has never hired itself out as a mercenary, either for cash or for canal concessions. Equally right was it in recognizing the *de facto* Government at Panama. It is always lawful, and generally imperative, to recognize facts, and it was a fact that that was the only existing Government on the Isthmus. The Colombian Government there had ceased to exist. It had been expelled. It had departed. The Colombian troops had not been driven out by us. They had gone because they found themselves alone and helpless amid a universally hostile population. They recognized the accomplished fact. The Panama Government was in entire and undisputed authority, and was ready to fulfil and was fulfilling the actual functions of government. The only possible procedure for the United States was to recognize that fact.

Nor is the rightfulness of our later recognition of the *de jure* independence of Panama to be impugned. It was done promptly, ten days after the Panamanian Declaration of Independence. There seems, however, to be no ground for the characterization of "indecent haste" which has been applied to it. There is no more generally accepted principle in international law than that every nation is its own judge of the time when it is fitting to recognize the independence of another. In our own revolution, France recognized our independence years before it was actually established, while Russia refused to recognize it until years after it had been established and had been recognized by the very Power from which we had won it. Both acted well within their legal rights. The United States recognized the revolutionary Republic in Brazil in 1889, no less promptly than it did the Republic of Panama, although there was much less assurance of its stability. The long delay in recognizing the independence of the South American Republics in the early part of the last century has been cited as a precedent which should have been regarded in the case of Panama. There was little if any analogy between the cases. The contrast between South America then and Panama now is enormous. Considering the difference in speed of communication, and in extent and completeness of our knowledge of the countries concerned, it is scarcely too much to say that a day gives as ample time for deliberation now as a year did three-quarters of a century ago.

In recognizing the independence of Panama we were lawfully recognizing an accomplished fact. If it be said it was a fact made possible only by our own conduct and attitude, the same may be said of other republics, which exist only because of our protection. Colombia herself would probably not have maintained her independence had it not been for the policy of the United States, especially as set forth and endowed with concrete force in the Treaty of 1846. In the act of recognition then, as in that of intervention, the United States fully observed its legal obligations to the Republic of Colombia.

3. It was justified on the ground of equity to Colombia. We must remember, what is too often overlooked, that while law is positive, equity is relative. We must fulfil legal obligations strictly and impartially, even toward the least deserving and least worthy. But we are privileged to consider the character, the conduct, and the deserts of the applicant for equity. He who seeks equity must deal equitably. The very word itself implies that. It is an elementary justice, based not on legal prescription, but upon the mutual merits of the parties to the controversy. What, then, were Colombia's deserts? So far as Panama was concerned, they were slight indeed. She had treated Panama most inequitably. She had forcibly abrogated the Constitution of 1863, and had subverted Panama's undoubted rights thereunder, without Panama's consent — just as though forty-four of our forty-five States should combine to deprive the forty-fifth of its equal representation in the Federal Senate without its consent. It had not only done that and persisted in it, but for many years it had systematically oppressed and plundered Panama, making the Isthmus the "milch cow of Colombia," as it used to be said Cuba was of Spain. Upon dispassionate and impartial review of the record, it was impossible to withhold sympathy from Panama in her controversy with the Bogota Government.

If, however, we were to go by on the other side, saying that such matters were none of our business, we could not ignore the fact that Colombia had treated the United States badly in more than one important respect. In 1880 this Government found it necessary to warn Colombia against making the concessions which she then proposed to make to France, as — to quote Mr. Secretary Evarts, on July 31, 1880 — "introducing interests not compatible with the treaty relations which we maintain with Colombia." Colombia then proposed — I quote from President Arthur's message of 1881 — "to the European powers to join in a guarantee which would be in direct contravention of our obligation as the sole guarantor of the integrity of Colombian territory." In other words, while enjoying, at her own request, our protection, Colombia was intriguing against our interests with the very Powers against which she had sought and was enjoying our protection. We may pass by the assumption that Colombia vigorously used all possible influence against the Nicaragua Canal enterprise so as to compel us, if possible, to adopt the Panama route at such terms as she might extort, for that is a matter of belief and common fame rather than of concrete record.

But we may justly complain that she acted inequitably toward us in rejecting the canal treaty which her minister negotiated with us in 1902–3. Mark that she had a legal right to reject it. That is indisputable. Her legal right to reject it was as absolute as our right to reject other treaties which our Government has negotiated, but which have not met with the approval of the Senate. She had, let us say, the same right to reject it that we had to negotiate it, or that we had afterward to make another treaty with Panama. Her rejection was legal, but it was not equitable; or, at any rate, it was no more equitable than our subsequent recognition of, and negotiation with, Panama. If she stood upon her strict legal rights in rejecting the treaty, we had as good a title to stand upon our strict legal rights in recognizing Panama.

But we may go beyond that, and say that her rejection of the treaty was positively inequitous — if I may coin that useful word, to express a slightly different shade of meaning from "iniquitous," though indeed "iniquitous" might serve as well. Two facts of record are sufficient to prove the indictment. One is the explicit and repeated offer made by General Reyes in behalf of the Bogota Government, of which he was the prospective next chief, to resurrect and ratify the dead canal treaty, by martial law or dictatorship, in return for our resubjugation of Panama to the Colombian yoke. The other is the confessed, deliberate plan of the Bogota Government to repudiate the concession lawfully given to the French Panama Canal

Company and to confiscate that company's property, which it would then sell to the United States for a round sum.

Let us note the details of that precious scheme. The charter or concession of the French company required the completion of the canal by October 31, 1904, failing which the concession and title would be forfeited to Colombia. It was obvious that the canal could not be completed by that time, so the company secured from the President of Colombia an extension of time of six years more. The plan of the Colombian Congress was to declare that extension invalid, thus repudiating the act of its own President, and then to confiscate the unfinished canal and abrogate the French company's concession on October 31, 1904. That was the real reason why the canal treaty was rejected, and why the suggestion of reopening negotiations for a new treaty was made. Colombia did not want to refuse our treaty. She wanted to make the treaty. But she wanted to postpone doing so until after the French company's concession had been forfeited, when she could herself secure the $40,000,000 which the United States was willing to pay for the unfinished canal, instead of having that convenient and much-coveted sum go into the pockets of the French shareholders. She would have accepted the treaty gladly after she had confiscated the canal.

Now the bearing of all that upon the question of our policy is simply to show upon how little ground Colombia could plead for better treatment as a matter of equity. Colombia, wearing the brand of a would-be spoliator, could not well come into court with a complaint that she had been despoiled. Upon the ground of equity she had nothing more to claim. She had been treated as well as she deserved, and better. Her only valid claim must be for legal justice, and in the making of that claim it might be well for her to take heed lest the court of civilization should declare to her: "Thou shalt have justice, more than thou desirest." It will not serve to say we would not have treated a great, strong nation thus. I am not sure of that. The record of our dealings with some of the greatest Powers of the world suggests that we have been no less independent in our bearing toward them than toward the lesser ones. On the other hand, we might equally well ask if Colombia would have acted thus toward a nation that was not rich, that was not urgently desirous of building the canal, or that was a little more in the habit of using the "mailed fist." We must, it is said, have one law alike for all nations, great and small. That is quite true.

What, then, would we have done had England recognized the independence of the Confederacy in 1862? The cases are not analogous. The Confederacy was never, either physically or legally, in as strong a position as Panama. I say that advisedly. The United States never scuttled out of the Southern States and abandoned them to secession, as Colombia did out of Panama, but from the very beginning exerted its fullest possible power to suppress the rebellion and to restore and preserve the Union. The Confederate States had no such constitutional defence of secession as that which Panama had in the fact of former independence forcibly destroyed without her consent. The European Powers did promptly recognize the Confederate States as belligerents. In that they were simply recognizing a fact, and, however distasteful it was to us, we had no cause for complaint.

There is another point which those who seek to raise this argument from analogy invariably overlook. It is this: That the United States had never, by treaty or otherwise, recognized international interests in the Southern States as Colombia had in Panama. In the Treaty of 1846, Colombia specifically recognized the fact that other nations, above all the United States, had natural and lawful interests in the Isthmus of Panama, which might in certain contingencies be paramount to Colombia's own interests there. Those interests were peculiar to the Isthmus, and did not extend to the rest of Colombia. For it is to be remembered that the provisions of that treaty, including our rights of intervention and our duty of protection and guarantee, did not apply to the whole of Colombia, but only to the State — that is, the Isthmus — of Panama. "The guarantee extends only to the Isthmus," wrote Mr. Bidlack, our Chargé d'Affaires who negotiated the treaty, to Mr. Secretary Buchanan in 1846. In that circumstance the separate status of Panama, as contrasted with the rest of Colombia, was recognized, and so were recognized the peculiar and even paramount interests of other countries in that territory. I quote from President Polk's message transmitting that treaty to the Senate for ratification: "The treaty does not propose to guarantee a territory to a foreign nation in which the United States will have no common interest with that nation. On the contrary, we are more deeply and directly interested in the subject of this guarantee than New Granada herself, or any other country."

Let us suppose, to make an analogy which does not now exist between our Civil War and the Panama revolution, that at some date prior to 1861 the United States had stipulated by treaty with England that the cotton trade from our Southern ports should never be interrupted or embarrassed, and that England should have the right to intervene whenever necessary to keep that trade free and open. In such case it seems to me that England would have had a legal and moral right to intervene in 1861–62, to break the blockade of our Southern ports and to prevent the United States from reëstablishing it. The United States never made such a treaty. It would never have made one. But Colombia did make the Treaty of 1846. There is the radical difference between the two cases.

It is said that the application of the *lex talionis* does not indicate the loftiest motives. Granted. But there were other motives for our policy which were high and noble enough to satisfy the most exalted doctrinaire. At the present moment the argument is simply this, that neither law nor equity requires a nation to go out of its way to be generous to an unworthy object, even though that object be a weaker nation. Weakness gives no immunity, and is not a charter to license any more than strength is a charter to oppression. A strong nation should use its strength nobly. A weak nation should use its weakness no less nobly, seeking in morals the strength it lacks in material resources.

4.   It was justified under both law and equity to other nations. Our Government has violated no item of international law. It has invaded no rights of other countries or of their citizens. It dealt fairly, lawfully, even generously, with the French Canal Company. It patiently awaited and accepted the adjudication of the French courts in whatever legal controversies arose over the transfer of the company's property. It has shown a scrupulous regard for the letter and spirit of international law, and for international equities. It has, moreover, fulfilled the implied duties which rested upon it as a result of its traditional policy. Under the Monroe Doctrine this country would not let other nations meddle in American affairs. It thus incurred a moral responsibility for those affairs. Thus it would not let European Powers guarantee neutrality and peace upon the Isthmus, and freedom of transit over that important route. Therefore it was morally bound itself to make such a guarantee, and to make it effective. It has done so. It would not permit any other nation to construct a canal across the Isthmus. Therefore it incurred itself the moral obligation to construct one. It is now proceeding to do so. The United States thus shows itself to be no dog-in-the-manger, but a Power that is as ready itself to do as to forbid others to do.

The question of "international eminent domain" has been adverted to many times. It is perhaps not altogether pertinent, for the reason that the United States was not compelled to resort to the application of such a principle. It is not to be denied, however, that such a principle exists, and that it has more than once been practically applied in the history of the world. Every "concert of the Powers" for the coercion of one or more nations involves its application. It was under that principle that Bosnia and Herzegovina, and Crete and Samos and The Lebanon, were removed from unbridled Turkish rule. It was upon the same principle that the joint control and the international tribunals were established in Egypt. It would scarcely be an exaggeration to say that the same principle was involved in the opening of The Sound to free navigation. There need be no hesitation in saying that if there had been no other way to secure the Panama Canal, the Powers of the world, or the United States alone, would have been amply justified in proceeding under that principle. But the principle is so delicate a one, and so easily liable to perversion and misuse, that there is cause for gratitude in the accomplishment of the world's desire at Panama without resort to it. If that principle, or the contemplation of it as a possibility, did to any degree enter into the case in confirming the United States in its policy or in affording justification for that policy, then instead of condemning our Government, the world must give it commendation for having to that extent made use of so delicate and even perilous a principle with so much discretion, and with results so invariably beneficent.

For what is, after all, most clear in the whole business is this, that the United States has acted unselfishly and for the good of the world. I say it has acted unselfishly, because it has sought no self-aggrandizement, no conquests, no acquisitions of territory, no extension of sovereignty. It has sought, and has secured, nothing but the privilege and power of constructing a canal which will be for the equal use and benefit of all nations. If it has in doing so exacted a grant of perpetual control over a part of the territory of another state, it has thus done only what was necessary for the safeguarding of the canal. It is inconceivable that any other nation on earth would have undertaken the construction of the canal and its protection and neutral maintenance on any basis of less authority. I say it has also acted for the good of the world, because it has assured fulfilment of the world's legitimate desire in the only way in which it could be satisfactorily fulfilled; because it has assured the speedy opening of what will be one of the greatest highways of peaceful and beneficent commerce; and because it has established a paramount influence for peace and justice in a land that for a century has known little of either peace or justice.

The opening of the Suez Canal marked an epoch in history, though it was followed by profligacy, controversy, and war. In Panama these latter evils ran their vicious course before the United States assumed control. It will be this country's privilege, in pursuance of the just and equitable policy already established, to make their recurrence forever impossible, and to make the future of that great enterprise an era of continued equity and unbroken peace. Thus governed, the benefits of the Panama Canal to the whole world may surpass those of the Suez Canal as much as the Atlantic and Pacific Oceans surpass in size the Mediterranean and the Red Seas. The policy that is leading, and that alone could certainly have led to such a consummation, may be carped at and impugned by some who see it through the distortion of too close and too partial a vision. In the clear, comprehensive, and just perspective of history, its terms no less than its results will be its abundant and perpetual vindication.

20

AMERICA AS CARIBBEAN PROTECTOR

One of the more pressing diplomatic problems in the early twentieth century was American policy toward the weak and underdeveloped Caribbean republics, many of which were economically unstable and beset by civil tension. This was especially true of Santo Domingo, whose situation, incurring threats from foreign creditors, evoked President Theodore Roosevelt's famous corollary to the Monroe Doctrine, which announced an American policy of preventive intervention in order to eliminate the need for foreign interference in territories under the shield of the Monroe Doctrine.

DEFAULTING OR DEEPLY IN DEBT TO EUROPEAN POWERS —

BACK IT UP WITH ARMS.

One of the most convincing arguments in favor of the Roosevelt corollary was that of the career diplomat and international lawyer, John Bassett Moore (1860–1947). Moore began his career in the Department of State as a law clerk, rising to Third Assistant Secretary of State, a post he held until 1891. From then, until 1924, he was a Professor of International Law and Diplomacy at Columbia University. Moore's other governmental posts included Assistant Secretary of State (1898) and Secretary to various conferences, i.e., Samoa (1887), the North Atlantic Fisheries (1887–8), and the Spanish-American Peace Commission (1898). From 1912 to 1938, he was a member of The Hague Permanent Court of Arbitration, and in the 1920s he sat as judge on the Permanent Court of International Justice at The Hague.

Moore wrote extensively, including books on extradition, *History and Digest of International Arbitrations* (6 volumes, 1898), *American Diplomacy, Its Spirit and Achievements* (1905), *A Digest of International Law* (8 volumes, 1906), and edited the works of James Buchanan (12 volumes, 1908). The article on Santo Domingo that follows raises the interesting question; if the United States had relationships with a remote island group such as Samoa in the South Pacific, in which her interests were relatively slight, would it not be sensible to aid in the rehabilitation of a nearby underdeveloped country?

SANTO DOMINGO AND THE UNITED STATES

John B. Moore

On Saturday, the 21st of January, there appeared in a late edition of an evening newspaper, in the city of New York, a telegraphic report from Santo Domingo, the capital of Santo Domingo (officially known as the Dominican Republic), that Commander A. C. Dillingham, U.S.N., whose presence at Santo Domingo on a special mission had previously been announced, and Mr. Dawson, the American minister, had concluded with the Dominican government an important agreement. In further dispatches from Santo Domingo, published in the press on the morning of Sunday, the 22d of January, it was stated that the agreement was in the form of a protocol; that, under it, the United States was to guarantee the integrity of the Dominican territory, undertake the adjustment of foreign claims, administer the finances on certain lines, and assist in maintaining order; and that the arrangement was to take effect on the 1st of February.

From these statements the inference was widely drawn that there existed an intention to treat the protocol as a perfected international agreement, as if it did not fall within that clause of the Constitution of the United States which empowers the President to make treaties by and with the advice and consent of the Senate. Promptly, on the 22d of January, however, a formal statement was issued by Mr. Loomis, Assistant Secretary of State, in which the paper reported to have been signed at Santo Domingo was described as a "memorandum of a proposed agreement;" and the significance of this phrase has since been more fully disclosed by the announcement made in the Senate by Mr. Cullom, chairman of the Committee on Foreign Relations, that no treaty or agreement had been "fully executed," but that the "proposed contract," or whatever it might be called,

FROM *The American Monthly Review of Reviews*, XXXI (March, 1905), pp. 293–98.

was "in the way of execution, for the purpose of sending it to the Senate." The statements of Mr. Loomis and Senator Cullom require no confirmation; but it may be observed that some of the clauses of the protocol, as signed at Santo Domingo on the 20th of January and published in the *Gaceta Oficial* of the next day, were of such a nature that the agreement must necessarily have been regarded at Washington as tentative rather than definitive.

Since we are assured that the administration has not proposed and does not propose to assume important obligations toward Santo Domingo, by means of an international agreement, without consulting the Senate, we are relieved from the necessity of participating in the constitutional discussions by which the question of policy has unfortunately been so largely obscured and supplanted. The question of methods, provided they be constitutional, is one of detail. The end in view may, no doubt, be accomplished by a treaty; nor can there be any doubt that it could be as fully accomplished by a joint resolution of Congress, without any elaborate agreement with the Dominican government; but these are matters into which it is not my purpose to enter. The essential fact before us is, that the United States has at length been brought face to face in Santo Domingo with a situation which calls for definite and specific action, and which cannot be evaded. The simple truth is that government has broken down in Santo Domingo. In spite of the unsurpassed riches of its forests, fields, and mines, the country has gradually descended from stage to stage of fratricidal contests and political and social disorders, till it has apparently become incapable of unassisted self-regeneration. With revenues which, if they were properly collected and administered, would be ample for all legitimate purposes, the government is obliged daily to borrow at ruinous rates the money required for its ordinary expenses, and the only creditor who is repaid is the daily lender. To the payment of principal and interest of the general debt, domestic and foreign, nothing is devoted. . . .

THE GREAT INTERESTS AT STAKE

That conditions so destructive and dangerous should, if possible, be abated is manifest. Nor are the interests at stake small. To say nothing of the vast concern of the Dominicans themselves in the establishment of law and order, the accumulated foreign commercial and industrial interests are so considerable that their sacrifice is not to be contemplated. The American vested interests alone are commonly valued at $20,000,000. The great sugar estates are owned chiefly by Americans and Italians. It is estimated that around San Pedro de Macoris, where in the late disturbances the estates were much damaged by roving bands, American investments in the sugar industry amount to $6,000,000. Extensive banana plantations are also owned by Americans; the United Fruit Company holds more than 18,000 acres, representing an investment of more than $500,000. There are two completed railroads, one of which is owned by British subjects, while the other, running from Puerto Plata to Santiago, was chiefly constructed and is now held and operated by the Company of the Central Dominican Railway, an American corporation. The exportation of woods is chiefly in the hands of Americans. The oil fields of Azua are being developed by an American company. The wharf privileges of the three principal ports are owned by foreigners — Americans and Italians. Four great commercial houses are owned or controlled by Germans, and one by Italians. One of the two steamship lines that regularly ply between Dominican and foreign ports is that of the American firm of W. P. Clyde & Co., while the other is French. It is sometimes suggested that, when citizens of a country go abroad and engage in business, they must be held to assume all the risks of disorder and injury in the country to which they go, and can look to the local authorities only, no matter how inefficient or malevolent they may be, for protection; but it suffices to say that no respectable government acts on any such theory.

PROTECTION OF THE CREDITORS

While commercial and industrial interests in Santo Domingo require protection, so also do the interests of the country's creditors. These interests deserve just consideration, but the problem they present is not so difficult as is sometimes supposed. The Dominican public debt is often said to amount to from $32,000,000 to $35,000,000, but it would be impossible to substantiate these figures except by including unliquidated claims at an enormous overvaluation. The Dominican bonded debt held on the Continent of Europe, — chiefly in France and Belgium, and to a small extent in Germany, — amounts to about $14,817,697, exclusive of overdue interest aggregating about

$750,000. Under a contract made with the Dominican government in 1901 by committees of bondholders in Paris and Antwerp, and ratified by the Dominican Congress, — a contract which has received the support of the French and Belgian governments, — interest is payable on the principal of the bonds at a fixed sum per annum, on a sliding scale; but the bonds are redeemable at fifty cents on the dollar. It is not improbable that the entire debt could, with the consent of the French and Belgian governments and the bondholders, be capitalized on that basis, if the establishment of a sinking fund and the payment of a reasonable rate of interest were assured by the administration of the revenues by the United States. There are also holdings of Dominican bonds in England which the British Government has heretofore manifested its intention to protect; but as these bonds are held by interests allied with the San Domingo Improvement Company of New York, they are now protected by the international award rendered on the 14th of July last, under the protocol between the United States and the Dominican Republic of January 31, 1903. Under this protocol the Dominican government agreed to pay, in full settlement of all claims of the San Domingo Improvement Company and its allied American companies, and for the transfer of all their properties, rights, and interests, the sum of $4,500,000, on terms to be fixed by three arbitrators, who were also to prescribe the manner in which the moneys should be collected. The gross amount to be paid was fixed in the protocol at the instance of the Dominican government. The bonds of the American companies were thrown in at fifty cents on the dollar and other claims were compromised or relinquished. The arbitrators (Judge George Gray, the Hon. John G. Carlisle, and Señor Don Manuel de J. Galvan) fixed the amount of the monthly installments, in which the principal sum was to be paid, and awarded that, in case the Dominican government failed to make the requisite payments, they should be directly collected, by an agent to be appointed by the United States, at Puerto Plata, and, in case the revenues there should be insufficient, or in case of any other manifest necessity, or if the Dominican government should so request, then at the ports of Sanchez, Samana, and Montecristi.

In addition to the bonded debt, there is a floating interior debt of about $3,230,000, not including arrearages of interest. Of this debt about $2,500,000 belongs to resident merchants of European nationality, the larger part being held by the representatives of a deceased Italian merchant named Vicini. There are also liquidated German, Spanish, and Italian claims (other than Vicini), amounting to about

[handwritten marginal note: THE DEBT WOULD BE CUT IN ½ SO LENDERS WOULD BE ASSURED OF A STABLE RETURN RATHER THAN EXORBITANT DEBT W/ NO GUARANTEE OF RETURN]

LIQUIDATED- MEANS DEBTS WHICH HAVE BEEN DETERMINED =
AMT. WHICH HAS TO BE PD.
BONDED- HOW
MANY BOND
ISSUES WOULD
HAVE BEEN RECORDED.
So THAT INTEREST IS
OWED.

$375,000, which are secured by definite contracts and the assignment of specific revenues. The total bonded and liquidated debt of the republic amounts to about $25,000,000. Beyond this there are the unliquidated claims to which I have heretofore adverted.

UNDETERMINED AMTS.

HOW FINANCIAL OBLIGATIONS
HAVE BEEN "DODGED"

For the payment of the interest on bonds embraced in the French-Belgian contract, the monthly revenues of the southern ports of Santo Domingo and San Pedro de Macoris are pledged to the amount of $25,000, and agents of the bondholders are authorized to receive the money as well as to advise the Dominican government in financial matters. Other creditors also hold specific pledges of the revenues. These pledges have, however, in the past few years proved to be worthless. Nothing was paid on the American award till the latter part of October last, when the agent appointed by the United States took charge of the custom house at Puerto Plata.

In this relation it is important to understand the condition of things in the Dominican Republic with regard to the collection of the revenues. Many years ago the government, being unable to raise money on ordinary security, adopted the practice of vesting the power of collection in its creditors. Duties are settled in pagarés, or promissory notes, duly indorsed, and payable usually in a month or two months. In order to secure loans, these pagarés were handed over to the creditor, who collected the money directly from the importer or exporter. This expedient, which was designed to protect the creditor against the government itself as well as against its enemies, was in vogue when the government in 1888 sought financial relief in Europe. Such relief was obtained from Westendorp & Company, bankers, of Amsterdam, who in that year underwrote and issued, at 83 ½ per cent., 6 per cent. gold bonds of the Dominican government to the amount of £770,000 sterling, the government creating a first lien on all its customs revenues, and authorizing the Westendorps to collect and receive at the custom-houses all the customs revenues of the republic. Under this contract, which was ratified by the Dominican Congress, the Westendorps created in Santo Domingo an establishment, commonly called the "Regie," which collected the duties directly from the importer and exporter and disbursed them, the Westendorps sending out from Europe the necessary agents and employees. It was further stipulated that the Westendorps should, in case of necessity, have the right to constitute a European commission, which it was understood was to be international in character. The power of collection and disbursement was exercised by the Westendorps down to 1893, when it was transferred to the San Domingo Improvement Company, of New York, which continued to exercise it till January, 1901, when the company was, by an arbitrary executive decree issued by President Jimenez, excluded from its function of collecting the revenues, though its employees were permitted to remain in the custom-houses till the end of the year. ✓

THE GOVERNMENT NOT REALLY BANKRUPT

As an assurance to the foreign creditor, whose legal security was thus destroyed, Jimenez constituted in the same decree a "Commission of Honorables," with whom the sums due to foreign creditors, including the American companies, were to be deposited; but their capacity as depositaries was not destined to be tested. Late in 1901, it became known that out of the reported revenues of the year, amounting to $2,126,453, the percentages for the domestic debt had *TO RESIDENT FOREIGNERS* not been set aside, and that no payment had been made on the floating interior debt, but that the Jimenez "revolutionary" claims had been paid without previous warrant of law, and that there existed *4 YRS. AGO. HENCE* a deficit. Since that time, with the exception of comparatively small *INTEREST IN ARREARS* amounts, nothing whatever has been paid to the foreign creditor. *+ PRINCIPAL +* The omission, however, has not been due to lack of revenues. It *INTERIOR DEBT* has been due to conditions which, if all the debts of the republic *MOUNTS UP.* were with one stroke wiped out, would continue to prevent the *- ONLY PAYING* government from meeting its ordinary expenses. The revenues have *DAILY EXPENSES.* been seized and dissipated by the government and its enemies in "war expenses," and in the payment of *"asignaciones"* and "revolutionary claims."

It is misleading to call the Dominican republic bankrupt. The public debt, if properly adjusted, would scarcely amount to more than a third as much per capita as that of some other countries of lower commercial and industrial capacity. On the other hand, the taxes, which are almost exclusively confined to customs duties, amount to little more than $4 per capita, as compared with $5 in

Haiti, $6 in Salvador, $7.50 in Roumania, $8 in Greece, $9 in Costa Rica, $10 in Portugal, and $15 in Uruguay. The Dominican Republic figures as a bankrupt, not for want of resources, but simply because its revenues either are not collected, or, if collected, are worse than thrown away.

THE SUPPORT OF SOME STRONG POWER NEEDED

That foreign governments will stand by and permit such conditions to continue cannot be expected. They have already manifested their desire to intervene. The interests of their citizens, including the creditors of the Dominican Republic, render interposition in some form inevitable. There are certain writers who have sought to maintain that intervention, at any rate by force, is inadmissible in the case of public debts, no matter what may be their origin. Force, it is said, has been abolished for the purpose of collecting private debts, and should also be abolished for the purpose of collecting public debts. The analogy would be excellent if it had any foundation, but it appears to rest on nothing but the assumption that because imprisonment for debt has been abolished, the use of coercion to compel the payment of private debts no longer exists. This inference is altogether erroneous. While the body of the debtor may not be taken, his property is laid hold of by legal processes having behind them the whole force of the state, and is devoted to the discharge of his obligations. I do not wish, however, to advocate the use of force as a general method of collecting international claims, or the assumption by the United States of the functions of a debt-collecting agency; nor in reality is this question in any proper sense involved in the present discussion. The question of debts and claims is but one of the incidents of the situation, the primal fact being that the Dominican Republic, by reason of its feeble and distressful plight, requires the succor and support of some strong power, in order that it may be enabled to fulfill its necessary duties. The Dominican government has itself invoked the assistance of the United States, and the question simply is whether the United States shall not only refuse such aid, but also forbid any other interested power to give it.

There can be no doubt that the mass of the Dominican people long for relief. No one can fail to be impressed with their courtesy,

[handwritten marginalia] ✱ TO ME, HELPING A COUNTRY PAY ITS DEBTS IS MORALLY SUPERIOR TO HOLDING THE TERRITORY UNDER THE NAME OF "PROTECTORATE" OR "ANNEXATION"

[handwritten] CRUXY KOSTION

AM. QUALITIES.

integrity, and willingness to labor; and, when not excited by ambitious and desperate leaders, they are peace-loving. If given an opportunity to till their fields and carry on their industry, unharmed by the pestilence of revolution, they would, with a proper system of public education, which they have heretofore lacked, exhibit a capacity for a higher civilization; and they have among them accomplished men, who, if law and order could once be firmly established, so that their voice could be heard, would make capable rulers.

IMPERIALIST VOCABULARY.

It is manifest that we have here a perfect example of the conditions described by President Roosevelt in his last annual message, in which, reiterating the sentiments expressed in his Cuban letter, he said:

> It is not true that the United States feels any land hunger or entertains any projects as regards the other nations of the Western Hemisphere save such as are for their welfare. All that this country desires is to see the neighboring countries stable, orderly, and prosperous. Any country whose people conduct themselves well can count upon our hearty friendship. If a nation shows that it knows how to act with reasonable efficiency and decency in social and political matters, if it keeps order and pays its obligations, it need fear no interference from the United States. Chronic wrong-doing or an impotence which results in a general loosening of the ties of civilized society, may in America, as elsewhere, ultimately require intervention by some civilized nation, and in the Western Hemisphere the adherence of the United States to the Monroe Doctrine may force the United States, however reluctantly, in flagrant cases of such wrong-doing or impotence, to the exercise of an international police power.

ROOSEVELT COROLLARY

"ACTION MUST BE TAKEN BY THE UNITED STATES."

There may be persons who, afflicted with a sort of xylophobia, can see in this statement, which may fitly be termed the Roosevelt corollary from the Monroe Doctrine, only another obtrusion of the "Big Stick." It is true that this corollary, if broadly construed, might lead the United States into extravagant measures; but the same thing may be said of every general statement of policy. The Monroe Doctrine itself, by reason of the generality of its terms, is susceptible of extravagant constructions; and yet there is no principle in the support of which, when properly applied, the American people are

Continuation of Monroe Doctrine Policy.

more united. The vital principle of the Monroe Doctrine is the limitation of European influence and control in the Western Hemisphere. If a situation similar to that now prevailing in Santo Domingo existed in a European country, it would be dealt with by a combination of European powers or by some one power acting alone as their delegate. In Santo Domingo, European powers have material interests similar to those of the United States; but, in view of its settled policy, the United States would now be unwilling either to permit the measures necessary for the reëstablishment of order and credit to be taken by European powers or to take them itself in conjunction with such powers. The situation, in a nutshell, is that either the United States must take the necessary action or it must not be taken at all. According to the Roosevelt corollary, action must be taken, and it must be taken by the United States. A ready test of whether this position should be commended or condemned may be furnished by putting into concrete form the converse proposition, which would run substantially as follows, "Chronic wrong-doing, or impotence which results in a general loosening of the ties of civilized society, though much to be deplored, must in America be permitted to continue unchecked, since it is not the policy of the United States either to interfere with such things itself or to permit any other power to do so.". . .

To-day, public opinion in the United States would be adverse to . . . a concert with European powers on an American question; besides, fortunately, in the present situation in Santo Domingo, the government of the country asks for the aid of the United States, so that no question as to the use of force against the titular government arises. The measures to be taken by the United States would in no wise be hostile to the Dominican government or its people. Their territorial integrity would be respected, but their finances would be adjusted; their administration of the revenues would be reformed, so that the custom-houses would no longer form centers and sources of supply of revolutions; and their government, while it would be enabled to discharge its obligations, would also be placed on a constitutional and legal basis.

After four years of effort through diplomatic and consular agencies to maintain a government in Samoa, the United States, from 1889 to 1901, under a treaty ratified by the Senate, endeavored to maintain, in conjunction with Germany and Great Britain, a cumbersome and unworkable tripartite administration in that distant island group. This artificial contrivance broke down of its own weight; but since 1901, when all the islands except Tutuila, which was reserved to the United States, passed under the single administration of Germany, order and tranquillity have prevailed. The tripartite experiment is not to be commended; but if the United States could take such risks with regard to a remote island group in the South Pacific, in which its interests were comparatively slight, it does not seem to be an extravagant thing to lend its aid to the rehabilitation of a neighboring community in which its interests have always been conceived to be of exceptional importance.

COLLECTORS WILL GET 5% INTEREST PER ANNUM.

NOT JUST AN AMERICAN TALENT. INTERESTING STATEMENT. COULD NOT SEE T.R. MAKING IT.

21

THE AMERICAN QUEST FOR INTERNATIONAL PEACE

Although the United States and England never entered into a formal alliance until the formation of the North Atlantic Treaty Organization in 1949, a rare harmony based upon sentiment and self-interest characterized the relationships between the two English-speaking nations. With the decline of British power and the concomitant rise of German and Russian power and their disdain for non-Anglo-Saxon lands, England turned to the "Great Rapprochement." The camaraderie of 1898 continued with British acquiescence to the Roosevelt Corollary, and an extremely cooperative feeling with regard to the settlement of the Alaskan boundary and the policy of an American controlled Isthmian canal.

Edwin Doak Mead (1849–1937) was one of the great advocates of such American-British international cooperation, especially in the area of the peace movement. In 1886 he began his interest in literary activities as an employee of the famous Boston publishers, Ticknor and Fields. Later he studied in English and German universities and the rest of his life was devoted to lecturing and literary work. Mead was chiefly distinguished for his life-long work in the cause of peace. Among his writings were *The Literature of the Peace Movement* (1910), *The American Peace Party and Its Present Aims and Desires* (1913), *Heralds of Peace* (1910), *The Limitation of Armaments* (1907), *The Results of the Two Hague Conferences* (1911), and *Washington, Jefferson and Franklin on War* (1913). At the outbreak of World War I, Mead visited leaders of civic thought in the belligerent nations in the interest of peace, and they all agreed on only one point, namely that this war must be the last war. Mead was also one of the last surviving links with New England's

ANGLO-SAXON FRIENDSHIP.

great literary past, for not only did he know many of the nineteenth century *literati,* but he was also active as editor of the *New England Magazine* (1889–1901), the International Library, and the Old South Leaflets. In the realm of the peace movement, he directed the World Peace Foundation and was a delegate of the American Peace Society to many international congresses.

The selection below, written in 1909, reflects the usual pre-World War I euphoria of the peace enthusiasts and reveals that even prior to the outbreak of war in 1914, age-old American distrust of Britain had in large measure been replaced by a cordial understanding that presaged our diplomacy during the years of neutrality that followed Sarajevo.

THE INTERNATIONAL DUTY OF THE UNITED STATES AND GREAT BRITAIN

Edwin D. Mead

MUST LOOK AT ARBITRATION+
VENEZUELAN CRISIS OF 1895

To those who are devoted to the cause of international progress, to the workers especially for fraternity and co-operation between England and the United States, there are few books in the library more pregnant than the two volumes which give the full reports of the two American Conferences on International Arbitration which were held at Washington in April, 1896, and January, 1904. These two Conferences, separated by an interval of eight years, were memorable gatherings, marked by profound feeling and clear and commanding purpose. They were called at critical times, they were attended by noteworthy bodies of the ablest thinkers of the country, and they culminated in significant resolutions, which should not be forgotten, but which leaders of opinion in both the United States and Great Britain should keep constantly before their respective peoples until they are realized in treaty and law. It is a main purpose of the present paper to recall attention to these memorable but too largely forgotten chapters of history, for the strong reinforcement

FROM *World Peace Foundation Pamphlets,* Vol. 1, No. 4, Pt. 4 (Boston, 1911).

which they furnish to the demand for a broader arbitration treaty between these two great nations at this time.

Some serious menace is often necessary to rouse men and nations to seriousness. Such a menace came in the United States with the sudden crisis in the Venezuela situation, in December, 1895. The possibility of strained relations, to say nothing of war, between the United States and Great Britain was something that most good Americans had long ceased to dream of; and the amount of jingo sentiment which certain words in President Cleveland's message proved the occasion of calling into expression from selfish and reckless politicians at Washington and in many parts of the country was a shock. Thoughtful and earnest men everywhere realized the importance of such authoritative action as should make another such menacing situation impossible. In Chicago, Philadelphia, New York, Boston, Washington, New Orleans, St. Paul, San Francisco and St. Louis, prominent and patriotic citizens came together and framed addresses to the people. The Chicago men said in their address, issued on the fifth of February, 1896, "Let the people of the United States make the coming birthday of George Washington even more glorious by inaugurating a movement for cementing all the English-speaking people of the world in peace and fraternal unity. Let the people of all cities and towns of the Union, at their meetings on that day, express their views, to be made known to both the President of the United States and the Queen of Great Britain, as to the establishment by the two Governments, by formal treaty, of arbitration as the method of concluding all differences which may fail of settlement by diplomacy between the two powers." The friends of arbitration in Philadelphia invited the men of other cities to join them in a convention at Philadelphia on Washington's Birthday. "The object of this Conference," they said, "is the advancement of the cause of international arbitration and especially, as a timely application of that principle, the creation of a permanent court of arbitration for the peaceful adjustment of difficulties which may arise between the United States and Great Britain. The time is evidently ripe for such a movement, in view of the recent crisis and of the strong popular expressions from leading Englishmen . . . of friendship towards this country, and the desire to secure a settlement of future troubles between us by peaceful and reasonable methods, rather than by force. A frank and cordial response from our people to these friendly overtures may at least pave the way for the establishment in practice of a great principle."

The Boston meeting resolved "that the time has come when

a complete system of arbitration between the two nations should be matured." The citizens' meetings elsewhere declared themselves in similar strain. "The cause of humanity and the cause of conscience demand that the English-speaking peoples should settle their international differences without resort to the abitrament of the sword."

The resolution adoped in New York embodied the following: "Whereas, The United States and Great Britain, akin in language, juripudence, legal methods and essential love of right, are already accustomed to arbitrate their disagreements, and have emphatically declared themselves in favor of such arbitration — Congress by the action of both Houses in 1890, and the House of Commons by its vote in 1893 — therefore, Resolved, That we earnestly desire such action by our National Legislature and the Executive, as shall make permanent provision for some wise method of arbitration between the two countries, it being our hope that such a step will ultimately lead to international arbitration throughout the civilized world."

The Philadelphia Conference was held on February 22, in Independence Hall, with eminent men in attendance from every part of the country. A letter was read from President Cleveland; and from the Anglo-American Arbitration Committee in London came the message, "Hearty greetings to our American kinsmen who are celebrating Washington's Birthday. We join with you in doing honor to your national hero, by advocating fraternal union, through a permanent court of arbitration, for the peaceful and honorable adjustment of all differences arising in the English-speaking family.". . .

The resolutions adopted at Philadelphia declared: "That the common sense and Christian conviction of America and England agree that the time has come to abolish war between these two nations which are really one people," and urged both Governments to adopt a permanent system of judicial arbitration. The movement for an early general conference at Washington was earnestly supported; and the call for this Washington conference, signed by leading men of all the cities, was promptly issued. "In confining the present movement to the promotion of arbitration between the United States and Great Britain," it was stated in the call, "we are not unconcerned for the wider application of the principle involved. But, taking into consideration the importance and the value of practical results, it has seemed wise to concentrate our immediate efforts upon the attainment of a permanent system between the two great English-speaking peoples."

The Conference met at Washington on the afternoon of April 22, and continued until the evening of the next day. . . . "We come here," said Mr. Edmunds, [Senator from Vermont] in his presidential address, "in order that we may deepen the channels and strengthen the mighty course of civilization, of religion and of humanity, by doing what we may to aid our Government and, so far as influence and example will go, our kindred Government over the sea, to come to a footing of practical arbitration that shall stand as the permanent means of peace between us, and finally between all nations." . . .

Carl Schurz, in a comprehensive and eloquent address, called upon the United States for brave leadership in the arbitration movement. It was a natural leader, owing to its peculiar position and strength, safely aloof from the feuds of the Old World, with no dangerous neighbors threatening its borders, and no need of vast armaments on land and sea to maintain its peace or protect its integrity. . . .

No one characterized more severely the crisis which had prompted the Conference than President [Charles W.] Eliot [President of Harvard University]. To thousands of sober-minded men in this and other countries, the Venezuela message to the President, the preceding papers of the Secretary of State which had since been made public, and the reckless talk of many men in Congress had been a surprise and a shock. During the last eight or ten years, indeed, we had heard from both political parties "the advocacy of a policy entirely new among us, absolutely repugnant to all American diplomatic doctrines, imported straight from the aristocratic and military nations of Europe — the doctrine called jingoism — a detestable word for a detestable thing. It is the most abject copy conceivable of a pernicious foreign idea; and yet some of our public men endeavor to pass it off among our people as American patriotism. A more complete delusion, a falser representation, cannot be imagined. The whole history of the American people runs directly counter to this notion. Can anything be more offensive to the sober-minded, industrious, laborious classes of American society than this chip-on-the-shoulder attitude, this language of the ruffian and the bully?" He closed with an earnest plea for such an education in the schools of America as should counteract this grave new mischief. "We want to have the children of this country, the young men who are rising up into places of authority and influence, taught what the true American doctrine of peace has been, what the true reliance of a great, strong, free nation should be — not on the force of arms, but on the force of righteousness. It is not by force of arms that we can best commend to the peoples of the earth the blessings of liberty and self-government. It is by example — by giving persuasive example of happiness and prosperity arrived at through living in freedom and at peace. I trust that in all our public schools these principles may be taught as the true American doctrine on this subject. It has been said here that we have been taught in our schools about the battles of the nation, but have not been taught about the arbitrations of our nation. Let us teach the children what is the rational, sober-minded, righteous mode of settling international difficulties. Let us teach them that war does not often settle disputes, while arbitration always does. Let us teach them that what is reasonable and righteous between man and man should be made reasonable and righteous between nation and nation." ...

Such was the memorable 1896 American Conference on International Arbitration. It is doubtful whether a more thoughtful or significant body of men ever met in conference in America. ...

It was eight years before the second American Conference on International Arbitration met in Washington, on January 12, 1904. In the interval much had happened. The Alaska boundary settlement had removed the most irritating and difficult question pending between ourselves and Great Britain. The Irish-American opposition, which had proved so unfortunate in 1897, had been largely eliminated by the adjustment of one of the great contentions between England and Ireland. The result of the arbitration of the Venezuela dispute had put an end to the frictions and suspicions there. The Hague Conference had been held, and the International Tribunal established, providing the machinery necessary and favorable for international arbitration. Finally, on the 14th of October, 1903, a treaty had been signed by Great Britain and France, by which the parties agreed to submit to the Hague Tribunal all differences not affecting the vital interests nor the independence or honor of the two countries. The leaders of the peace and arbitration movement in this country felt that the United States must not longer postpone a new effort for an arbitration treaty with Great Britain; and on December 4, 1903, the National Arbitration Committee issued its call for the meeting in Washington on January 12. Not so large a gathering as that of 1896, this second Conference brought together nearly two hundred of the leading international men of the country, many of them the same men who had taken part in the earlier Conference; and letters of endorsement came from five hundred more, and from many commercial and other bodies. Representatives of commercial bodies took a more prominent part in the Conference than in 1896; and organized labor found expression through an eloquent speech by Samuel Gompers and a letter from John Mitchell. ...

More than once during the Conference had the practice in treaties of excepting questions of "honor" from arbitration found sharp condemnation. "What we have to do," said one, "is to build up a true sense of national honor. The only thing which constitutes national dishonor is the thing which involves national degradation; and if the true sense of honor be involved in a controversy, we who are the parties to such a controversy ought not to be ashamed to submit the question of honor to an international tribunal." "It is upon this very class of questions," said another, "that nations ought to seek the interposition of a sane third party; they are themselves probably least of all competent to pass judgment upon that point, and an impartial tribunal would enable them to get rid of the controversy." To this point Mr. [Andrew] Carnegie addressed himself in an eloquent passage in his speech. "The most dishonored word in the English language," he said, "is honor. Fifty or sixty years ago honor would have required you to march as Hamilton did to meet Aaron Burr. To-day the gentleman belonging to the race that speaks the English tongue would be degraded if he fought a duel. Honor has changed. No man can be dishonored except by himself. So with nations. As long as the republic herself acts honorably she remains stainless. Who abolished the duel? Our own English-speaking race. Let us now take the next step forward and abolish international duels; let us have the nations' differences settled by the supreme court of humanity."

→ MOVE TOWARD INTERNATIONAL CODE OF HONOR

— CRUX OF U.S. SPREADING THE WORD — THE U.S. LAW.

Perhaps the two most pregnant addresses of the day were those of Hon. John W. Foster, the president of the Conference, and Hon. George Gray, the chairman of the Committee on Resolutions. Mr. Foster discussed the claim that national honor and territorial questions are subjects which a nation should not arbitrate, from the standpoint of the actual history of Great Britain and the United States. . . .

During the year following this Washington Conference of January, 1904, Secretary Hay negotiated arbitration treaties with Great Britain and several other nations, essentially upon the lines of the Anglo-French treaty. These treaties the Senate did not ratify; and it was not until 1908 that treaties of substantially the same character, negotiated by Secretary Root with various nations, were ratified. Meantime it is to be feared that our people have for the most part forgotten these great Conferences of 1896 and 1904, which brought together the most important bodies of our American international thinkers ever assembled, and gave the most important expression

[handwritten margin note: WHO CONSTITUTES ARBITRATERS?]

ever given to the best international sentiment of the country, gave that expression unanimously in both Conferences, and in both gave it to the same effect, — that all differences between the United States and Great Britain which fail of adjustment by diplomatic negotiations be referred to arbitration, and that provision to the same effect be made as soon as possible with other nations. Our people cannot afford to forget this memorable action, endorsed by the leading citizens and organizations of every character throughout the country. Their failure to remember it and to follow it up earnestly and persistently is failure to remember the warning closing words of Mr. Edmunds, the president of the first great Conference: "It is important to say that no great movement in the progress of the world has been accomplished by temporary or spasmodic emotions and efforts. The triumph of truth, the triumph of education, the triumph of peace, so far as it has gone, have been attained only by persistent endeavor." The two great Washington Conferences concerned themselves primarily, the first Conference almost exclusively, with the relations of England and America; but it was with confidence that any broad policy adopted by these two great nations would quickly be adopted by other nations. . . .

[handwritten margin note: SO GERMANY WOULD BE THE LOSER IF SHE DID NOT ADOPT THE TREATIES.]

There is no need of multiplying general essays, as in the case with other nations, upon the natural and peculiar fraternity of England and America and the duty of keeping that fraternity strong and vital and putting it to high use for the world's good. The arguments . . . are "old and hackneyed — hackneyed, however, only in the sense that they are often repeated, because they often spring from the heart to the lips." The two Washington Conferences were themselves the natural outcome and expression of this sense of the peculiar bond between England and America. The men gathered on those great occasions were all believers in the universal scope and application of international arbitration; but all felt the peculiar duty and advantage of beginning with England, and beginning in a great and prophetic way — agreeing to refer to arbitration every difference which might arise, not settled by diplomacy, with no anxious or jealous reservations of territorial questions, or questions of "honor" and "vital interest." No interest would ever be so vital, no honor so great, as the appeal to reason and to law rather than to force and pride.

Those prophetic and memorable resolutions have not been realized; and there is to-day no other obligation so great upon the United States and Great Britain, if this peculiar fraternity which we are eloquent about is a vital thing, as to realize them, for our own good and the world's good. The failure and fault are not Great Britain's, but our own. Mr. Carnegie was entirely right in saying in his address at the 1904 Conference: "Great Britain longs for such a treaty as we propose to offer here." ...

But there has been one trouble with ... arbitration treaties, almost all of them. It is precisely the thing perceived and unanimously condemned by the sagacious and prophetic men of the two great Washington Conferences. The financial and foolish reservations in them about "vital interests" and questions of "honor" and the rest prove maelstroms mighty enough to engulf any number of ships, — oceans rather big enough to float any number of battleships for which the pride and ambition of any selfish and supicious people choose to pay, regardless of the clear logic and the moral imperative of the Hague conventions. The logic of those conventions, it cannot be too often repeated, clearly prescribes the steady decrease of the machinery of the nations for the arbitrament of their differences by war commensurate with the present gradual and already so great increase of the machinery for their arbitrament by law. This is so manifest that only obvious and serious new dangers could excuse nations parties to the Hague conventions from the limitation and then mutual reduction of their armaments. Yet the immense lessening of danger and the immense strengthening of security to almost every nation in these years has been accompanied in almost every one by an immense increase instead of decrease of armaments. It seems a paradox, and would be if this were entirely a world of rational and earnest men. But this is a world in which pride and ambition, self-seeking and adventurism make up a very large part of the compound. All manner of false patriotism, base politics, professional vanity, commercial greed and vested interests are bound up with the present showy and costly system of naval armaments especially; and every excuse and argument that can be used to prolong its life will be magnified and made the most of.

Now the territorial reservations and "vital interest" and "honor" reservations in the arbitration treaties give the ambitious big navy men in England and America and everywhere else just what they want. "The Hague tribunal is very well, but no nation is obliged to have recourse to it unless it obliges itself by arbitration treaty. The multiplying treaties of obligatory arbitration are all very well, but they make reservations of 'vital interests' and the rest, and it is for every nation to determine for itself in every case what its vital interests are. Hence the need for battleships remains just where it was before; and let us have more and more of them!" Their favorite

> SECURITY →
> ↑ ARMS

BUILDING ↑ BATTLESHIPS

AMERICA CAN'T JUST ENFORCE HER WILL ON ANY NATION W/OUT RUNNING INTO REPERCUSSIONS

contention that, the bigger and more numerous the battleships, the better the conditions for peace between two rival nations, finds rather confounding recent commentary in the Anglo-German rivalry, each added Dreadnought proving not a new bond or pledge of peace, but a new provocation and danger rather. But our big navy philosophers are not hunting for commentaries, but for appropriations.

The talk of these men, be it conceded, is largely hypocrisy; but that makes little practical difference. The governments in the main are serious, honest, faithful and peaceful, sure to construe their treaty obligations in a broad and honorable, not in a technical and petty way; and so far has the sense of international obligation now advanced, that any important conflict of interests arising between any two of the really important nations is practically certain of adjustment, where specific provision for adjustment does not exist, by means mutually agreed upon in the exigency. The theory that this is still a world in which mere wantonness controls any great nation is a theory to be dismissed to the limbo of things which are no longer even "respectable nonsense."

But when all this is said, the actual circumstances, the prevalent arguments and their pernicious influence make it incumbent upon the nations, and especially incumbent upon the United States and Great Britain as leaders in the arbitration movement, to take decisive steps to remove the present mischief and firmly secure the advance of the last ten years. To develop our international law and courts, and still go on piling up our costly and menacing war machinery, as if the courts had not been called into existence to supplant the armies and the navies, is to accuse ourselves either of infidelity or gross incompetence. . . .

So clear has it become that the adequate broadening of the scope of arbitration treaties is the imperative next step in the movement for international justice, that the International Peace Bureau at Berne has sent out a circular letter to all its members in the various countries urging concerted effort the present year, the tenth anniversary of the first Hague Conference, in behalf of treaties between all nations of the same form as the Denmark-Netherlands treaty. It is a wise and timely prompting. What nations can act upon it so easily and with such powerful effect as Great Britain and the United States? There exists for these nations one other transcendent opportunity and obligation. The Second Hague Conference adopted a plan for the establishment of a Court of Arbitral Justice, leaving to the nations the adjustment by mutual negotiation of the method of selecting the judges. Any two or more nations may unite to

inaugurate such a court, leaving others to join at will. Secretary Root
has had this great step peculiarly at heart. It is a step of cardinal
moment. Why will not the United States and Great Britain take
it together? Let them ask Germany to unite with them in it. These
three chief of nations are now unhappily, in their unworthy naval
excesses, chief disturbers of the world's tranquillity and confidence.
Let them rise together to a nobler rôle through union for the advance
of international justice and reason. . . .

It is for the United States to coöperate with Great Britain to
ensure the last — and all else will follow. Upon the relations of the
two countries themselves there is not a cloud. The clouds which
once were there rose from false history and false education. President
Eliot did not insist too warmly in Washington upon peace teaching
in the schools. For a century our boys and girls were fed on such
accounts of the American Revolution, in their school-books, as made
them all haters of the very British name. Now they know well that
in 1775, as in 1861 and always, there were two Englands, and that
the best England — the England of Chatham, Burke and Fox, of Barre,
Grafton and Conway — was all with us in our great struggle. Trevel-
yan tells the story of the struggle, at once England's struggle and
ours, better than we have yet told it for ourselves. Samuel Plimsoll,
by his citations to us a dozen years ago from a score of the best
known and most popular English text-books, showed us that the
boys and girls in the English schools get as plain teaching as our
own about George the Third and Lord North, and that Washington
and Franklin are their heroes, too; and Freeman, in Chicago, on
Washington's birthday, makes his subject "George Washington, the
Expander of England," — expander of England because he enforced
on England in a way taken to heart the costly but imperative lesson
as to the necessity of just and generous dealing with her colonies
in order to the growth and the very integrity of her empire. Our
students inform themselves about our own American Commonwealth
from the pages of Mr. Bryce, as we think English students will
inform themselves about their own from the pages of Mr. Lowell.
The long and inevitable period of irritation and alienation between
the two great English-speaking peoples has forever passed, and the
time foretold by Whittier has come, —

"When closer strand shall lean to strand,
  Till meet, beneath saluting flags,
  The eagle of our mountain-crags,
The lion of our Motherland!"

It means — and it is to hasten the efficiency and influence of it that Britain and America are called — a new age for Teutondom, for Christendom, for mankind, —

"The golden age of brotherhood
Unknown to other rivalries
Than of the mild humanities,
And gracious interchange of good."

We celebrate this year the centenary of the birth of Tennyson, who gave to the great cause of the "federation of the world" and "universal law" its dearest and noblest verse. Just as its prophecy of "the parliament of man" finds its fulfilment at The Hague, we have celebrated the tercentenary of the birth of Milton. It was Tennyson who gave to Milton his noblest title, the "God-given organ-voice of England." "What can war but endless war still breed?" was the question of the "organ-voice" to the "war-drum's throb" of the seventeenth century, as it is still to ours. But the voice proclaims: "Peace hath her victories no less renowned than war," with a fulness and assurance to-day impossible then; for the intervening years have been crowded with victories, none of them so renowned as those of the last decade. The "war-drum's throb" is being drowned by "the organ-voice"; and the final and decisive victory is near. It is for the men who speak Milton's speech and think Milton's thoughts to unite in such action to-day as shall ensure the victory to-morrow.

BIBLIOGRAPHICAL ESSAY

This list of suggested readings is intended as a guide to selected writings on American expansion and foreign relations from the close of the American Civil War to the beginning of World War I. Excluded are primary sources (for example, contemporary journals, newspapers, reminiscences, government reports). Most monographs dealing only in part with the period 1865–1914 are omitted, and only a few periodical articles are cited.

A number of popular textbooks will be useful in examining the general foreign relations of the period: Thomas A. Bailey, *A Diplomatic History of the American People* (8th ed., 1969); Samuel F. Bemis, *A Diplomatic History of the United States* (5th ed., 1965); Julius W. Pratt, *A History of United States Foreign Policy* (2nd ed., 1965); Richard W. Leopold, *The Growth of American Foreign Policy: A History* (1962); Robert H. Ferrell, *American Diplomacy: A History* (1969). See also Foster R. Dulles' brief and very general *Prelude to World Power: American Diplomatic History, 1860–1900* (1965) and his *America's Rise to World Power, 1898–1954** (1955); Pratt's *Challenge and Rejection: The United States and World Leadership, 1900–1921** (1967); and John A. S. Grenville and George B. Young, *Politics, Strategy, and American Diplomacy: Studies in Foreign Policy, 1873–1917* (1966). The latter work rather interestingly sketches Benjamin Harrison as "strong" and knowledgeable in the ways of diplomacy. The opening chapter on Admiral Stephen B. Luce is helpful in establishing newer understandings of the revived navy.

The pertinent sketches in Bemis, ed., *The American Secretaries of State and Their Diplomacy* (10 vols., 1927–1929) are still useful. The official compilation of American diplomatic correspondence dating from the Civil War is *Papers Relating to the Foreign Relations of the United States* (renamed in 1931, *Foreign Relations of the United States*).

To conserve space, data concerning the publisher's name and place of publication have been omitted for all but a few titles.

Books available in paperback editions are shown with an asterisk [*] following the title.

On the Secretaries of State during the Gilded Age (1865–1890) see in addition to *The American Secretaries of State* collection, Glyndon G. Van Deusen, *William Henry Seward* (1967), a detailed and adequate account of Seward's dreams of empire and accomplishments; Allan Nevins, *Hamilton Fish* (1936); Brainerd Dyer, *The Public Career of William M. Evarts* (1933); Chester L. Barrows, *William M. Evarts* (1941); Alice F. Tyler, *The Foreign Policy of James G. Blaine* (1927) is old but still the best monographic treatment; and Charles C. Tansill, *The Foreign Policy of Thomas F. Bayard: 1885–1897* (1940).

On general post-bellum expansion, see Joe Patterson Smith, *The Republican Expansionists of the Early Reconstruction Era* (1933). On the first annexation, see Van Deusen's *Seward* and the very full account by Victor J. Farrar, *The Annexation of Russian America to the United States* (1937). Convenient explanations of anti-expansionism are given in Donald M. Dozer, "Anti-Expansionism during the Johnson Administration," *Pacific Historical Review,* XII (1943), 253–75 and the older article by T. C. Smith, "Expansion After the Civil War, 1865–1871," *Political Science Quarterly,* XVI (1901), 412–36.

In addition to the Grenville and Young volume, the revitalization of the navy is treated by Daniel J. Carrison, *The Navy from Wood to Steel, 1860–1890* (1965) and Walter R. Herrick, *The American Naval Revolution* (1966). Older works on Admiral Mahan are still useful: William Livezey, *Mahan on Seapower* (1947) and W. D. Puleston, *Mahan* (1939).

For American-Canadian relations, the following works are useful: Donald F. Warner, *The Idea of Continental Union: Agitation for the Annexation of Canada to the United States, 1849–1893* (1960); Lester B. Shippee, *Canadian-American Relations, 1849–1874* (1939); and Charles C. Tansill, *Canadian-American Relations, 1875–1911* (1943). Warner's book is especially revealing, emphasizing the role of economic crises in annexationist agitation north of the border. He shows clearly how weak such feeling was in the United States, except of course for Blaine! Thomas N. Brown's *Irish-American Nationalism, 1870–1890** (1966) describes Fenians and other Irish revolutionaries and their effect on American-British relations. See also Brian Jenkins, *Fenians and Anglo-American Relations During Reconstruction* (1969). Such issues as the fisheries, fur seals, reciprocity, and the Alaskan boundary, which vexed American-Canadian goodwill, are treated in terms of their effect on Canadian unity in Robert C. Brown, *Canada's National Policy, 1883–1900: A Study in Canadian-American Relations* (1964).

The fullest treatment of American-Samoan relations is George H. Ryden, *The Foreign Policy of the United States in Relation to Samoa* (1933). On general Latin American-American affairs, Dexter Perkins's detailed *The Monroe Doctrine: 1867–1907* (1937) is the standard work. R. H. Bastert, "A New Approach to the Origins of Blaine's Pan American Policy," *Hispanic American Historical Review,* XXXIX (1959), 375–412, is useful in analyzing Blaine's motivation for issuing the call for an Inter-American Conference (chiefly to divert attention from past blunders). Herbert Millington, *American Diplomacy and the War of the Pacific* (1948) is quite helpful. *No Transfer* (1961) by John A. Logan, Jr., demonstrates that this policy was linked to the Monroe Doctrine only as late as Grant's administration. For a general overview of relations with Hawaii, see Sylvester K. Stevens, *American Expansion in Hawaii, 1842-1898* (1945) and Merze Tate, *The United States and the Hawaiian Kingdom: A Political History* (1965). For a brief survey of American interest in Africa, consult Clarence Clendenen, Robert Collins, Peter Duignan, *Americans In Africa 1865-1900** (1966).

Two works provide a corrective to the notion that the period of the 1870s and 1880s was the "nadir" of overseas interest: David M. Pletcher, *The Awkward Years: American Foreign Relations under Garfield and Arthur* (1961) and Milton Plesur, "Rumblings Beneath the Surface: America's Outward Thrust, 1865-1890" in H. Wayne Morgan (ed.), *The Gilded Age: A Reappraisal** (1963). Both authors conclude that expansionism was never very overt, but was rather nascent. The Gilded Age period served as a connection between the aggressive diplomacy of Reconstruction and the spirited times of the 1890s. See also the essay on foreign policy by Paul S. Holbo, "Economics, Emotion, and Expansion: An Emerging Foreign Policy" in the latest edition of *The Gilded Age** (1970). This author's full attitudinal study of the period 1865-1890 is presently being readied for publication.

The literature on foreign relations in the nineties is lengthy. For a general treatment and convenient survey, see Foster R. Dulles, *The Imperial Years** (1956). On the second Cleveland administration, see G. R. Dulebohn, *Principles of Foreign Policy under the Cleveland Administrations* (1941). For Hawaii, see Stevens' and Tate's works already cited and Julius W. Pratt, *Expansionists of 1898** (1936) which states convincingly that the primary reason for the Hawaiian Revolution of 1893 was the desire of the white community for a more stable government. Two works by W. A. Russ, Jr. are acknowledged as the standard treatments: *The Hawaiian Revolution, 1893-1894* (1959) and *The Hawaiian Republic, 1894-1898* (1961). See also Ralph C. Kuykendall, *The Hawaiian Kingdom, 1874-1893: The Kalakau Dynasty* (1967).

On the Spanish-American War, consult Joseph E. Wisan, *The Cuban Crisis as Reflected in the New York Press: 1895-1898* (1934) for a fine treatment of public opinion; Walter Millis, *The Martial Spirit: A Study of Our War with Spain* (1931), a most fascinating and humorous account; Frank Freidel, *The Splendid Little War* (1958), an interesting collection of pictures and text; Pratt's *Expansionists of 1898,* excellent on opinion toward annexation as well as a provocative study of the intellectual preparation for expansionism, the spirited stand of most religious groups, and the "small" concern of business for adventuresome overseas policies; Ernest R. May, *Imperial Democracy: The Emergence of America as a Great Power* (1961), a significant volume based upon European as well as American archives. May asserts that Great Power status came only after 1898 because only then did the other powers so regard the United States. He feels that McKinley's final decision for war was the result chiefly of domestic opinion. Walter LaFeber, *The New Empire: An Interpretation of American Expansion, 1860–1898** (1963), who like Pletcher and Plesur, not only describes the Gilded Age as a time of expansionist preparation, but contrary to Pratt, feels that big business did not oppose the Spanish-American War. This work treats the global interests of most of this country's politicians, who reflecting the agricultural and industrial overproduction, were steadily seeking commercial empire as opposed to actual territory. For example, LaFeber discloses the business backing Cleveland received for his nationalistic posture toward Great Britain during the Venezuela Crisis; indeed, for LaFeber, the possible loss of markets dictated this policy. As far as the war feeling went, business was not of one mind on hostilities, McKinley dominated both Congress and the yellow press, and again commercial motivations dictated policy — not so much the desire for war, but for the fruits war would bring. McKinley's hard-headed purpose was seen, LaFeber asserts, in the President's view of the Philippines as an economic springboard for Asiatic commerce. H. W. Morgan's *William McKinley and His America* (1963) is a most descriptive and convenient survey. Morgan's brief survey, *America's Road to Empire: The War with Spain and Overseas Expansion** (1965) is a fine summary. Pratt's *America's Colonial Experiment: How the United States Gained, Governed, and In Part Gave Away a Colonial Empire* (1950) deals with American policies in its post-1898 empire; see also Frederick Merk, *Manifest Destiny and Mission in American History** (1963) which asserts that the Manifest Destiny of the 1890s was quite antithetical to the continental variety of fifty years earlier; also relevant is Fred H. Harrington, "Literary Aspects of American Anti-Imperialism, 1898-1902," *New England Quarterly,* X (1937), 650–67. A fresh, incisive, and philosophical view of the entire question of imperialism and its many elements is contained in Ernest R. May, *American Imperialism: A Speculative Essay** (1968). A recent case study exploration of anti-imperialism is Robert L. Beisner, *Twelve Against Empire: The Anti-Imperialists, 1898–1900* (1968), a survey of a dozen Republicans who lost the battle against empire because they were too splintered and not in touch with fresh trends. W. M. Armstrong's *E. L. Godkin and American Foreign Policy, 1865–1900* (1957) is a pertinent study of The *Nation's* editor, his anti-expansionism, and anti-Blaine feelings.

America's improving relations with Great Britain at the end of the nineteenth and during the early twentieth centuries are described by several writers. Alexander E. Campbell, *Great Britain and the United States, 1895–1903* (1960) deals with topics — for example the Venezuela problem — from a British point of view. He also shows that despite earlier British reluctance at an American-owned and fortified isthmian canal,

Britain ultimately gained from such an arrangement. See also Charles S. Campbell, Jr., *Anglo-American Understanding, 1898–1903* (1957); Richard H. Heindel, *The American Impact on Great Britain, 1898–1914* (1940); Lionel M. Gelber, *The Rise of Anglo-American Friendship: A Study in World Politics, 1898–1906* (1938); and R. G. Neale, *Great Britain and United States Expansion: 1898–1900* (1966). The latter book dates the rapprochement before 1898, feels it was of little importance in preventing Great Power intervention in the war, and discounts the British influence on the origin of the Open Door Policy. Bradford Perkins, *The Great Rapprochement: England and the United States, 1895–1914* (1968), concludes that the British Navy did the most to head off European intervention in the Spanish-American War and that the famous rapprochement in part involved British encouragement of America in imperialistic ventures.

For Far Eastern affairs in the early twentieth century, see A. Whitney Griswold, *The Far Eastern Policy of the United States** (1938), probably still the best treatment; Tyler Dennett's critical *John Hay* (1933); Paul A. Varg, *Open Door Diplomat: The Life of W. W. Rockhill* (1952), a very full and careful treatment of the diplomat's contributions which shows his prowess as an Oriental scholar; and Charles S. Campbell, Jr., *Special Business Interests and the Open Door Policy* (1951). Thomas J. McCormick, *China Market: America's Quest for Informal Empire, 1893–1901** (1967) sees the United States' commercial interests in Asia as a response to domestic unhappiness. In his discussion of the Russian relationship to the promulgation of the Open Door Policy, McCormick provides a revisionist interpretation. Internal tensions, as opposed to the desire for markets, also explains expansionism according to Marilyn B. Young, "American Expansion, 1870–1900: The Far East" in Barton J. Bernstein (ed.), *Towards a New Past: Dissenting Essays in American History** (1968). A clear statement of our involved Chinese relationships is found in Charles Vevier, *The United States and China, 1906–1913* (1955) and a new study by Paul A. Varg, *The Making of a Myth: The United States and China, 1897–1912* (1968). For Japanese-American tensions, see the very readable Thomas A. Bailey, *Theodore Roosevelt and the Japanese-American Crises* (1934) and his earlier study, *Roosevelt and the Russo-Japanese War* (1925); P. J. Treat, *Diplomatic Relations Between the United States and Japan, 1895–1905* (1938); Tyler Dennett, *Roosevelt and the Russo-Japanese War* (1925); and Eugene P. Trani, *The Treaty of Portsmouth: An Adventure in American Diplomacy* (1969). An interesting account of Japanese-American problems in California is contained in Roger Daniels, *The Politics of Prejudice: The Anti-Japanese Movement in California and the Struggle for Japanese Exclusion** (1962). Raymond A. Esthus, *Theodore Roosevelt and Japan* (1966), shows that Roosevelt's support of Japan against her Asiatic enemies was good American policy since this country was otherwise so weak in the Orient. This view supplants earlier statements of, for example,

Bailey and Dennett. Incidentally, Esthus used Japanese sources to excellent advantage in addition to American ones. Charles E. Neu, *An Uncertain Friendship: Theodore Roosevelt and Japan, 1906–1909* (1967) agrees with Esthus, maintaining that Roosevelt's Japanese policy was shrewd and skilled, that Japan was America's best defense in the Orient. W. R. Braisted, *The United States Navy in the Pacific: 1897–1909* (1958) is a corrective to the notion that all big-navy schemes originated with Roosevelt and offers a detailed survey of the desire for naval bases. Robert A. Hart, *The Great White Fleet: Its Voyage Around the World, 1907–1909* (1965), gives a detailed, colorful, and critical treatment of the Roosevelt gamble in sending old ships which were really dependent upon foreign fleets for protection.

On Korea, see Fred H. Harrington, *God, Mammon, and the Japanese: Dr. Horace N. Allen and Korean-American Relations, 1884–1905* (1944). On American-Latin American relations in the first decade and a half of the twentieth century, the following works are standard: Perkins' *Monroe Doctrine, 1867–1907,* useful and essential for all topics within these dates; Wilfrid H. Callcott, *The Caribbean Policy of the United States, 1890–1920* (1942); David F. Healey, *The United States in Cuba, 1898–1902* (1963); Allan R. Millett, *The Politics of Intervention: The Military Occupation of Cuba, 1906–1909* (1967). On the canal issue, see Gerstle Mack, *The Land Divided: A History of the Panama Canal and Other Isthmian Canal Projects* (1944); Dwight C. Miner, *The Fight for the Panama Route* (1940); and Sheldon Liss, *The United States and the Panama Canal* (1967). On American-Caribbean economic policy, there is Dana G. Munro, *Intervention and Dollar Diplomacy in the Caribbean: 1900–1921* (1964), which deemphasizes economic reasons for interventionism. For the Wilson period, consult Selig Adler, "Bryan and Wilsonian Caribbean Penetration," *Hispanic American Historical Review,* XX (1940), 198–226, an analysis of why interventionism continued under Wilson despite his denunciation of the Roosevelt and Taft policy; Arthur S. Link, *Wilson the Diplomatist: A Look at His Major Foreign Policies** (1957); the pertinent parts of his *Woodrow Wilson and the Progressive Era: 1910–1917** (1954); *Wilson: The New Freedom** (1956); and *Wilson: The Struggle for Neutrality, 1914–1915* (1960). Link's statements are, as always, balanced and judicious. For Wilson's Mexican troubles, consult Howard F. Cline, *The United States and Mexico** (rev. ed., 1963); Robert E. Quirk, *An Affair of Honor: Woodrow Wilson and Occupation of Vera Cruz** (1962), a criticism of Wilson's self-righteousness and precipitous actions; and Kenneth J. Grieb, *The United States and Huerta* (1969).

On the First Moroccan Crisis, see Eugene N. Anderson, *The First Moroccan Crisis, 1904–1906* (1930). The best monograph on its subject is Calvin D. Davis, *The United States and the First Hague Peace Conference* (1962). The standard study of reciprocity with Canada and

Taft's failure is L. Ethan Ellis, *Reciprocity, 1911: A Study in Canadian-American Relations* (1939).

The remaining titles deal in a general way with American foreign relations in the first years of the twentieth century. Perhaps the most important and most scholarly monograph on Roosevelt's diplomacy is Howard K. Beale, *Theodore Roosevelt and the Rise of America to World Power** (1956). Covering a number of diplomatic events rather interestingly and something of a standard is Alfred L. P. Dennis, *Adventures in American Diplomacy, 1896–1906* (1928). Thomas A. Bailey, "America's Emergence as a World Power: The Myth and the Verity," *Pacific Historical Review*, XXX (1961), 1–16, concludes rather interestingly and perhaps questionably that the United States achieved world status when it declared independence in 1776, not in 1898 when we became a landed empire. William E. Leuchtenburg, "Progressivism and Imperialism: The Progressive Movement and American Foreign Policy, 1898–1916," *Mississippi Valley Historical Review*, XXXIX (1952), 483–504, shows the close and even enthusiastic connection between the progressive movement and imperialism, while Barton J. Bernstein and F. A. Leib, "Progressive Republican Senators and American Imperialism, 1898–1916: A Reappraisal," *Mid-America*, L (1968), 163–205, challenges this thesis.